A LOVE FOR FOOD

A LOVE FOR FOOD

RECIPES AND NOTES
FOR COOKING
AND EATING WELL

Daylesford
with
Sheila Keating

Photography by
Sarah Maingot

daylesford

Fourth Estate • London

First published in Great Britain by
Fourth Estate
a division of HarperCollins*Publishers*
77–85 Fulham Palace Road
London W6 8JB
www.4thestate.co.uk

Designed by Emery Barnard

A catalogue record for this book is available from the British Library

ISBN 978-0-00-727479-6

MIX
Paper from
responsible sources
FSC www.fsc.org **FSC® C007454**

Printed and bound in Spain by Graficas Estella

Contents

1   *Carole Bamford: The Beginning*

7   Grazings

47   Soups

69   *Jez Taylor: The Market Garden*

77   Salads

125   Vegetables

159   *John Longman: The Cheese Room*

165   Savoury tarts and pies

197   Fish

221   *Richard Smith: The Livestock*

227   Meat

271   Puddings

307   *Eric Duhamel: The Bakery*

313   Bread

343   Cakes and Breaks

375   *John Hardwick: The Kitchens*

379   Staples

413   *Tim Field: The Environment*

419   Weights and Measures

420   Acknowledgements

421   Index

The Seasons

Everything we do at Daylesford is governed by the natural rhythm of the seasons, from the animal husbandry to the taste of the milk and cheese, which changes subtly as the herds move from pasture to pasture. Spring, summer, autumn and winter are our constant watchwords, each season eagerly anticipated, each bringing particular treasures straight from the market garden into the kitchens. From the first purple sprouting broccoli and rhubarb into the colourful summer riot of tomatoes and berries, and on through the autumnal pumpkins, squash and orchard fruits, we make the most of everything we grow or source seasonally, in as many dishes as possible. And when we have a glut, it is all hands to the deck, making jams and chutneys and pickles, in order to capture the essence of one season to enjoy in another.

Of course some produce has an extended season, or more than one season, or it grows for most of the year, so there will be different combinations of fruit and vegetables to enjoy as the seasons change.

Other marriages are available to us for all too brief a time, so are not to be missed, and you will find some of these on the following pages.

Spring

Crushed New Potatoes with Olives, Capers and Herbs	127
Pearl Barley, Asparagus and Pea Shoot Risotto	156
Oddington Goat's Cheese and Asparagus Tart	170
Rhubarb Queen of Puddings	287
Rhubarb and Ginger Jam	404

Summer

Broad Bean, Pea, Mint and Feta Toasts	12
Chilled Pea and Mint Soup	51
Broad Bean, Bulgar Wheat and Herb Salad	79
Smashed Broad Beans, Peas and Mint	129
Gooseberry Fool with Shortbread	273
Gooseberry and Elderflower Jam	405

High Summer

Daylesford Summer Wine Cup   40

Plum Brandy   41

Chilled Tomato, Cucumber and Fennel Soup   52

Grilled Peaches, Spelt, Pea, Rocket and Mozzarella Salad   82

Tomato and Feta Salad with Mint and Lemon Dressing   89

Three Tomato Tart   179

Red Tomato Chilli Jam   399

Strawberry and Vanilla Conserve   406

Autumn

Blackcurrant Vodka   41

Celeriac and Apple Soup   60

Butternut Squash, Honey and Sage Soup   62

Griddled Butternut Squash, Goat's Cheese and Olive Salad   97

Pickled Pear and Hazelnut Salad, with Chickpeas, Quinoa and Daylesford Blue Cheese   101

Mushroom, Celeriac, Truffle Honey and Toasted Pine Nut Salad   118

Wild Rice, Red Cabbage, Apple and Toasted Cobnut Salad   121

Woodland Mushroom Shepherd's Pie   136

Spiced Pumpkin, Butter Bean and Spinach Casserole   143

Butternut Squash and Kale Tart   177

Wootton Estate Game Pie   191

Venison Cottage Pie with Beetroot and Apple Salad   268

Poached Apple and Pear Jelly with Crumble Topping and Prune Cream   282

Vanilla Rice Pudding with Apple and Blackberry Compote   290

Blackberry and Apple Crumble Tart   295

Squash, Honey and Sage Bread   316

Spiced Apple Cake with Streusel Topping   350

Apple and Chilli Chutney   394

Butternut Squash Chutney   397

Winter

Sloe Gin   41

Purple Sprouting Broccoli, Spelt, Crispy Garlic and Toasted Almond Salad   109

Jerusalem Artichoke and Cavolo Nero Tart   178

Venison and Cranberry Pies   189

Mulled Wine and Orange Trifle   279

'It seemed so simple and obvious that it was all about the soil.'
Carole Bamford, The Beginning

What we are really trying to do here at Daylesford is to take a step back in time and re-learn the skills and values of our grandparents' generation, when country people had a kitchen garden or an allotment and ate whatever they grew. If they had a smallholding or farm, they raised crops to feed whatever animals they had, which in time would be slaughtered to feed the family. You might have a few hens for eggs, or a pig, or a cow to milk, so you might make butter and cheese, and it was all healthy and fresh and self-sustaining.

I grew up in the countryside in the Midlands, not on a farm, but close to farming, and the way we shopped was very simple. On Sunday we had a joint of meat or a chicken, which was a real treat that you had once every two weeks or so. Monday would be leftovers day, then on Tuesday we would shop afresh for the week, at the butcher's shop, the bakery and the cheesemonger's, and the fishmonger's on Friday, which was always fish day. Everyone in the shop knew your name and what you liked, and it is that personal connection with food and the people who grow it and raise it that we are trying to achieve at Daylesford.

I really didn't mean for the project to have grown as it has done; one thing just led to another. It started with wanting to make a difference, on a small, family level, after two chance incidents. The first was when we were living and farming at Wootton in Staffordshire thirty-six years ago. I was in the garden with my eldest child, Alice, who was only six months old. I was pushing her in the pram and we went to look at some roses I had planted a few days before, and found they were wilting. This was the seventies, when like everyone we had big fields, because all the hedgerows had been taken out, and it turned out they were spraying Roundup on the farm. I didn't even know what Roundup was, but I soon learned it was a very powerful herbicide, and that the toxins had carried in the air from the fields and affected the roses. As a new mother, I was horrified. That was the beginning of thinking that we couldn't carry on farming as we were.

Then, a little later, I was at an agricultural show, again with Alice in the pushchair, and the Soil Association had a little tent there. The organic movement was quite a small, niche thing in those days, but I went inside and talked for about an hour and a half to a man who was so inspiring; it was a real open-window moment. That night I said to my husband, 'We can't carry on farming as we are. We are ruining the soil and the environment with chemicals, for our babies, and for future generations. We have to stop and think about what we are doing.' It seemed so simple and obvious to me that it was all about the soil. Unless you look after the health of the soil, you don't have good plants, and so you aren't producing healthy food for us or for our animals. So we went to see the farm manager, who didn't really believe it was possible, but I was quite determined, and after a few years he realised it was the right thing to do.

That was the start. We were farming deer, Aberdeen Angus cattle, sheep and chickens, then we came to Gloucestershire in 1992 and again, the first thing we did was convert the land to become organic. It took a long time for it to clean itself, because of the chemicals that had been used previously, but suddenly wonderful things started happening, wild flowers and plants that hadn't been seen before began appearing in the undergrowth; I remember particularly seeing so many different kinds of violets growing. Everything comes back to the soil, and ours began to be rich and dark and alive with worms: a totally different colour to soil that has had chemicals in it.

I think there is no other way to farm, but organic has become a difficult word, because it has been abused – I don't want to eat organic food that has come into the supermarket from 3,000 miles away and has been picked at the wrong time of year. So we prefer to talk about food that is local, seasonal and sustainable.

When we arrived at Daylesford we also inherited a dairy herd, so we were able to have our own milk – there is something wonderful about fresh farm milk that has a flavour you remember from childhood. And so I thought, 'Why don't we make cheese?' But how on earth was I to find a cheesemaker? I bought a copy of the Specialist Cheesemakers' Association magazine and rang the editor, who happened to live in Chipping Norton, and he said, 'It's funny you should call. There is an American cheese-maker called Joe Schneider . . .' Joe's passion was British farmhouse cheese, and he was the first person I employed. We put together a plan and he started making our first Cheddar, which we matured for ten to eighteen months, greased with our own organic lard from our cattle and wrapped in organic muslin, and I hand-wrote the first labels. We wanted to take the artisan process as far as we could and be correct and ethical to the nth degree. We were very lucky, in that the Cheddar won a gold award the first year. I love our Cheddar and I am very proud of it. I like to see the cheeses in the maturing room, and the constant checking to see how they are coming along. Cheese-making is truly the work of the hands.

One of the things I love to do is go to the shows and livestock auctions with Richard, our farm manager, and as the farm has grown we have been able to support more and more heritage crops and breeds of animal, including Cotswold, Ryeland and Kerry Hill sheep, and South Devon cattle. And the lovely thing is we now have our own rare-breed Gloucester herd of cows, which are dual-purpose beef and dairy animals, and which we took over from a farmer who had died. Richard said, 'Some of them aren't well. I think I will just take the good ones.' But I said, 'No, take them all.' Some didn't make it, but we have since built up the herd, and the beef is wonderful, as it has so much marbling, which makes it really flavoursome and tender. And having the herd also means that we can make our own Double Gloucester and Single Gloucester cheese. The Single Gloucester is very special, because it is a very old cheese that was only made in farmhouse kitchens, not to be sold, and it had virtually disappeared. Now we are one of the few farms that make it. It has a very delicate flavour, not immediately commercially appealing, perhaps, but I love it.

Joe was a true artisan, very skilled and passionate, like John Longman, who now makes the cheese, and all the people on the team, from Richard, who is so down-to-earth, and dedicated to all that we do; to Jez who is in charge of the market garden and a real character. He has expanded the garden to twenty acres and introduced wonderful winter salad leaves and micro-leaves which the chefs love, because they give such a burst of flavour. Then there is Eric, our baker – there is nothing he doesn't know about flour and bread-making. Every day in the bakery they are not only making bread, but cakes and tarts and biscuits – many of the things we are most proud of, and, like the team who work with John Longman in the dairy, our bakers are the unsung heroes of Daylesford. I truly value all these people and I am so lucky to have them, because they are really committed, hardworking and genuine characters. What they do isn't just a job to them; they really believe in what we are trying to achieve.

A whole tapestry of people have helped and supported me right from the beginning, especially Carlo Petrini, who founded the Slow Food Movement. He speaks Italian; I speak English, but we understand each other! He inspired me so much with his love of food, his support for artisans and sustainable systems, and each year he would send us two students from the university he set up in Bra, in northern Italy. And Patrick Holden, who was then President of the Soil Association, would come down to the farm to advise us on what to do. When I had to find a way to present and package all the things we made, to sell in the shop, someone suggested I talk to designer Teresa Roviras. I went to her house and on the table in the kitchen was a big cardboard box of organic vegetables, just delivered: so I knew immediately she was the right person. We did everything using recycled paper and vegetable dye, and even sent out the first turkeys in sacking. And Teresa's husband, Spencer Fung, who is a wonderful architect, designed all the interiors of the buildings on the farm, using wood from the estate.

In the same year that we produced our first cheese, we set up a little bakery in one of the barns, where Emmanuel Hadjiandreou, our first artisan baker, made sourdough, often with herbs or vegetables from the garden. And that is how the farmshop began, just with an idea of selling some of our bread, cheese and meat, locally. We were about to open around six weeks before Christmas, and it was so cold, I rather panicked, worrying about all these people coming out to a wintry barn, so we thought, 'Why not do some soup and a sandwich to keep them warm?' I never intended to open a proper café. But again, the project just grew. As more people came to the farmshop, they wanted to stay for lunch.

The food I have always wanted to eat is very simple, and the recipe books I treasured most when I was first married and learning to cook were the kind where you wrote notes in the margin, and were full of down-to-earth, nourishing food for the family. Some of the recipes we now use in the farmshop and kitchens are old favourites, or recipes that have been in my family for a long time, and I developed many of them, such as our Christmas pudding and cake, with Betty Thornton, who was a wonderful baker and worked with us for many years.

I have always felt that we can learn from Italy and Sicily, because there the cooking is all about using wonderful ingredients and letting them speak for themselves. There is a market that I have been to often in Catania in Sicily, which is held in the most incredible marble hall and is like a medieval piece of theatre. The colours of the fruit and vegetables and the fish and the carcasses of meat hanging are a true feast for the eyes … and in the restaurants there I have eaten some of the simplest, most memorable food. But why not do the same with British ingredients?

There is nothing like a salad of different shapes and colours and flavours of English tomatoes, which have their own special taste; a fully ripe, freshly picked English strawberry, or a heritage apple from the orchard. Old English varieties can be difficult, because they are more susceptible to disease, and there will be years when you barely have a crop, but they are worth it, purely for the taste.

I have been very lucky in that I have had very good chefs in my life, and it has been interesting to watch Tom Aikens and Tom Kitchin, initially, and then our executive chef, John Hardwick; our head chef, Gaven Fuller; and Vladimir Niza, who launched our cookery school – all of whom came from Michelin-starred backgrounds – changing their perspective and enjoying seeing at first hand the way the fruit and vegetables are grown, and the meat and venison is produced. For a chef it is a very different challenge to create menus around what is available at any time of year on the farm, rather than phoning a supplier. When we were planning the café I said to Tom Aikens, 'Don't cook for a while, just go and research the best table birds, so we know which chickens we should be rearing, and look at different breeds of lamb, from a cooking point of view.'

John Hardwick, who is a great character, and a wonderful chef, has been in charge of the kitchens for over eleven years now, and the talented Gaven has been head chef for over eight – he was working in a country house hotel locally, and already ordering ingredients from the farm, before he joined the kitchen. And I think our food really represents that emphasis on fresh, seasonal, healthy food – or at least 80 per cent healthy, 20 per cent naughty. We are also very proud of our 'real meals' – freshly prepared dishes for people to finish off at home – that are created in the Black Barn on the farm every morning by our dedicated team led by Andy Wheeler. Andy is an absolute rock; so committed to what he does that he has been known to walk for hours through a blizzard to make it into the kitchens, and the recipes for some of our favourite recipes from the Black Barn appear in this book.

Fish is difficult for us, because we can't produce it ourselves, but Tim Field, our very knowledgeable and enthusiastic environmental expert, is there to make sure we do the right thing, and we are always learning. And there is other produce that we can't rear or grow, but we also like to celebrate, such as asparagus from the Vale of Evesham, and the best of European produce too. I like the first early French asparagus, which comes in just before the English crop. And I happen to love chestnuts, but I really think the best come from Italy, because they tend to dry out less quickly than our English ones.

Of the home-grown produce, the things I find most exciting are often the simplest: the winter black radishes, thinly sliced with some good sea salt and delicious butter. Purple sprouting broccoli is a favourite and I always look forward to it. Once it comes into season I don't mind if I eat it for weeks, in all kinds of different ways. I look forward, too, to the first forced rhubarb, and the damsons in autumn, which feel so English; and I love it when all the marmalades and chutneys are being made. The idea of making marmalade on a cold day, with the fire going, takes me right back to my childhood. And in autumn, too, there are little treasures from the trees: wet walnuts and cobnuts. Sometimes there is a bumper crop, sometimes none, but there is nothing nicer than a glass of wine and some wet walnuts – just delicious.

In 2008, we created the Summer Solstice garden, which is now a part of the market garden, for the Chelsea Flower Show – everyone on the farm still talks about it, because, my goodness, it was ambitious, and there was such a lot of work involved! Richard grew a special field of wheat, which we managed, somehow, to get to London – it was the first time anyone had had a field of organic wheat at Chelsea before – and it was planted with traditional wildflowers: cornflowers, poppies, chamomile, ragged robin and ladies' smock, which you rarely see in fields these days. We wanted to bring alive all the old country skills that we are in danger of losing, so there were proper laid hedges, and we had willow-weaving around the raised beds, which were full of vegetables, herbs and fruits; we even had medlar trees. It was all very English. We had rainwater being collected, and a wormery. Spencer designed the pavilion using recycled wood and logs from the farm, with solar panels, and a wood oven, where one of our bakers baked bread. The idea was to encapsulate the journey of sustainable food from the fields to the table, and everything in that garden had meaning. I chose bread for the theme, because it is so fundamental to life. In the wooden table in the 'kitchen' we had carved into the table: 'Give us this day our daily bread.'

After the show, we brought the garden back to the farm and rebuilt it in the market garden, and now we run courses there, often for schoolchildren, who come to see the farm, and learn about what we do.

There is an old saying that I particularly like, which is along the lines of: 'The earth is not a gift from our parents; we are only borrowing it from our children.' What began with Alice and my worries about the future of our environment for her and for all our children has now come full circle, in that she has started growing fantastic produce bio-dynamically. She works as a film-maker and all these years I didn't know how much she was watching and taking things in, so it really surprised me. But she saw the food being grown and realised that it was a good and fun thing to do . . . and now, too, I have my grandchildren to take around the farm. They love to see the sheep-shearing and the spring lambs, and at Christmas we go to see the turkeys, which are very funny and follow you around. The children understand that this is where their food comes from . . . and that makes me very happy.

GRAZINGS

Just good things to eat
Crisp fresh vegetables and dipping sauces
for a lazy summer's day
Comfort food on toast to curl up
with by the fire
A dish of baked eggs
Terrines and paté

This is really a collection of favourite things that are rarely far from the kitchen menu and make a great brunch, sharing plate, starter, lunch or supper. Some of them feature ingredients from the garden that pop into season briefly and that we want to make the most of before they disappear; many are served on charred and toasted bread, which can be made smaller and daintier for picking up with fingers and nibbling with drinks, or left chunkier, to eat with a knife and fork. There is an art to making the perfect bruschetta-style toast that is crispy on the outside, and soft on the inside – for chef John Hardwick's notes on how to do it, see page 15.

There are also a couple of terrines, which pair beautifully with chutney, piccalilli or red tomato chilli jam (see pages 389–400 for recipes). Terrines do take a little bit of effort, but they are great things to make ahead when you have friends coming round, as all the work is done in advance. The thing to do is make a big terrine – more than you need in one go – then it will keep in the fridge for the rest of the week, ready to be spooned out on to crusty bread or toast for a quick lunch or supper.

Garden Vegetables with Hot Cheddar Sauce and Salsa Verde Mayonnaise

This is simply about celebrating the bounty of the summer garden on any given day. 'It really sums up Daylesford for me,' says chef John Hardwick. 'The vegetables can change as the season goes on, and you might want to add baby beetroots when they are young, tender and sweet. We tend to keep the root vegetables to just carrots and beets, however, so that the overall feeling is light, rather than too earthy.' The only thing to consider is that there is no hiding place for the vegetables, so everything you choose has to have real freshness and flavour.

We serve the crudités on a board, with some boiled eggs nestling in amongst them, and a pot each of hot Cheddar sauce and cold salsa verde mayonnaise. Everyone has different ideas on how to achieve the best boiled egg, but our way is to start with the eggs at room temperature, so that they have less chance of cracking. Then lower them into boiling water – not cold – as this allows you to time them more accurately, from the moment they go in. For a medium-sized soft-boiled egg that you can dip soldiers into, boil for 5 minutes; for a medium egg – which is what you want here – that has a vibrant, slightly soft yolk – boil for 7 minutes. If you want a really hard egg, for example, for egg mayonnaise, boil for 10 minutes. If you are peeling the eggs, as here, then as soon as you take the pan off the hob, put it under the cold tap until the eggs are cool, which will prevent a grey-blue line forming around the yolks. A pinch of salt in the cooking water helps stop the whites of the eggs clinging to the shells, and makes peeling easier.

4 medium eggs

a pinch of sea salt

1 bunch of asparagus, woody ends removed

2 bunches of baby radishes, trimmed

1 bunch of baby carrots, trimmed, stalks left on

2 handfuls of sugar snap peas

2 baby gem lettuces, halved lengthways

3 stalks of vine cherry tomatoes (about 20 tomatoes)

5 or 6 spring onions, trimmed

4 slices of good bread, preferably sourdough

1 handful of pea shoots

1 quantity of Cheddar sauce (see page 387), to serve

½ quantity of salsa verde mayonnaise (see page 382), to serve

Have the eggs at room temperature. Bring a medium pan of water to the boil and add a pinch of sea salt (this will make the eggs easier to peel). Gently lower in the eggs and simmer for exactly 7 minutes. Take off the heat and rinse them immediately in cold water to prevent discolouring, then peel the eggs.

Arrange the prepared vegetables on a board or platter.

Toast the bread until crisp – either under the grill, or, if possible, on a medium hot griddle pan until both sides are nicely charred. Cut each slice into 3 fat soldiers and arrange with the vegetables.

Halve the eggs and add to the platter, then sprinkle with the pea shoots.

Warm the Cheddar sauce over a low heat, stirring constantly, and as soon as it is warm (before it starts to simmer), remove it from the heat to avoid curdling and pour into a small pot. Have the chilled salsa verde mayonnaise in a separate pot and serve both alongside the crudités.

Four Toasts

Summer vegetables, hot crab, sardines and mature Cheddar all take on a different dimension on top of crunchy toasted bread.

Broad Bean, Pea, Mint and Feta Toasts

These are really colourful, bright, fresh bruschetta-style toasts that capture early summer, and are great to put out on a big board or platter with drinks. They are so quick and easy to make that if you don't have a griddle pan, or the time, you can simply grill the bread (under a medium grill, so you can do it relatively slowly) rather than griddle it first and finish it in the oven. However, if you want to be perfectionist about it, this two-stage toasting is the secret to getting the bread beautifully crispy on the outside, so that it won't turn mushy when you add your topping, but not so hard that you think you are going to break your teeth when you bite into it. By brushing the toast with oil and rubbing it with garlic first, you seal in these flavours but stop the toast being greasy when you are eating it with your fingers. (See the notes on page 15 for more hints on how to get toasts just right.)

After you have zested and squeezed the juice from the lemon half, a nice touch is to grill or griddle the other half, at the same time as the bread, until it just chars, then add it to the serving platter.

150g podded broad beans

110g fresh or frozen peas

1 small bunch of fresh mint, finely shredded

juice and zest of ½ a lemon

4 tablespoons extra virgin olive oil

75g feta cheese

sea salt and freshly ground black pepper

4 slices of sourdough bread (about 1cm thick)

1 clove of garlic, cut in half

1 handful of fresh pea shoots

Preheat the oven to 180°C/gas 4.

Have ready a bowl of iced water. Bring a small pan of water to a rapid boil and drop in the beans. Cook for 30 seconds, then lift them out with a slotted spoon (leaving the water in the pan) and plunge them into the iced water. Add the peas to the boiling water. If they are frozen, cook as before, for just 30 seconds, then drain them well under the cold tap and transfer them to a bowl (if you are using fresh peas, they will need to cook for about 5 minutes to become tender). Lightly crush the peas with the back of a fork.

Once the beans are cold, slip off the outer skins (discard these) and add the beans to the bowl of peas, together with the mint, lemon juice and zest, and 2 tablespoons of the olive oil. Finally crumble in the feta, mix gently and season with salt and plenty of black pepper.

Either heat a grill or get a griddle pan smoking hot on the hob. Lightly char the bread on both sides, then transfer to a baking tray. Rub each slice of toast with the cut surface of the garlic, drizzle with 1 tablespoon of the remaining oil, and season with a little salt and pepper.

Put into the preheated oven for about 6 minutes, or until crisp on the outside but still soft on the inside. Remove from the oven, halve each slice of toast and arrange on a board or platter. Top with the broad bean mixture, add a few pea shoots, and drizzle with the remaining olive oil.

Notes on toasts

Toast is as English as can be, but Italian bruschetta is toast taken to a different level. Bruschetta, at its simplest, is toasted bread rubbed with a little garlic and drizzled with really good olive oil, plus a few flakes of sea salt. Just that. But obviously you can also add whatever toppings you like.

The bread is either grilled (under a medium grill, so you can do it fairly slowly) or preferably griddled, rather than done in a toaster. Bread toasted this way is always crispier than in a toaster. However, if it is griddled I also like to put the toast into the oven briefly to reinforce it, so that when you add the oil, tomato, or whatever topping you choose, you have the brilliant, slightly charred, crispy crusts but keep the softness inside. Not everyone does the oven stage, but for me this is the way to get the best result. If you just griddle the bread, you get the nice charry lines, but not so much crispiness, so your topping can make the toast mushy; whereas if you just put the bread into the oven, you miss out on that charry flavour. I like the best of both worlds. In the case of the pea, bean and feta bruschetta on page 12, which are made to eat with drinks, we rub the toast with olive oil and garlic before putting it into the oven, so you have those classic tastes without the oiliness that can sometimes make bruschetta difficult to eat with your fingers.

It is crucial to start with the right bread. You want a good, open-textured bread with bubbles through it: sourdough is just right. You can cut it about a centimetre thick, and it will be crunchy on the outside, but thick enough to stay good and soft in the centre.

If you were to use a dense bread – for example our rye bread – and cut it this thick, it would become rock hard, so as a rule of thumb, if you are using a dense bread, slice it more thinly. We also make very thin, light, oven-baked toasts, which we use in chicken Caesar salad (page 122) and to serve with a light pâté such as the smoked mackerel one on page 36, as it is nice to pair it up with something equally light (and crispy).

Some of the things on toast in this chapter are classically British, like rarebit, or Dorset crab, and because you need to put the topping in the oven or under the grill, they are only toasted on one side first or not at all; however, thanks to the heat from the grill or oven, as well as bubbling up and browning the topping, you will end up with a crispy-based, soft-centred toast.

John Hardwick

Hot Dorset Crab on Toast

This makes a lovely, simple, but indulgent light lunch, with a really satisfying contrast in textures: a little crustiness from the cheese on top, then you crack through to the gooey crab, and finally hit the crispness of the toast.

Always buy fresh, unpasteurised, hand-picked crabmeat. By combining some of the more flavoursome brown meat with the very delicate white meat, you have a mixture that can hold its own inside the creamy, slightly mustardy mayonnaise and under the cheese topping.

300g fresh white crabmeat

200g fresh brown crabmeat

80g mayonnaise

2 teaspoons English mustard

juice of ¼ of a lemon, plus 1 whole lemon, quartered, to serve

sea salt and freshly ground black pepper

a little oil, for greasing

4 slices of good bread, preferably sourdough

2 tablespoons finely grated Parmesan cheese

2 tablespoons finely grated Cheddar cheese

1 tablespoon chopped fresh flat-leaf parsley

2 tablespoons extra virgin olive oil

4 small handfuls of mixed salad leaves

4 tablespoons French dressing (see page 381)

Preheat the oven to 180°C/gas 4 and lightly oil a baking tray.

In a bowl mix together the crabmeat, mayonnaise, mustard and lemon juice, and season well.

Preheat the grill, or heat a griddle pan, and lightly toast the bread on one side only. Arrange on the prepared baking tray, toasted side down, then generously spread each slice with the crab mixture and sprinkle with a little of each cheese. Put into the preheated oven for about 8 minutes, until the cheese melts and turns golden brown. Take out of the oven, sprinkle with the chopped parsley, drizzle with extra virgin oil and add a twist of black pepper. Serve with the salad leaves, tossed with the dressing, and a wedge of lemon.

Sardines on Toast, with Tomato, Basil and Caper Relish

February and March is the best time for sardines, as that's when they are at their most plump and plentiful, so they are a great source of cheap protein.

The easiest thing is to ask your fishmonger to butterfly the sardines for you – i.e. to take off the head and remove the central bones. However, if you want to do it yourself, buy fish that has been gutted, cut off the heads, snip off the fins with a pair of kitchen scissors, and then, with a sharp knife, extend the slit along the belly where the sardines have been gutted, all the way to the tail. Turn the fish over on a board and gently and evenly press down with your fingers all the way along the backbone, to release the bones. Don't push too hard or you will damage the flesh. Turn the fish back over again, and you should now be able to lift up the backbone and pull it away, cutting it off at the tail end. Just feel the flesh for any obvious small bones, and if necessary pull these out with tweezers.

If you want a bigger kick to the relish, use a smaller, hotter chilli.

4 slices of good bread, preferably sourdough

12 fresh sardines, butterflied, i.e. central bones and head removed (see introduction, above)

3 tablespoons olive oil

sea salt and freshly ground black pepper

1 clove of garlic, cut in half

extra virgin olive oil for drizzling

3 large vine tomatoes

6 small handfuls of rocket leaves

For the tomato caper relish:

3 tablespoons olive oil

1 large red onion, thinly sliced

a pinch of coriander seeds

a pinch of fennel seeds

50ml white wine vinegar

40g caster sugar

1 teaspoon finely chopped long red chilli

5 large red vine tomatoes, chopped

4 tablespoons capers

juice and zest of 1 lemon

1 handful of fresh basil, leaves roughly chopped or torn

19

Heat the olive oil in a pan, then put in the red onion, coriander and fennel seeds and cook gently over a low heat until the onions have softened, but are not coloured. Add the vinegar, sugar, chilli, chopped tomatoes and 200ml of water. Bring to a simmer and continue to cook gently, stirring occasionally, until the tomatoes have broken down and all the liquid has evaporated. Stir in the capers, lemon juice and zest, and the basil, remove from the heat and leave to cool, then taste and season as necessary.

Preheat the oven to 180°C/gas 4.

Either heat a grill or get a griddle pan smoking hot on the hob. Lightly char the bread on both sides, then transfer to a baking tray and put into the preheated oven for about 6 minutes.

Meanwhile, rub the sardines with olive oil, and season. Either put them under a hot grill or, preferably, cook on a hot griddle for 2 minutes on each side, until lightly charred and cooked through – check by gently pressing the flesh with the back of a fork and if it starts to flake it is ready.

Rub each slice of toasted bread with the cut side of the clove of garlic, and drizzle with extra virgin olive oil.

To serve, slice the tomatoes and divide between six plates. Put a slice of toast on top and spoon some tomato relish on to it, followed by 2 sardines. Garnish with rocket leaves, drizzle everything with some more extra virgin olive oil and add a few twists of black pepper.

Welsh Rarebit and Chutney

A good Welsh rarebit is all about the balance of strong, mature Cheddar and the spice and heat that comes from mustard and Worcestershire sauce. If you use a subtle-tasting cheese, its flavour will be lost in the spiciness; but conversely, if you don't add enough spiciness, you are really just talking about cheese on toast. As with all the things on toast in this chapter, you want crunchiness on the outside, but softness in the centre.

Some people toast the bread first, then pile the cheese mixture on top and grill it, but we prefer to do the whole thing in the oven – that way you avoid either soggy or rock-hard toast. You do have to start with good bread, though: open-textured and not too dense, with a good crust and some character of its own, so a sourdough is perfect. The topping is just spooned on to the bread, but because it sits on an oiled baking sheet, in the 10 minutes that it is in the oven the bottom of the bread turns nice and crunchy, the top of the rarebit glazes and the bread is also cooked, so it forms a firm but soft layer underneath the unctuous cheese.

The apple and chilli or butternut squash chutneys on pages 394 and 397 go especially well with the rarebit.

The cheese mixture can be kept in the fridge for up to a week if you don't want to use it all in one go.

100ml milk

500g mature Cheddar cheese, grated

2½ tablespoons plain flour

2 tablespoons English mustard

1½ tablespoons Worcestershire sauce

2 eggs, plus 2 egg yolks

sea salt and freshly ground black pepper

a little olive oil, for greasing

6 slices of good bread, preferably sourdough

6 tablespoons chutney (see recipes on pages 394–397)

6 small handfuls of mixed salad leaves

3 tablespoons French dressing (see page 381)

Preheat the oven to 190°C/gas 5.

Put the milk and grated cheese into a pan over a gentle heat and let the cheese melt slowly. Gradually add the flour, mustard and Worcestershire sauce and stir constantly until all are incorporated and you have a smooth sauce. Remove the pan from the heat and allow to cool, then beat in the whole eggs and yolks and season.

Grease a large baking sheet with a little olive oil.

When ready to serve, spread a nice thick layer of the cheese mixture on each slice of bread and arrange on the prepared baking sheet.

Put into the preheated oven for about 10 minutes, until golden brown on top and slightly crispy underneath.

Serve with a good dollop of chutney and the salad leaves, tossed in the dressing.

Cold Rose Veal with Tuna and Caper Mayonnaise

This is based on the Italian classic *vitello tonnato*, and is an old favourite of Carole Bamford: 'One of the first things I learned to make when I got married.' It is a dish you can make all year round, but it especially lends itself to a long, lingering summer lunch, when you can serve it alongside a selection of cold dishes such as the tomato, feta, lemon and mint salad (page 89), the crunchy mixed raw vegetable salad (page 91), chicken Caesar salad (page 122), and one of the savoury tarts on pages 165–83.

750ml white wine

½ a medium onion, sliced

½ a medium carrot, chopped

3 cloves of garlic

1 teaspoon fresh thyme leaves

900g rump of veal

250g mayonnaise

100g tinned tuna, drained

juice of ½ a lemon

1 tablespoon chopped fresh flat-leaf parsley

2 tablespoons small capers, chopped

sea salt and freshly ground black pepper

4 small handfuls of rocket leaves (or micro-leaves, if you can find them)

extra virgin olive oil, for drizzling

Put the wine, vegetables, garlic and thyme into a large pan with 1.5 litres of water and bring to the boil. Put in the whole rump of veal and simmer gently for 15 minutes. Take the pan from the heat and leave the veal to cool down in the cooking liquid (stock).

Meanwhile, in a bowl, mix together the mayonnaise, tuna, lemon juice, parsley and capers and season well.

Lift out the cooled veal from the stock and slice it very thinly. Divide between six plates and spread a little of the mayonnaise over each slice.

Scatter the leaves over the top and finish with a drizzle of extra virgin olive oil, some sea salt and freshly ground black pepper.

Rita's Baked Eggs and Onions

Over the years we have had a number of cooks from Barbados in the Daylesford kitchens, and this is a dish made famous by Rita, a lovely, jolly Bajan lady whom everyone loves. No matter who makes it, it will never be quite like Rita's.

It is a pure comfort brunch or light lunch dish, especially if you serve it with wholemeal or basmati rice (about 500g, cooked and drained). When you mix baked eggs with the rice, it just works, in a similar way to a kedgeree, and turns it into more of a meal than a grazing.

sea salt and freshly ground black pepper	850ml milk
8 eggs	1 tablespoon Dijon mustard
175g butter	50g Gruyère cheese, grated
4 large onions, thinly sliced	120ml cream
80g plain flour	20g Parmesan cheese, grated

Preheat the oven to 180°C/gas 4.

Bring a medium pan of water to the boil and add a pinch of sea salt (this will make the eggs easier to peel). Gently drop in the eggs and simmer for exactly 10 minutes. Take off the heat, rinse the eggs immediately in cold water to prevent discolouring, then peel them.

Melt 75g of the butter in a separate pan. Add the onions and cook over a low heat with a lid on for about 10 minutes, until softened, then season well, remove from the heat and leave to cool.

Melt the rest of the butter in a small pan over a low heat. Add the flour, whisking to a smooth paste, then cook very slowly without colouring for 5 minutes. Gradually whisk in the milk and stir until thickened and smooth. Add the mustard and Gruyère, and when the cheese has melted add the cream. Taste, season as necessary, then take off the heat.

Divide half the softened onions between four ovenproof
shallow dishes or cast iron skillets (alternatively you can
just use one larger shallow ovenproof dish). Slice 4 of the
hard-boiled eggs and arrange on top, then spoon over
a third of the cheese sauce. Repeat the layers, finishing
with the remaining cheese sauce, and sprinkle with the
Parmesan.

Bake in the preheated oven for about 15 minutes (if using
a single dish it may take longer), until hot and golden
brown on top. Remove from the oven and leave to stand
for 5 minutes to cool slightly and allow the flavours to
merge before eating.

Bubble and Squeak with Fried Egg

It's a classic after Christmas, or any time you have had a roast dinner and have potatoes and vegetables left over – but we like to keep bubble and squeak on the menu throughout autumn and winter, when we have plenty of root vegetables and brassicas in the market garden – and there is something comforting about bubble and squeak that evokes wintry days and warm fires. Whether you are starting from scratch or using up cooked vegetables, the key is to chop the vegetables and colour them in a pan before mixing them with mashed potato to get the roasted flavour and crunchy edges which make bubble and squeak so moreish (even if you have roast potatoes to add to the mix, you need a little mash to bind everything together).

Of course you can make a loose bubble and squeak, just piling the mixture into the pan and moving it around so that it is hot all the way through, and you have lots of crispy brown surfaces. However, if you shape the mix into cakes you can make them in advance and chill them in the fridge for a while, which also helps to set and hold the cakes together when you fry them.

You could use a light olive oil, but rapeseed has an interesting flavour and can be taken to a higher temperature without losing its character, and is eco-friendly.

3 large potatoes, such as Sante or the red Romano, peeled and cut into 6

½ a medium swede, peeled and cut into 6

sea salt and freshly ground black pepper

about 6 tablespoons rapeseed oil

60g butter

1 medium onion, sliced

1 clove of garlic, chopped

70g Savoy cabbage, thinly sliced

150g Brussels sprouts, chopped

1 head of broccoli, separated into florets

2 tablespoons chopped fresh flat-leaf parsley

250g fine polenta

4 eggs

good tomato ketchup, to serve (see page 401)

salad leaves (optional), with a little French dressing (see page 381), to serve

Put the potatoes and swede into a pan and cover with cold, slightly salted water. Bring to the boil, then turn down the heat and simmer until just tender. Drain in a colander, then put into a large bowl and mash.

Heat 2 tablespoons of the oil and half the butter in a non-stick frying pan and put in the onion, garlic, cabbage, sprouts and broccoli. Cook gently for about 15 minutes, until golden brown and softened. Add to the mashed potato and swede, together with the chopped parsley, and season well.

Form the mixture into 8 'cakes', transfer to a plate or tray, let them cool, then put them into the fridge for 1–2 hours.

When ready to cook, preheat the oven to 130°C/gas 1.

Have the polenta ready in a shallow bowl. Dip each cake in it to coat, shaking off any excess.

Heat 2 more tablespoons of the oil with the rest of the butter in a non-stick frying pan and fry the cakes in two batches, until golden brown on both sides and hot in the middle, putting the first batch into the oven to keep warm while you cook the second batch. Add a little more oil if necessary.

Meanwhile, heat the rest of the oil and fry the eggs to your liking. Serve on top of the bubble and squeak, with a good dollop of tomato ketchup and, if you like, some salad leaves, tossed in French dressing.

Notes on eggs

I love eggs – probably eat way too many of them, but a bunch of boiled eggs is lunch for me, quite often. They are such a wonderful, inexpensive source of protein. But an egg isn't just an egg. In my view, the stocking density for even free-range systems is too high. If you have 15,000 birds in a henhouse, you can encourage them to go outside all you like, but they are not going to be bothered to climb over 300 of their friends to get to the pop hole and go free ranging; they have food and water inside, why do they need to go anywhere else? As a result of the hen's inactivity and diet, the average supermarket egg has a pale yolk, and tastes quite bland and neutral. Whereas if a hen is outside the majority of the time, foraging and scratching around, eating grass and clover, plucking at insects, as it would do if you kept it in your back garden, then that egg will have a rich golden yolk, and a real flavour that many people have forgotten.

We have various breeds of hen, including the Blue Legbar, whose eggs are instantly recognisable because they have shells that are naturally coloured from blue through to turquoise to a pale khaki green, and we probably get fewer eggs per bird than many farmers, but the hens have over-sized ranges to run around and forage in, and spacious houses to shelter in at night. Then every few months the houses and runs are moved to new, fresh pasture, leaving behind naturally manured and nutrified ground for Jez's crops.

Richard Smith

Pan Haggerty with Mustard, Egg and Caper Mayonnaise

This makes a great winter brunch with a fried egg on top. Potatoes, onions and cheese are a great combination, and pan haggerty is the traditional Northumberland version of it, to which we add bacon, then serve it with some salad leaves tossed in French dressing, and a mustard and caper mayonnaise, so that the tartness of the dressing and the capers counters the richness of the cheese and bacon.

You want a quite silky-textured potato, such as Maris Piper or Desiree, for this.

700g potatoes (see introduction, above), peeled

50g butter

1 medium onion, finely chopped

75g smoked streaky bacon (or pancetta), chopped

2 cloves of garlic, finely chopped

150g Cheddar cheese, coarsely grated

2 tablespoons chopped fresh flat-leaf parsley

olive oil

4 small handfuls of mixed salad leaves

a splash of French dressing (see page 381)

For the mayonnaise:

2 eggs

150g mayonnaise

50g wholegrain mustard

50g capers

2 tablespoons chopped fresh flat-leaf parsley

sea salt and freshly ground black pepper

Preheat the oven to 180°C/gas 4.

Leaving the peeled potatoes whole, put them into a pan and cover with slightly salted cold water. Bring to the boil, then turn down the heat to a simmer and cook for about 15 minutes, until the potatoes are still firm and slightly undercooked. Drain in a colander and when cool enough to handle, grate them, coarsely, into a large mixing bowl.

While the potatoes are cooking, bring a medium pan of water to the boil and add a pinch of salt (this will make the eggs easier to peel). Gently lower in the eggs and

simmer for exactly 10 minutes. Take off the heat and rinse immediately in cold water to prevent discolouring, then peel the eggs and grate them roughly into a bowl. Add the mayonnaise, mustard, capers, parsley and seasoning and mix well. Keep in the fridge while you cook the pan haggerty.

Melt the butter in a small pan, then add the onion, bacon and garlic and cook gently until the onion is soft but not coloured. Take off the heat and cool a little, then mix into the grated potato, together with the cheese and chopped parsley, and season with salt and plenty of pepper.

Form the mixture into 4 cakes. Heat the oil in a non-stick frying pan that will transfer to the oven, then put in the cakes and gently brown them on each side. Transfer to the oven for about 10 minutes, until crisp on the outside and soft and cooked in the middle.

Serve each pan haggerty with a handful of salad leaves, tossed in the dressing, on top, and a spoonful of the mustard caper mayonnaise on the side.

Corned Beef Hash with Brown Sauce

This is a twist on the classic New York brunch dish, made with very English beef, and though it can be done with tinned corned beef, that tends to be a lot fattier. So the proportions here are really designed for the homemade corned brisket on page 262. You can eat the brisket hot one day, then shred what is left and set it in its cooking juices, mix with cooked potato, spice up with some Worcestershire and Tabasco sauces and fresh chilli, fry until golden, top with a fried egg and serve with brown sauce. Great for a lazy, late Sunday morning. Usually corned beef hash is made with cubed cooked potato, mixed with the beef and then fried loosely until crispy, whereas in our version we mix the chopped meat into mashed potato and form it into cakes before frying.

We make our own brown sauce and, if you want to do the same, there is a recipe on page 402.

750g corned beef (see page 262)	1 tablespoon Worcestershire sauce
500g potatoes, peeled and quartered	1 tablespoon chopped fresh flat-leaf parsley
sea salt and freshly ground black pepper	2–3 tablespoons plain flour
100g butter	2 tablespoons olive oil, plus a little extra for frying the eggs
2 onions, finely chopped	
¼ fresh red chilli, deseeded and finely chopped	6 eggs
a dash of Tabasco sauce, to taste	6 tablespoons brown sauce, to serve (for homemade, see page 402)

If the corned beef has been in the fridge, take it out and bring to room temperature.

Preheat the oven to 180°C/gas 4.

Put the potatoes into a pan and cover with cold, slightly salted water. Bring to the boil, then turn down the heat and simmer until just tender. Drain through a colander, then put into a large bowl and mash.

Chop the corned beef and mix with the mashed potato.

Heat half the butter in a small pan, then put in the onions and cook gently for 5 minutes, until softened. Mix into the potato and beef, along with the chilli, Tabasco, Worcestershire sauce, parsley and some salt and pepper.

Have the flour ready in a shallow bowl. Form the corned beef mixture into 6 round cakes and dust each with a little flour, shaking off the excess.

Heat the remaining butter with the olive oil in a frying pan and cook the cakes, in batches if necessary, over a medium heat until hot and golden brown on both sides. Lay them on a baking tray and put into the oven for 5 minutes, to heat right through to the middle.

Meanwhile heat some more olive oil in a separate frying pan and fry the eggs. Serve each cake with a fried egg on top and brown sauce on the side.

Smoked Mackerel Pâté with Daylesford Toasts

This is the ultimate, quick, easy, tasty pâté, traditionally served with light, crunchy toasts. Ours (which we also make for chicken Caesar salad, using seeded bread) are somewhere between thin crostini and classic melba toasts. Our version is made with sourdough bread, very thinly sliced, then brushed with olive oil (you can add a few thyme leaves if you like) and crisped in the oven.

700g smoked mackerel fillets, skin removed

200g crème fraîche

2 tablespoons chopped fresh flat-leaf parsley

juice of 1 lemon

a pinch of cayenne pepper

sea salt and freshly ground black pepper

1 small loaf of good bread

3 tablespoons olive oil

8 small handfuls of mixed salad leaves

3 tablespoons French dressing (see page 381)

2 lemons, cut into quarters

Put the mackerel fillets into a food processor and blend until smooth. Scoop out and put into a bowl. Add the crème fraîche, parsley, lemon juice and cayenne and mix together well, then taste and season as necessary. Spoon into six small serving pots or ramekins and put into the fridge to chill for at least 2 hours, or overnight.

When ready to serve, preheat the oven to 180°C/gas 4.

Cut the bread into wafer-thin slices – approximately 2mm thick – and lay them on a large baking tray. Drizzle each slice with a little olive oil and season with a pinch of salt and freshly ground black pepper. Bake for 6–8 minutes in the preheated oven until very crisp and golden brown. Leave to cool.

Toss the salad leaves lightly with the dressing and divide between six plates. Add a pot of chilled pâté and a wedge of lemon, and serve with a basket of the toasts.

Ham Hock Terrine with Piccalilli

Ham hocks – the 'ankle' of the pig – are often forgotten about, but they are wonderful and flavoursome. You just have to work a bit harder with them. We like to serve this terrine in the autumn, with the nicely matured piccalilli that was made from the summer glut of vegetables in the market garden, and some charred and toasted sourdough.

You need to start this a couple of days before you want to serve it, as the ham hocks need to be soaked for 24 hours, and the finished terrine will need to rest in the fridge overnight.

3 ham hocks	juice and zest of 1 lemon
2 heads of garlic	2 tablespoons capers, drained
3 sticks of celery, roughly chopped	2 tablespoons Dijon mustard
1 leek, roughly chopped	sea salt and freshly ground black pepper
2 carrots, roughly chopped	6 gelatine leaves
1 big bunch of fresh flat-leaf parsley, stalks and leaves chopped separately	12 tablespoons piccalilli (for homemade see page 390)

Soak the ham hocks in water for 24 hours, then drain and rinse them. Put them into a large pan and add enough fresh cold water to cover the ham by 5–7cm. Add the vegetables and parsley stalks. Bring to a simmer and cook for about 3 hours, until the ham is very tender, topping up with boiling water as necessary so that the liquid level doesn't drop below the top of the ham.

Lift out the hocks (reserving the cooking liquid) and flake the flesh, removing all the fat and gristle. Put into a bowl with the chopped parsley leaves, lemon juice and zest, capers and the mustard. Mix well and season.

Put the gelatine leaves into a bowl of ice-cold water until soft (the water must be cold or the gelatine will dissolve). Take out, squeeze, and put to one side.

Line a terrine tin with clingfilm and spoon in the ham mixture.

Strain the ham cooking liquid and measure 1.2 litres of it into a pan (top up with water if you do not have enough). Bring to the boil, then take off the heat and stir in the squeezed gelatine leaves, continuing to stir until completely dissolved. Leave to stand for 15 minutes, until tepid, then pour over the terrine so that all the ham is just covered.

Put into the fridge to chill overnight. When ready to serve, slice the terrine – this will be easiest with a sharp, serrated knife – and serve with the piccalilli.

Notes on tipples

Surrounded as we are at Daylesford by fruit from hedgerow to orchard, we can't resist using it in drinks as well as in our cooking, baking, bread-making and dairy produce. There is nothing better on a hot day than a glass of fresh lemonade, a fruit and wine cup, served from a big glass jug or bowl when friends come around; and we like to keep up the old English tradition of seasonal fruit liqueurs. Even when we put water carafes on the table, we like to fill them with long strips of cucumber, or a mix of cucumber, lemon slices and mint.

Lemon Refresher

This is a proper old-fashioned recipe. The Epsom salts and acids you can get in any chemist, and they are there to make a few bubbles and zing, in contrast to the more usual flat homemade lemonade.

Peel the rind from 5 large unwaxed lemons with a vegetable peeler, and put into a large earthenware bowl. Cut the lemons in half and squeeze the juice into the bowl, too. Add 800g caster sugar, 25g Epsom salts, 12g citric acid and 8g tartaric acid. Measure 1 litre of boiling water and pour over the top, then stir with a wooden spoon until all the sugar has dissolved. Cover the bowl with clingfilm and leave overnight in the fridge.

The next day, have ready two sterilised litre bottles (see page 388). Strain the liquid through a conical sieve into the bottles, seal and keep in the fridge (for up to a month). Serve over ice in tall glasses garnished with sprigs of fresh thyme.

Daylesford Summer Wine Cup

For a jugful big enough for about 12 glasses, you need 1 punnet of strawberries, stalks removed and halved; plus ½ a pineapple, skin cut off; 2 ripe peaches, stoned; 2 apples, cored, and 1 mango, peeled – all of these need to be chopped quite small (about 1cm). You also need a few extra halved strawberries, and some more neatly cut, small pieces of the other fruit, to garnish, plus about 12 sprigs of mint.

The Summer Wine Cup needs a little sugar syrup to sweeten it, but how much you put in is really up to you. The best thing to do is make up more than you need and then add a little at a time, until you are happy with the depth of sweetness. We make our syrup in the ratio of one part sugar to two parts water.

Make the sugar syrup first by putting 12 tablespoons sugar into a pan with 360ml of water and heating, stirring, until the sugar has dissolved and you have a clear syrup. Take off the heat and leave to cool.

Put all the fruit into a large bowl, then pour in 2 bottles of dry white wine, 2 tablespoons each of Maraschino (cherry) liqueur and Grand Marnier, and add your sugar syrup to taste. Put into the fridge for 48 hours, to marinate, then strain through a fine sieve into a large glass jug containing some ice. Add the fruit garnish and mint sprigs.

Seasonal Liqueurs

We make Blackcurrant Vodka, Plum Brandy and Sloe Gin as the fruit becomes available. For the sloe gin, the best time to pick the fruit is after the first frost, as the sloes will be a lot sweeter and will have more flavour.

All the liqueurs are made using the same method. We divide a litre of the appropriate alcohol between two large (2 litre) sterilised kilner jars (see page 388), together with the fruit (350g blackcurrants, washed and stalks removed, for the vodka, 660g plums or damsons for the brandy, and 450g sloes, washed and pricked, for the gin); and granulated sugar (200g for the vodka; 330g for the brandy, and 210g for the gin).

Then we seal the jars and leave them to stand in a cool, dark place (for example a garage) for 10 months, shaking the jars every month for the first 4 months to fully dissolve the sugar. After 10 months, we strain the liqueur through three layers of muslin cloth into a jug, then pour through a funnel into a sterilised bottle or bottles and seal, making sure this is airtight. The liqueur is now ready for drinking.

Venison Terrine with Tomato and Chilli Jam

This is a terrine that has the feel of autumn/winter about it. There is something about the pairing of juniper and venison that evokes winter woods and log fires. The addition of tomato and chilli jam makes a combination that is a big favourite of Rosie Henderson who, amongst her many roles at Daylesford, helps run the farmshop. 'Such an amazing mix of flavours,' she says. 'If you make the tomato and chilli jam (see page 399) when the tomatoes are at their best in the summer, the flavours will have softened out and mingled nicely by autumn, ready to serve alongside chunky slices of the terrine.'

Venison is one of the healthiest meats, with negligible fat content, but in order to keep the terrine moist you do need some fat, hence the pork belly.

125g butter, plus a little extra for greasing the terrine

2 shallots, finely chopped

2 cloves of garlic, chopped

200ml port

700g venison shoulder, chopped

550g pork belly, chopped

1 teaspoon freshly grated nutmeg

1 teaspoon ground ginger

3 juniper berries, crushed

70ml double cream

3 eggs, beaten

70g fresh breadcrumbs

sea salt and freshly ground black pepper

450g sliced smoked streaky bacon

12 tablespoons tomato and chilli jam (see page 399), to serve

12 slices of good toasted bread, preferably sourdough, to serve

Preheat the oven to 180°C/gas 4.

Melt the butter in a medium pan, add the shallots and garlic and cook gently over a low heat for 5 minutes, until slightly softened but not coloured. Add the port, bring to a simmer and bubble until reduced by half. Remove the pan from the heat and leave to cool.

In a food processor, using the pulse button, or with a hand mincer, mince the venison and pork together and transfer to a large bowl. Add the cooled onion mixture along with the spices, cream, eggs and breadcrumbs and season well. Before you put it into the terrine, you need to check the seasoning. Do this by frying a tiny piece of the mixture in a hot frying pan until the meat is cooked. Taste it, then season again accordingly.

Grease a terrine with a little butter and line it, widthways, with the bacon slices. Make sure each slice butts up against the previous one (you don't need to overlap the slices, or the bacon layer will be too thick). The slices need to overhang the edge of the terrine by about 7–8cm on either side, so if they are not long enough, use 2 slices, butted head on in the centre of the terrine.

Carefully spoon in the terrine mixture and fold the overhanging slices of bacon over the top. This time, you do need to overlap the ends slightly, as the top of the terrine will be subjected to the highest heat, and the slices will shrink and pull apart otherwise. Cover the top of the terrine with foil, put it into a roasting tin and fill the tin with enough hot water to come halfway up the outside of the terrine, creating a bain-marie.

Put into the preheated oven for 1¾ hours, until cooked through. To test, run the cold tap over a metal skewer, so that it is very cold. Insert into the centre of the terrine, leave it there for 5 seconds, then quickly remove it and carefully press it to the back of your hand. If the skewer is still cold, the terrine is not ready. If the skewer is warm, it is ready. If the skewer is about to burn your hand, then the terrine is overcooked. Leave to rest and cool down for 1 hour so that the heat from the outside of the terrine transfers to the centre, resulting in even cooking throughout. Once cold, put into the fridge for 24 hours.

To serve, slice the terrine and serve with the tomato and chilli jam and a basket of the toasted bread.

SOUPS

Summer in a bowl of refreshing pea and mint
or tomato and cucumber
Detox broth bursting with ginger and fresh herbs
Earthy beetroot and bacon
Autumnal celeriac and orchard apples
Comforting butternut squash with honey and sage
A minestrone for all seasons

Soup is one of our favourite ways of celebrating the calendar in the market garden: chunky, quite substantial root vegetable soups for winter; blended ones, made with tomatoes, greens and herbs, which can be chilled, for summer.

The truth is that, like any dish, you can only get out of a soup what you put in, so it is all about choosing really fresh ingredients, rather than treating the soup-pot as a home for tired old vegetables. So soups always begin with Jez, who will come into the kitchen laden with whatever is in abundance in the market garden and say: 'There you are: I've done your menu for you.'

Unless you are making something like a minestrone, which is all about using chunks of a medley of different vegetables, the secret is to keep to two or three key flavours, so that rather than ending up with something indistinct, you really taste every ingredient.

Notes on soup

The smaller you can chop your vegetables the better – about 1cm – rather than leaving them in big chunks, as this allows the soup to cook more quickly and keep its flavour, goodness and colour. Also, if the pieces are to stay whole, rather than be blended, as in a minestrone, when you put your spoon into the bowl you want to scoop up a good selection in one go. Although it might seem tedious, try to cut pieces all of the same size, too, so they cook evenly.

Take care when you use celery in a soup – don't be tempted to put masses in, unless of course you are making celery soup – and be especially careful not to let it cook for too long, because it becomes quite pungent and overpowering. My grandfather always had a pot of soup simmering on the stove, and all I remember when I went into the kitchen was the smell of celery! Even if I were to make a celery soup, I would put in something potent that could stand up to the flavour and break it up a little: like cubes of blue cheese crumbled in at the end.

Soup needs a good stock. If you just use water you don't get the same depth of flavour. For years we used our rich chicken stock for all the soups, but more and more people like the lightness of a vegetable stock, so we will make a big pot of it from around a dozen or more different vegetables from the garden. Vegetable stock, especially, is such an easy thing to make at home, and a great way to use up that couple of carrots, lone leek, or wedge of butternut squash. You can make plenty, then freeze it in bags or ice-cube trays (see pages 416–18 for stock recipes).

Earthy root vegetables like beetroot and carrot quite often need a little sharpness to give them a lift. More often than not a dash of lemon juice is a good way of bringing out your flavours (in any soup, really) even more: you won't taste it specifically, but it will add a little extra zing. And when you season your soup with salt and pepper before serving, do this gradually, especially with the salt. Taste a spoonful, add a little cautious seasoning, stir the soup, leave it for a minute or so, taste it and season lightly again if necessary. Do this a few times, tasting three or four spoonfuls until you are happy. It is always advisable to go easier on the seasoning than you might do for a sauce, as you will only be eating a little of this, along with other elements on the plate. Remember you are going to be eating a whole bowlful of soup, and it is very easy to taste just a spoonful, season the soup, think it is fine, then find that, towards the end of the bowl, the cumulative effect is making it taste too salty.

John Hardwick

Chilled Pea and Mint

This is the simplest of soups to celebrate summer. It is lovely to make when you have fresh peas; however, all the podding does take time, and there is absolutely nothing wrong with a pea that has been frozen as soon as it is picked – in fact, when it comes to soups and purées, frozen peas can be preferable, as they give you that really intense bright, summery green colour.

Andy Wheeler, our soup and casserole guru, who makes this soup in small batches in the Black Barn to sell in the farmshop, reckons that this is also lovely eaten hot.

600ml good vegetable stock (see page 416)

750g frozen or fresh peas

200ml double cream

juice of ½ a lemon

2 tablespoons chopped fresh mint leaves, plus extra to garnish

sea salt and freshly ground black pepper

a little extra virgin olive oil to serve (optional)

Bring the stock to the boil in a medium-sized pan and add the peas. Bring back to the boil, then remove from the heat and stir in the cream, lemon juice and mint.

Liquidise until smooth, then taste and season with salt and pepper.

Cool and put into the fridge until chilled. Serve in chilled bowls and, if you like, drizzle with a little olive oil, and scatter with the mint leaves.

Chilled Tomato, Cucumber and Fennel

Everything in this summer garden soup is raw, but as well as the bright, fresh flavours, the pleasure comes from the different textures. Some of the tomatoes are blended with the oil and vinegar, and the cucumber, fennel, pepper and celery are chopped finely and mixed through to lend a nice crunch in amongst the softness. This is one occasion when it is really worth taking the time to cut all the vegetables into small cubes – about half a centimetre – as not only will it make the soup look its best, but the idea is that everyone spoons up a delicate sprinkling of each vegetable in every mouthful, rather than suddenly coming across a huge chunk of fennel or celery.

You want really sweet cherry tomatoes. Gardener's Delight are easily accessible ones, but throughout the summer Jez sends the kitchens heritage tomatoes in every shape and colour from the market garden – so sometimes the soup will be very red, at other times more orangey – but it really doesn't matter, as it's all about the flavour.

800ml tomato passata

150g cherry tomatoes roughly chopped, plus 4 ripe red vine cherry tomatoes, chopped small (about 0.5cm)

6 tablespoons olive oil

2 tablespoons balsamic vinegar

juice of ½ a lemon

¼ of a fresh red chilli, deseeded and finely chopped

1 clove of garlic, crushed

1 teaspoon sugar

1 cucumber, deseeded and chopped small (about 0.5cm)

1 fennel bulb, chopped small (about 0.5cm)

½ a red pepper, deseeded and chopped small (about 0.5cm)

½ a yellow pepper, deseeded and chopped small (about 0.5cm)

½ a green pepper, deseeded and chopped small (about 0.5cm)

1 stick of celery, chopped small (about 0.5cm)

2 tablespoons chopped fresh flat-leaf parsley

3 tablespoons shredded fresh coriander

sea salt and freshly ground black pepper

a little extra virgin olive oil

In a large jug, combine the passata, roughly chopped tomatoes, olive oil, balsamic vinegar, lemon juice, chilli, garlic and sugar with 500ml water. Pour into a blender – in two batches if necessary – and blend until smooth.

Mix the rest of the chopped vegetables and tomatoes together in a large bowl, pour the blended tomato mixture over them and put into the fridge to chill for 1–2 hours.

Just before serving, chill six bowls.

Take the soup out of the fridge, stir in the parsley and coriander, taste and season as necessary, then serve in the chilled bowls, drizzled with a little extra virgin olive oil.

Beetroot, Bacon and Crème Fraîche

One of our award-winning soups, almost psychedelic in its vibrant pinkness. It is one for the autumn, when the big winter beetroots are around, and their earthiness combines beautifully with the smokiness of the bacon and the crème fraîche, which has a little more acidity than cream, so adds a touch of sharpness, but also some sweetness, and gives the soup a lift, drawing out the flavour of the beetroot rather than adding richness.

We use vegetable oil in this, as the bacon needs to be crisped up first, before the vegetables are added, and vegetable oil holds up at a higher heat better than olive oil.

This is another favourite of Andy Wheeler, who makes it all the time in the Black Barn, and is a big fan of beetroot: 'It's a vegetable that is not used nearly enough,' he reckons. 'Beetroot and smoky bacon are two ingredients that are made for each other, and the crème fraîche at the finish gives it a nice smoothness. I often make this soup at home on a Saturday lunchtime and we have it with bread that I bake in the morning. My daughter loves it, and for one Christmas lunch with the family I even served it as a starter and put in some scallops, quickly seared in a pan, with some strips of grilled smoked bacon on top. John Hardwick looked at me in horror when I mentioned the combination of scallops and beetroot – but it was really good!'

2 tablespoons vegetable oil

150g smoked streaky bacon, finely chopped

2 onions, finely chopped

500g raw beetroot, peeled and chopped

juice of ½ a lemon

1 sprig of fresh thyme, leaves only

1 litre good chicken stock (see page 417)

100g crème fraîche

sea salt and freshly ground black pepper

Heat the oil in a large pan (one that has a lid), add the bacon and sauté until golden brown.

Add the onions, reduce the heat, put the lid on the pan and cook for about 10 minutes until softened.

Add the beetroot and continue to cook, with the lid on, over a medium to low heat for another 10 minutes, stirring to prevent sticking.

Add the lemon juice, thyme leaves and stock and bring to the boil, then reduce the heat and simmer with the lid on for about 25 minutes.

Add the crème fraîche and bring back to the boil, then remove from the heat. Liquidise, taste and season as necessary before serving.

Chicken (or Turkey), Ginger and Vegetable

This is a great detox broth that really feels as though it is doing you good. It is a handy recipe for making a day or so after you have roasted a chicken, as you can turn the carcass into stock, and shred any slivers of leftover meat into the soup. It is also perfect to make with turkey for Boxing Day. We put it on the menu in January, and people love it after the indulgence of Christmas.

You can put in the vegetables in any proportion you prefer – and if you don't have them all it doesn't matter, but the greater the mixture the more flavoursome, and healthier, the broth will be.

If you want to make turkey stock, crush the carcass with your hands, to break the bones, and put them into a large pan with 2 large white onions, peeled and halved; 2 carrots, peeled and halved; 2 heads of unpeeled garlic, just cut in half; a small bunch of fresh thyme; and a tablespoon each of peppercorns and sea salt. Cover with cold water, bring to the boil, then reduce the heat to a simmer, and skim off any grease and scum on the surface. Then simmer gently for 2–3 hours.

2.5 litres good chicken stock (see page 417) or turkey stock	500g cooked chicken or turkey meat, torn into thin strips
400g shredded mix of red onion, carrots, cabbage, leeks, celeriac or celery, and kale	sea salt and freshly ground black pepper
	3 tablespoons chopped fresh flat-leaf parsley
about 2cm fresh root ginger, finely chopped	2 tablespoons chopped fresh chervil

Bring the stock to the boil, add all the prepared vegetables and the ginger, and simmer for about 5 minutes, until all the vegetables are soft. Add the chicken or turkey and bring back to the boil, then take off the heat.

Taste and adjust the seasoning as necessary, and sprinkle with the herbs before serving.

Celeriac and Apple

Celeriac and apples are harvested at the same time in autumn, and they make a classic combination. You want a tart, full-flavoured apple, such as a Cox, or look for Bountiful, which Jez calls a nearly-cooking variety, which sweetens by October to suit dishes like this.

300g good, tart eating apples, see above

juice of 2 lemons

50g butter

500g celeriac, peeled and chopped

1 litre good chicken or vegetable stock (see pages 417 and 416)

150ml double cream

sea salt and freshly ground black pepper

Peel, core and chop the apples and put them into a bowl with the lemon juice.

Heat the butter in a large pan (one that has a lid) over a low heat until melted, then add the celeriac, put the lid on the pan and cook over a medium heat for 10 minutes, without letting the celeriac colour, stirring occasionally.

Add the apples and lemon juice, put the lid back on and cook for a further 5 minutes.

Add the stock and the cream and bring to the boil, then turn down to a simmer for about 10 minutes, or until the celeriac and apples are soft.

Liquidise, taste and season as necessary before serving.

Squash and Smoked Haddock Chowder

We serve this with grilled sourdough bread.

500ml good vegetable stock (see page 416)

1 thick 300g fillet of smoked haddock, skinned and boned

½ a red chilli, seeds removed

3 tablespoons butter

1 medium onion, chopped

½ a leek, roughly chopped

1 stick of celery, chopped (about 1cm)

1 clove of garlic, finely chopped

½ a small squash (peeled, halved and deseeded), cut into bite-size chunks

200ml milk

2 tablespoons cream

2 tablespoons chopped fresh parsley

sea salt and freshly ground black pepper

Pour the stock into a pan, bring to a simmer and drop in the fillet of haddock, together with the chilli. Simmer for 5 minutes, remove the pan from the heat and allow to cool slightly, then lift out the haddock and flake it. Strain the stock into a bowl and discard the chilli.

Melt the butter in a large pan (one that has a lid) and add the chopped onion, leek, celery and garlic. Cook over a medium heat for 5 minutes, until the onion is soft, but not coloured. Add the squash, then cover and continue to cook for a further 10 minutes, stirring occasionally. Add the stock, then bring to a simmer and cook for a further 10 minutes, until the liquid has reduced by half and the squash is starting to break up slightly.

Add the milk, cream and flaked haddock, bring back to a simmer again, then add the parsley. Taste and season as necessary, adding plenty of black pepper, and serve.

Butternut Squash, Honey and Sage

Another award-winning soup. John Hardwick reckons
this is his all-time favourite: 'Very rich – so you don't need
to serve enormous bowls of it – fantastically smooth and
silky, with a great colour and just the right element of
sweetness.'

Of the readily available squashes, you can't beat
butternut, which is full of flavour and has the right
texture and vibrant colour, whereas some varieties
have disappointingly dull-looking flesh. Of the heritage
squashes Crown Prince is also good, but avoid pumpkin
for this, as the flesh tends to be more watery.

80g butter	150ml double cream
1kg butternut squash, peeled, deseeded and chopped	juice of ½ a lemon
	75g honey
1 teaspoon sea salt	2 tablespoons finely chopped fresh sage
1.1 litres good chicken stock (see page 417)	freshly ground black pepper

Melt the butter in a large pan (one that has a lid) over a
low heat, then add the squash and salt. Cover with the lid
and sweat for 10 minutes over a low heat, until softened
but not browned.

Add the stock and the cream, turn up the heat and bring
to the boil, then turn down to a simmer for 5 minutes, or
until the squash is cooked through and soft.

Add the lemon juice, honey and sage, bring back to the
boil, then remove from the heat.

Liquidise, taste and season as necessary before serving.

Ten Vegetable and Two Grain Minestrone

You can make a version of minestrone all year round, with different combinations of vegetables – though it is good to keep to the base of carrot, onion, celery and courgette. The recipe below is one for late summer/autumn, when the swede and squash are in season together, but in high summer you can replace these with fresh peas, broad beans and green beans – it doesn't have to be exactly ten vegetables.

'There's a lot going on in this soup; there's nothing half-hearted about it,' says Black Barn chef Andy Wheeler, who makes small batches of it for sale in the farmshop. 'Because of the profusion of different vegetables, you want to have a taste of as many as possible in every mouthful, along with a little chicken and chorizo, so try to chop everything, including the meat, as neatly as you can, and quite small – about 1cm (this also allows the small cubes of chicken to cook through quickly).'

3 tablespoons pearled spelt

3 tablespoons pearl barley

1 tablespoon olive oil

½ a medium white onion, chopped

1 clove of garlic, finely chopped

sea salt and freshly ground black pepper

raw meat from 2 small chicken thighs, chopped

1 small cooking chorizo (about 100g), chopped

½ a small carrot, chopped

½ a stick of celery, chopped

¼ of a small swede, chopped

about 70g butternut squash or pumpkin, chopped

1 tablespoon tomato paste

¼ of a fresh red chilli, finely chopped

½ teaspoon smoked paprika

1 tablespoon plain flour

1 teaspoon fresh thyme leaves

1.3 litres good chicken stock (see page 417)

500g tinned chopped tomatoes

¼ of a small leek, chopped

½ a small courgette, chopped

2 kale or cabbage leaves, thinly shredded

a dash of red wine vinegar

½ teaspoon sugar

Put the spelt and pearl barley into a pan and cover with cold water. Bring to a simmer and cook for about 30 minutes, until the grains are tender, then drain in a colander and keep to one side.

Heat the olive oil in a large pan (one that has a lid), put in the onion and garlic, season with a little salt and cook for about 5 minutes over a low heat, until the onion is softened but not coloured. Add the chicken, chorizo, carrot, celery, swede and squash, put the lid on and continue to cook for a further 5 minutes.

Add the tomato paste, chilli, paprika, flour and thyme leaves and cook for a further 2 minutes, then add the chicken stock and tinned tomatoes. Bring to a simmer, then add the rest of the ingredients and cook for 5 more minutes, until all the vegetables are tender. Taste and adjust the seasoning, adding plenty of black pepper.

Leek and Potato

A very British, very comforting classic that will always be a part of the Daylesford repertoire – especially as leeks are a vegetable that thrives in the market garden. Around March/April they are young and tender and perfect for this soup, combined with floury potatoes, such as King Edwards or Cara, which will break down well in the stock.

It is a very simple soup, but because of that it can either be really satisfying, or bland and gloopy, if you use too much potato over leek, or leave it cooking for too long, so that it stews and looks rather grey and you miss the slightly peppery sharpness of the leeks coming through. Some people insist on only using the white of the leeks, but we don't believe in throwing away the green parts, which also help to keep the soup looking fresh and green. So we use plenty of both colours, chopped finely, and if the potatoes are also cut small, the leeks will hold their colour in the short time that the potato takes to cook. Because the ratio of each vegetable is so important in this case, the quantity of potato is given as a weight, rather than a rough number of potatoes.

In the café we often finish the soup with some grated mature Cheddar – a couple of tablespoons per bowl – and it really benefits from a good few twists of black pepper before serving. In the Black Barn, Andy Wheeler and his team make a version with the Cheddar actually blended into it. 'It gives a different sensation,' says Andy, 'because the cheese and soup emulsify and you get the Cheddar flavour right the way through. Just add a handful or so of grated cheese, to your taste, when you liquidise the soup.'

80g butter	500g leeks, finely chopped
2 onions, peeled and chopped	1.4 litres good vegetable stock (see page 416)
3 cloves of garlic, sliced	150ml double cream
2 teaspoons fresh thyme leaves	sea salt and plenty of freshly ground black pepper
200g potatoes, peeled and chopped (see above)	mature Cheddar cheese, grated, to serve (optional)

Melt the butter in a large pan (one that has a lid) over a low heat, then add the onions, garlic and thyme leaves. Put the lid on the pan and cook gently for about 5 minutes, until the onions have softened, stirring occasionally.

Add the potatoes and cook for a further 5 minutes with the lid on, then add the leeks and continue cooking slowly, still with the lid on, until the vegetables have softened.

Add the stock and the cream, bring to the boil, then turn down to a simmer and cook for 10 minutes.

Liquidise, taste and season as necessary before serving, with grated Cheddar if you like, and an extra twist or two of black pepper.

'Funny old things seasons . . .'
Jez Taylor, The Market Garden

When you grow fruit and vegetables, you seem to be forever saying, 'That was a funny old season,' because seasons generally are . . . crops might be early or late, magnificent or spoilt by some freak of weather. There is always some new challenge, so, particularly when you farm organically, you are constantly discovering and adapting. In the five years since I arrived at Daylesford we have extended the market garden from eight to twenty acres, because ultimately we are trying to be as self-sufficient and diverse in our growing as it is possible to be. We want to concentrate on interesting, often heritage crops that have to be grown and harvested by hand and that suit our 'terroir' – sounds a bit pretentious, doesn't it? But that is what growing, and especially organic growing, is all about: understanding and evolving a particular piece of ground, learning over time what grows best there; and nurturing the soil, preserving the micro-organisms, so that you leave the land in a good state to endure seasonal extremes, and for future generations.

In reality what we have at Daylesford isn't naturally the kind of prime, horticultural growing land that the big specialists in East Anglia have. There it is all flat fields, very consistent terrain, quite peaty, rich soils, so it is easy to plan, plant, manage, hoe and harvest mechanically with all their specialist kit. We have land that isn't flat, that has quite a lot of wind blowing through; we have mixed soils, and we harvest by hand.

The farm is on the site of an ancient river bed, and so there are river pebbles everywhere. It was a big, meandering river, so there are patches of field which are very sandy, others quite sticky clay, and there are significant dips which can flood and become boggy. Then on the slopes around, we have the traditional limestone shale normally associated with the Cotswolds. If you have waterlogged ground, a lot of the goodness will be washed out, much of the microbial, earthworm activity is knocked out, and if you keep going at it, rotovating it or driving on it, it becomes compacted, and suffers even more: which of course is the antithesis of the whole ethos of looking after the soil.

So when you have ground that can be quite vulnerable, you have to find your niche and celebrate and emphasise the crops that thrive, and that we can do brilliantly. Of course we can grow things like carrots, parsnips and potatoes well here, but we don't want to do things just because we can; we want to make a song and dance about crops that we are really good at, like specialist leaves and herbs, heritage tomatoes, soft fruit, such as goose-berries, blackberries, jostaberries, plums and particularly strawberries; leafy things like kale, spinach and chard, or purple sprouting broccoli; and the whole allium family: onions, garlic and leeks. We are brilliant at leeks. In a good year, we have 40–50,000 of them, pert and gorgeous, bang on the money, that we will harvest over a good nine months.

When I arrived here there was an asparagus bed, but it is hard to control the slugs, asparagus beetle and perennial weeds such as couch grass and creeping buttercup – and it only really makes sense if you are a specialist. We like to celebrate local food as well as what we can grow ourselves – so it is better for us to sell beautiful English asparagus from the nearby Vale of Evesham in the farmshop, when it comes into season, than battle to try and grow some of our own.

What we are doing here is exactly what I would do myself if I had my own smallholding

– just on a much bigger scale. My background is in the kind of 'rational peasantry' which, historically in the country, meant that local people would cultivate a bit of land, growing whatever they could, do a bit of haymaking, harvesting, beating, foraging, and generally accumulate as many skills as possible in order to survive and turn a buck.

I was born on Jersey, where my father worked for the Ministry of Agriculture, helping to develop outdoor tomatoes and early potatoes. Then my parents bought an old farmshop in Cleeve Prior, near the Vale of Evesham, and tried growing everything from sweetcorn to raspberries, before they stumbled across the idea of making hanging baskets, and turned the farm into a highly successful hanging basket nursery. I was always interested in growing, and food but, because I was good at science, for a mad moment I thought I wanted to be a food technologist, until I started study-ing the subject at Reading University, and it seemed to be principally about incorporating cheap ingredients into processed food and advertising it well. So I went back to horti-culture.

After I finished my degree, I rented two walled gardens near Reading for ten years where I grew specialist salad leaves and vegetables for restaurants and farmers' markets, developed a box scheme and set up my own business making cider and apple juice in Cleeve Prior, then selling it in Reading, as well as doing a bit of tree surgery and willow work. Once, when I was growing up, my father made a vast amount of apple juice, which was kept in the garage and went fizzier and fizzier and then sour, because we couldn't drink it all, but it was a formative moment for me, because it taught me you could do something amazing with unwanted apples. There used to be around 2,000 acres of apple, perry pear and

plum orchards in Victorian times in the Vale of Evesham, and though so many had been grubbed up and lost, some of the small farms still had fruit trees. So I would go around them all and say, 'Can I have your apples?' and they would either give them to me for free, or trade them for juice or cider. Eventually I became quite snobbish and only wanted to get my fruit from old, wild orchards. I also started grafting fruit trees, and so my legacy in Cleeve Prior is some 300 cider apple trees planted around my parents' nursery.

When the opportunity came up to be head gardener at Daylesford in 2008 I was doing a consultancy for the Eden Project in Cornwall, helping to develop a market garden there, and the timing was just right. It doesn't matter whether you are growing on a small scale or a big one, you can still be romantic about the opportunity to grow organic, diverse and sea-sonal food, hands-on, using age-old skills; to build your own team around you and be part of a traditional mixed farming system, with animals, the creamery and the bakery. And it is great to work closely with chefs whose skill is in pulling off brilliance with simple fresh produce, and who appreciate the value of turning gluts into preserves to use for the rest of the year.

And then, a year after I started at Daylesford, by some sort of serendipity, an orchard just happened to become available a couple of miles up the road, planted with different cider apple varieties, and with its own cider-making shed and press. So I sold up my cider business in Cleeve Prior, and now we make local Cotswold cider for Daylesford. In a day at the orchard we can make 1,000 litres. Once it has fermented to cider, at least ten months later, it is bottled and a small amount of sugar is added – the equivalent of a level teaspoon per bottle – which balances the acidity. And it is carbonated, which is the way most people want to drink cider.

Making cider is such a simple thing to do, but it feels bio-regionally right to use apples that would otherwise go to waste, from this 'terroir', and produce a drink with local characteristics that is really contemporary and very enjoyable. I think it goes with everything, and I use it instead of white wine when I am cooking.

An organic market garden is all about the diversity and safety of your food supply. Inevitably you are vulnerable to the vagaries of the weather, the temperature, too much rain, too little rain, but when you grow as many different crops and varieties as you can sustain, if one fails, you always have something else to fall back on. That way we don't suffer in 'funny old seasons' in the way that specialists can do.

Diversity also means that terrible weather conditions for one crop can create a window of opportunity to work on something else – for example in 2012 we had the best tomatoes ever. We grow around 2,000 plants in thirty different varieties, many of them heritage: black, green, yellow, orange, stripy; bell-shaped, pear-shaped, plum-shaped . . . and in that summer we harvested about 4 tonnes partly as a result of an awful, rainy strawberry season, when we couldn't pick the berries in July because it was too wet. Instead we used the time to take off all the leafy side-shoots from the tomato plants in the tunnels, so without these sapping energy from the plants, all their efforts went into flowering and the subsequent, fantastic fruit. Bad seasons can teach you good lessons.

We regularly take on Soil Association apprentices and trainees – my assistant, Kate, who is an absolute star, started as an apprentice – and it is great to be able to show young people a rich, diverse and fascinating food culture, and teach skills that are in danger of being lost, in case there comes a time when communities have to fall back on them: rational peasantry again. We never have idle hands. In agriculture it is very easy to become a cog in the machine of a big operation producing for the supermarkets and doing something mind-numbingly repetitive every day, but here there is always something different happening and new things to learn.

Before Christmas a few years ago the whole farm was covered in a foot of snow, so there was very little that we could do in the gardens. But we have a little willow plantation, so we fashioned big wreaths from willow and foraged around the estate for leaves and berries. The wreaths were so successful that now we make them every year. Once the cider is made, we have the wreath-making . . . and so the cycle goes on.

Growing crops is all about food for me. Of course it is, you might think, but if you were working in a big agricultural packhouse day in, day out, you might not make that same connection. All the things I grow I want to cook and eat – especially the whole squash and pumpkin family. We concentrate on the best culinary ones that are valued for their tasty flesh, in soups, roasted in chunks on their own or in a risotto, rather than the more spectacular Halloween varieties. The secret with squash is to store them in nice warm, airy conditions, then you can keep them right through to April/May. In an ideal world I would like a nice specialist squash and pumpkin store, similar

to the cheese room, where I could keep the humidity out – one day, maybe. Often I will make a big vegetable soup using squash at the beginning of the week, which will turn into a base for a spicy curry on another day.

What I love to grow and eat most, though – and what I am really known for – are unusual salad leaves. In my family salad is a meal in itself: the base will be mixed leaves, chopped up a little, then lots of bean sprouts, which are very easy to produce. I have a kilner jar next to the sink, and I put some mung beans, alfalfa or green lentils in the bottom, fill the jar with water, then leave them to soak overnight. The next day I close the jar, but without the rubber seal, so there is a gap for the water to run out. Then I lay the jar on its side, so the water can drain into the sink. I just flush the jar two or three times a day with fresh water and let it drain away, because the only thing that is not good for sprouts is to let them sit in a container full of water. Within a few days I'll have a jarful of sprouts.

To my leaves and sprouts in my salad bowl I'll add some red onion that has been finely chopped and steeped in cider vinegar for twenty-five minutes, to take out some of the bitterness. Then I'll roast some seeds in a dry pan: pumpkin in first, as they are the biggest, then sunflower, and when the pumpkin seeds start to pop, I put in some sesame seeds. When they start to turn golden I take the pan off the heat and mix the seeds with a little tamari (Japanese soy sauce), which gives a savouriness when you add the mix to the salad. Then there will be something like chopped cauliflower, grated carrot or finely chopped red cabbage for crunch and juiciness, and perhaps some chopped olives.

The dressing might be olive oil, balsamic vinegar, lots of garlic and chilli tomato jam (see recipe on page 399). I'll finish with some feta or toasted tofu for my wife Jo, who doesn't eat meat, and for myself and the children, some salami, or perhaps pieces of roasted meat from Sunday lunch. Whatever else I make – whether it is big Spanish omelettes, risotto, or shepherd's pie, there will pretty much always be a big salad on the side.

Every year we increase the number of salad leaves that we grow: outside in summer, and inside in the six tunnels in winter – though even into January we can still be harvesting 40 per cent of salad leaves, such as mustard, rocket and endive, outside; as well as those in the tunnels, all of which are unheated, but give natural warmth and protection. When you grow organically you always have to establish a four-year rotation, so that you don't have the same crop in the same location more than once every four years, which helps improve the structure of the soil, lowers the risk of disease and helps with pest control. So the leaves, like all the crops that we grow, are organised in families. Then we can create a rotation of brassica leaves, mustards and rocket; lettuce; endive, herbs, etc.

The key to growing winter salad leaves is to get the plants in the ground in the tunnels early so they have time to develop a good root system. The growing season is principally the period of time between the clocks changing, from the end of March to the end of October. If you suddenly think, 'Winter salads, must do something,' in mid-September, it is too late, but if you plant in mid-August, you can keep harvesting the leaves for six months, cutting a few leaves from each plant, and leaving behind the little rosettes in the centre, from where new leaves will grow. Then in April, the leaves come out in all but one of the tunnels (which we keep for delicate salads like rocket and mizuna). Within three weeks we will have moved from winter production to summer production and done all the tunnel planting of summer herbs like parsley, basil and coriander, and fruiting crops, such as tomatoes, chillies and cucumbers. I favour small, more European-style cucumbers, which we have learned to grow really well, and they produce little yellow star-shaped flowers, smaller than courgette flowers, which we harvest for the chef's 'bling'.

Because we can never cultivate right to the edge of the tunnels, we use up what would otherwise be wasted space by building raised beds, where we grow micro-leaves, like Red Frills mustard, and really peppery land cress, with amazingly pretty leaves, which look a bit like crayfish tails and which the chefs love. Around late February we have the greatest variety of leaves of all, everything from butterhead lettuce to radicchio, and Japanese mustards like mizuna and mibuna.

Because I think that a salad needs a touch of bitterness to get the tastebuds going, I love endive, but I know some people object to it because of the bitterness. However, that intensity of flavour is a response to UV rays, so the great thing about winter endive is that it doesn't develop the bitter taste as much. It calms down and is actually pretty sweet.

Every year we invest in more fruit bushes and trees, the most recent being rows of cherry trees, as I wanted a fruit for the kitchens to use that would be ripe after the strawberries have finished and before the blackberries and raspberries.

Raspberries are a tricky fruit, because picking them is very time-consuming and tedious, as the fruit is very soft and bunched together – whereas strawberries are so much easier. People love our strawberries, because we are one of a handful of growers that raise the plants outside in the ground. Ninety per cent of strawberry farms use growbags on tabletops in tunnels – but we want to celebrate a sense of place: 'terroir' again. All our plants – around 22,000 of them – are grown in the soil and we have six different varieties, which means that the season is extended naturally and the picking is spread out from early June to late July. In theory, that is. If you get a cold, wet, 'funny old season', of course that doesn't work and everything comes through together – but as I constantly say, in a diverse market garden there is always something else that can be done on the days when picking is impossible, whereas if you are a specialist grower, you suffer much more.

For me, the perfect strawberry shouldn't be all sweetness, you need some acidity, but mainly it has to be ripe. That is what we specialise in: ripe strawberries. It sounds obvious, but if you pick a strawberry when it is orange, it will last for a week in a display cabinet, but never become truly ripe, whereas when we pick ours, they are properly red, and will last for only about two days.

Our varieties are Honeoye, Alice, Fenella, Symphony, Christine and Cambridge Favourite, which I used to think was a great strawberry, very disease-resistant, but it can be quite soft – good for jam, though – and we make lots of jam. Our favourite these days is Honeoye, which comes through early, and is just the right size. It gets redder and redder and sweeter and sweeter, producing fruit which stays compact, even in a wet season, for the whole of June, before the likes of Symphony and Fenella take over in July.

Beyond the Summer Solstice Garden – where we give demonstrations in growing and cooking, and show off some of our skills, such as willow work – and beyond the composting area, are the propagation tunnels where Kate painstakingly records all the details of every seed that we sow.

Whenever possible, when you are trying to garden sustainably, you save seeds, and we have had success with some varieties of peas and climbing and borlotti beans. Plants like the fancy frilly mustards are also good to let go to flower and save the seeds, but seed-saving isn't always straightforward. Squash and courgettes, for example, are very promiscuous and can cross-pollinate with other plants, which might result in 'rogue' types. So we buy many of our heritage varieties from a small company who specialise in old varieties of seeds that grow particularly well in our climate.

The world of propagation is all about nurturing plants slowly from seed and gradually moving them through various stages of being kept warm and covered to the environment in which they end up growing, so that it isn't a shock to them – so the propagation tunnels are very exciting places. It doesn't matter how many years you have been growing fruit and vegetables, it is still magical when on a cold February day you sow the seeds of spring onions, chillies, peppers, tomatoes and herbs, and over the space of a weekend the tiny plants suddenly appear.

SALADS

Peaches and mozzarella
Griddled courgettes with cooling minted yoghurt
Tomatoes in rainbow colours
Crunchy ribbons of raw vegetables
A flurry of seeds, nuts, grains and fresh
garden herbs

Substantial salads that are either starters or meals in themselves are a huge feature of the kitchen menu at Daylesford. We build them up around seasonal produce from the market garden, and while some of them take a little bit of work, others are very simple.

More than the rest of the menu, the salads tend to reflect a touch of the Mediterranean or Asia in amongst the home-grown ingredients, since the British salad tradition is not that strong. It isn't so long ago that a salad in most homes featured little other than lettuce, cucumber, tomatoes, and perhaps some hard-boiled egg and spring onions, if you were lucky. The British climate hasn't traditionally been conducive to a huge repertoire of salads; however, in recent decades people have been looking for healthier, lighter food, and so will choose a creative, interesting salad over other dishes, particularly for lunch.

Salads love herbs: lots and lots of them, so even though the recipes might suggest half a bunch, don't hold back – a big flurry of freshly chopped herbs, some gently folded in and the rest scattered over a salad, is what gives that wonderful burst of freshness, flavour and colour from the first forkful.

Broad Bean, Bulgar Wheat and Herb

The first broad beans are harvested around the second week of June and will be small and very tender, and although the vivid green colour looks fantastic if you slip off the skins once you have cooked them, this can be quite fiddly – so if you don't have time, don't worry, the flavour will be just as good. By the end of the season the beans will be quite big and easier to skin, but their flavour will be beginning to be slightly bitter. So the optimum time is mid-season, when the beans are medium size, quite tender, not bitter, and not too hard to skin.

sea salt and freshly ground black pepper

225g bulgar wheat

400g freshly podded baby broad beans

½ a cucumber

½ a medium red onion, finely chopped

½ a plump red chilli, finely chopped

3 cloves of garlic, crushed

1 small bunch of fresh mint, leaves roughly chopped

1 small bunch of fresh flat-leaf parsley, roughly chopped

juice and zest of 2 small lemons

4 tablespoons extra virgin olive oil

Half fill a large saucepan with water, stir in 1 teaspoon of salt and bring to the boil. Add the bulgar wheat, return to the boil and cook for 8–10 minutes, until tender. Drain well in a sieve under running water until cold. Drain again and tip into a large serving bowl.

Have ready a bowl of iced water. Half fill a medium pan with water and bring to the boil. Add the broad beans and return to the boil. Cook for just 2 minutes, then drain and put them into the bowl of iced water. Leave for 5 minutes, then slip off their skins and add the beans to the bulgar wheat.

Cut the cucumber in half lengthways and scrape out the seeds with a teaspoon, then chop (about 1cm). Add to the

bowl of wheat and beans, along with the onion, chilli, garlic and herbs.

Add the lemon juice and zest, olive oil and plenty of freshly ground black pepper and mix until all the ingredients are thoroughly combined. Taste, adjust the seasoning as necessary, and serve.

Grilled Peaches, Spelt, Peas, Rocket and Mozzarella

This evokes long summer days, the kind when you can set a table outside, and put out a big bowl of this for family or friends, perhaps alongside some plates of prosciutto and other cured meats. This salad has evolved, from the grilled peaches that we used to serve whenever luxurious, creamy burrata cheese was available from Italy, into a celebration of summer garden produce, including green beans and peppery rocket, combined with buffalo mozzarella.

You need ripe peaches, but not so soft and juicy that they won't stand up to being grilled.

The spelt in the salad isn't meant to be substantial; it is little more than a handful of grains, just to add a scattering of nuttiness.

sea salt and freshly ground black pepper

4 tablespoons pearled spelt

4 ripe but firm peaches

2 teaspoons olive oil

150g green beans, trimmed

140g fresh or frozen peas

1 small bunch of fresh basil

6 small handfuls of rocket leaves

zest of 1 lemon

5 tablespoons French dressing (see page 381)

500g buffalo mozzarella

2 tablespoons extra virgin olive oil, to finish

Half fill a medium pan with water, add ½ teaspoon of sea salt and bring to the boil. Stir in the spelt and return to a simmer. Cook for 20–30 minutes, or until the spelt is just tender, stirring occasionally, then drain through a sieve under running water until cold.

While the spelt is cooking, cut the peaches in half and remove the stones. Cut each peach half into three and rub with the olive oil. Preheat a griddle pan over a high heat (or alternatively heat the grill).

Griddle or grill the wedges of peach for 2–3 minutes on each side, until lightly charred, then remove with tongs and transfer to a plate to cool.

Have ready a bowl of iced water.

Half fill a medium pan with water and bring to the boil. Add the beans, bring back to the boil and cook for 1 minute, then lift out with a slotted spoon (leaving the water in the pan) and put into the bowl of iced water. Leave for 5 minutes, then drain.

Return the water in the pan to the boil and add the peas. Bring back to the boil again, cook for about 5 minutes if fresh, or take off the heat after 30 seconds if frozen, then immediately drain in a colander and rinse under plenty of running water until completely cold. Tip into a large wide serving bowl or platter and add the drained beans and the spelt.

Scatter with the basil, rocket and lemon zest. Add the peach wedges, pour over the dressing and toss gently together. Season to taste and toss gently. Tear the mozzarella into bite-size pieces, scatter over the salad and drizzle with the extra virgin olive oil.

Asparagus, Spelt, Peas and Mint

English asparagus will be around for about 6 weeks, and at the beginning of the season it will be tender enough to use every part of the spears; but as the weeks go on it will become a little more woody, so you will need to take off the lower, white parts.

In this salad the spelt just adds a little texture and nuttiness, but you can leave it out, if you like.

sea salt and freshly ground black pepper

300g pearled spelt

2 bunches of slender asparagus

300g fresh or frozen peas

1 small bunch of fresh mint, roughly chopped

1 small bunch of fresh flat-leaf parsley, roughly chopped

5 tablespoons extra virgin olive oil

juice of 2 large lemons (roughly 5 tablespoons)

1 handful of pea shoots

Half fill a medium saucepan with water, add ½ teaspoon of sea salt, and bring to the boil. Stir in the spelt and return to a simmer. Cook for about 20 minutes, or until the spelt is just tender, stirring occasionally, then drain through a sieve under running water until cold. Drain well, then tip into a large serving bowl or platter.

While the spelt is cooking, cut the asparagus into 4cm lengths on the diagonal. Half fill a large saucepan with water and bring to the boil. Add the asparagus and bring back to the boil. Immediately take off the heat (you want the asparagus to be quite crisp), drain in a colander under running water until completely cold, and add to the spelt.

Cook the peas in the same way if frozen (if fresh they will need to simmer for about 5 minutes, until tender), and when cold add them to the spelt and asparagus, with the mint, parsley, olive oil and lemon juice, and toss well together. Season to taste and toss very lightly again. Scatter the pea shoots over the salad, fold in gently and serve.

Griddled Courgettes and Pine Nuts in Yoghurt and Mint Dressing

This is quite a chunky salad for the end of summer especially, when the courgettes are at their best. It makes a good light starter, as well as an accompaniment to grilled meat. Serve it at room temperature.

5 medium courgettes

4 tablespoons extra virgin olive oil

4 plump cloves of garlic, sliced into very thin slivers

juice of ½ a lemon

sea salt and freshly ground black pepper

1 small bunch of fresh mint, leaves roughly chopped

150ml natural yoghurt

50g pine nuts, lightly toasted in a dry pan

1 small bunch of fresh basil, leaves roughly torn

1 small red onion, very finely sliced into rings

Preheat the oven to 200°C/Gas 6.

Get a grill or griddle pan hot. Cut the courgettes in half lengthways and lay them cut side up under the grill, or cut side down on the griddle pan. Cook for 4–5 minutes, until lightly charred.

When the courgettes are cool enough to handle, cut them into chunks on the diagonal, roughly 2cm thick, then put them into a large bowl and toss with 2 tablespoons of the olive oil. Scatter over a large baking tray in a single layer and roast in the preheated oven for about 8 minutes, until tender.

Tip the hot courgettes carefully into a serving dish and add the garlic and lemon juice. Toss well together and season. Leave to cool a little.

To make the dressing, put the chopped mint into a bowl and add the remaining olive oil and the yoghurt. Taste and season as necessary, mix well, then spoon over the warm courgettes. Scatter with the pine nuts, basil and red onion and serve straight away.

Notes on tomatoes

I have a top ten list of tomatoes – some easy to find, some more unusual, heritage ones – which are all so popular that we also sell the plants so people can grow them in their own gardens. For a tomato salad I would choose either all cherry tomatoes of different colours, just halved, so you can keep their integrity; or all big, beef tomatoes, which I would slice – these meatier tomatoes are best combined with chunky ingredients, so they are fantastic in a classic tomato, mozzarella and basil salad.

Stupice – early season, cold-tolerant fruits that are red, but sometimes have green 'shoulders', and are golf-ball-sized, with a potato leaf and a good balance of sweetness and acidity – so they also make good sauces.

Purple Russian – purple, plum-shaped, sweet and fleshy, with low acidity and a soft skin. These come through quite early and the plants are really vigorous.

Black Cherry – not quite black, but a really dark purple, they are similar in flavour to Gardener's Delight (below) and look fantastic.

Green Zebra – this dark green and yellow stripy fruit is often picked early for its colour, but at the beginning of the season its flavour hasn't developed properly and it can be quite sharp. You need to resist picking it until it has gone the distance and ripened properly (though it will stay green). Then it is sweet and meaty.

Tigerella – really sweet, rich and tangy – and great to look at: orangey-red, with a yellow stripe.

Golden Cherry – small, yellow, thin-skinned and very sweet.

Sungold – these are a hybrid cordon variety, and one of the sweetest little orange tomatoes you can find.

Gardener's Delight - everyone knows this one: probably the most popular red cherry tomato, but full of flavour.

Marmande – this one is a slow burner, which often doesn't ripen until August, but is worth the wait. It is a big, ribbed, bulbous tomato, with really meaty flesh, great for slicing, and for sauces.

Jez Taylor

Tomatoes and Feta with Mint and Lemon Dressing

Another Daylesford classic: a very simple, light, Mediterranean-style salad for the height of summer that relies on the very best produce – salty cheese, sweet, big, juicy beefsteak tomatoes. 'Tomatoes,' says Carole Bamford, 'that have warmth and sunshine in them; and lots and lots of soft, fresh, fragrant mint leaves.' If you can find heritage Marmande tomatoes – which look like little red ribbed pumpkins, so much the better.

Leave the shredding of the mint leaves until the last minute, to prevent them from turning black.

300g mayonnaise

juice of 2 lemons

sea salt and freshly ground black pepper

8 large tomatoes, preferably heritage, plus a handful of cherry tomatoes

400g feta cheese, drained

1 small bunch of fresh mint

plenty of extra virgin olive oil

Mix the mayonnaise, lemon juice and a couple of twists of ground black pepper in a small bowl until thoroughly combined – it should have a pourable consistency.

Slice the tomatoes thinly and arrange on a serving platter. Season with a little more freshly ground black pepper and salt.

Crumble the feta into small chunks and scatter over the tomatoes.

Drizzle the salad with the lemon mayonnaise. Finely shred the mint leaves and scatter over the top, finish with a good slug of olive oil, and serve.

Tomato and Sourdough, with Red Pepper, Onion and Basil

This is based on the famous Italian salad from Tuscany, panzanella – one of those dishes that was originally concocted to use up bread that was a few days old. However, instead of adding stale bread, we lightly toast cubes of sourdough in the oven. This is a salad for the height of summer and is only as good as the tomatoes you use. Colourful, heritage varieties, full of flavour, to look out for include Green Zebra, Tigerella and Purple Russian.

2 thick slices of sourdough bread, cubed (about 2cm)

about 8 good flavoursome tomatoes

1 cucumber

1 medium red onion, finely sliced

1 large red pepper, deseeded and chopped (about 1.5cm)

3 cloves of garlic, crushed

1 small bunch of fresh basil, leaves torn

1 small bunch of fresh flat-leaf parsley, roughly chopped

sea salt and freshly ground black pepper

4 tablespoons extra virgin olive oil

2 tablespoons red wine vinegar

Preheat the oven to 190°C/gas 5.

Scatter the cubes of bread over a large baking tray in a single layer. Bake in the preheated oven for 7–8 minutes, until dry and only lightly coloured, then leave to cool.

Cut each tomato into 8 and put into a large bowl. Cut the cucumber lengthways in half. Scrape out the seeds with a teaspoon and chop (about 1.5cm). Add to the tomatoes, along with the red onion and red pepper. Scatter the toasted bread on top and add the garlic, basil and parsley. Season and toss lightly.

Mix 3 tablespoons of the oil with the vinegar, pour over the salad and toss well. Tip gently into a serving dish and drizzle with the remaining oil. Leave at room temperature for around 20 minutes to let all the flavours develop and soak into the bread, then serve.

Mixed Raw Vegetables and Cashew Nuts in Chilli, Soy and Ginger Dressing

'This is one of my favourite salads,' says chef John Hardwick, 'really fresh and light with a good kick from the dressing. It has evolved in the farm kitchens over many years, and it is the one that people most request the recipe for. It was first introduced by Kuttiya, our Thai chef, based on the classic noodle dish, pad thai, but without the noodles, and it has been endlessly played around with, changed and added to, according to what is best from the market garden. Because the whole idea is that the strips of vegetables should resemble noodles, this is one of the few dishes on the kitchen's menu that is quite showy, since we use a Japanese turning mandoline to shred the carrots and beetroot into curls.'

The only criteria is that all the raw vegetables must be crunchy, so things like kohlrabi, mixed beansprouts, fresh, firm cucumber and radishes can all be added.

The salad doesn't need salt and pepper, as the soy sauce provides saltiness, and the chilli gives peppery heat.

3 medium carrots

3 raw medium beetroots

¼ of a small red cabbage

¼ of a small white cabbage

1 small red pepper, deseeded and finely sliced

½ a medium red onion, finely sliced

1 small bunch of fresh mint, leaves roughly chopped

1 small bunch of fresh coriander, leaves only

25g cashew nuts, lightly toasted in a dry frying pan and roughly chopped

For the soy, chilli and ginger dressing:

100ml dark soy sauce

100g clear honey

juice of 4 large limes

1 tablespoon caster sugar

2 cloves of garlic, crushed and finely chopped

2cm piece of fresh root ginger, peeled and finely chopped

1 hot red chilli pepper, deseeded and finely chopped

75g cashew nuts

To make the dressing, put all the ingredients, apart from the cashew nuts, into a small pan. Bring to a gentle simmer, stirring constantly, and cook for 2 minutes, then remove from the heat and leave to cool.

Put the cashew nuts into a food processor, then add the cooled dressing and blitz until smooth. Keep to one side.

If you have a Japanese mandoline, use the attachment that cuts into curls to shred the carrots, otherwise use a flat mandoline with a medium attachment to shred them lengthways into spaghetti-like strips; or cut them into very fine, long julienne strips with a sharp knife. Put the shredded carrots into a large bowl. Peel and shred the beetroots in the same way and add to the carrots.

Remove any damaged outer leaves from the cabbages, as well as the central core, and discard. Shred the cabbages very finely and add to the bowl, along with the pepper, red onion, mint, coriander leaves and toasted cashews, and toss lightly.

To serve, drizzle with the dressing, toss lightly and tumble on to a serving platter.

Crunchy 'Chopped' Vegetables

This is a classic Daylesford recipe, which Carole Bamford loves because 'it can be made with whatever crunchy vegetables are good at any particular time of the year.' It does involve a lot of chopping, as everything has to be diced as small as you can manage – little more than the size of a match head – but the tiny pieces are the whole point of this salad. There isn't much pleasure in chomping your way through great chunks of raw carrot, radish, cauliflower, etc., but a bowlful of light, crunchy little cubes of mixed vegetables, united by the dressing, that can be forked up easily, makes a lovely refreshing starter.

2 large carrots	1 medium cauliflower
1 large cucumber, cut in half and deseeded	1 large red onion, finely chopped
4 sticks of celery	250ml French dressing (see page 381)
6 red radishes	
2 sweet red peppers, cut in half and deseeded	juice of ½ a large lemon
1 medium head of broccoli	sea salt and freshly ground black pepper

To cut the carrots into tiny dice, first slice them lengthways very thinly, using a mandoline or a sharp knife, then slice these strips again, into long thin batons, around 3mm wide. Finally cut the batons into dice of around 3mm. Put into a large bowl. Repeat with the cucumber and add to the bowl. Cut the celery, radishes and peppers into similar-sized dice and, again, add to the bowl.

Thinly slice the broccoli and the cauliflower heads on a fine mandoline or with a sharp knife, but stop when you reach the stalks. Discard the stalks, and add the chopped broccoli and cauliflower to the rest of the vegetables.

Add the sliced red onions, pour over the French dressing and lemon juice and leave to marinate for 30 minutes, no more or the vegetables will start to soften. Season to taste and serve.

Griddled Butternut Squash, Goat's Cheese and Olive

We make this with soft, creamy Oddington goat's cheese. It is a salad that plays on the contrast of colours and looks stunning layered up, rather than tumbled together.

1 large butternut squash, peeled, halved and deseeded

150ml extra virgin olive oil

fine sea salt and freshly ground black pepper

150g soft goat's cheese, such as Oddington

15g pumpkin seeds, lightly toasted in a dry pan

1 small bunch of fresh flat-leaf parsley, roughly chopped

For the balsamic onions:

3 medium red onions

3 tablespoons extra virgin olive oil

1 tablespoon good balsamic vinegar

50g caster sugar

For the black olive purée:

100g pitted black Kalamata olives

1 tablespoon capers

1 clove of garlic

3 tablespoons extra virgin olive oil

For the garlic and chilli dressing:

200g crème fraîche

1 clove of garlic, crushed

½ a plump red chilli, deseeded and very finely chopped

freshly ground black pepper

Preheat the oven to 200°C/gas 6.

To make the balsamic onions, peel the onions and cut each one into 8 wedges, keeping the root end intact so the wedges don't fall apart. Scatter over a shallow ovenproof dish and add the olive oil, balsamic vinegar, sugar and 3 tablespoons of water. Toss lightly together, then cover the dish with foil, put into the preheated oven and bake for 25 minutes. Remove the foil and cook for a further 5–10 minutes, or until the onions have softened and are lightly browned. Remove and leave to cool, but leave the oven on.

While the onions are baking, prepare the butternut squash. Cut the squash in half again, then cut into thick wedges (about 1.5cm). Heat a griddle pan, preferably (or otherwise the grill), and cook the squash for 1–2 minutes, turning once, until lightly charred on both sides. Transfer to a baking tray, brush generously with roughly a third of the oil and season. Put into the oven and cook for 10 minutes, then take out and turn the squash over. Brush with half the remaining oil and season generously. Return to the oven for a further 10 minutes, until softened and lightly browned, then remove and cool to room temperature.

To make the black olive purée, put all the ingredients into a blender and blitz to a coarse paste.

To make the dressing, put the crème fraîche into a bowl and stir in the garlic and chilli. Add enough cold water to make the dressing pourable (around 1–2 tablespoons) and season with a little ground black pepper.

To serve, arrange the butternut squash in a shallow serving dish in a single layer. Crumble the goat's cheese into chunky pieces and scatter them over the top, then drizzle the dressing over. Top with the balsamic onions. Dot with the olive purée and sprinkle with the toasted pumpkin seeds and parsley. Finally drizzle with the remaining oil and serve.

Variation: With Aubergine, Pomegranate, Feta and Pumpkin Seeds

Follow the recipe above, but omit the olive purée and substitute 3 medium aubergines for the squash. Trim the ends of the aubergines and cut into 1.5cm slices, then griddle or grill in the same way. Use 250g of drained feta instead of the goat's cheese, and sprinkle the seeds from a large ripe pomegranate (or 130g of seeds bought separately) over the salad along with the pumpkin seeds. Finish with fresh coriander, instead of parsley.

Pickled Pear and Hazelnuts, with Chickpeas, Quinoa and Daylesford Blue

In autumn/winter on the farm, the fresh pears that come in from the orchards go beautifully with Daylesford Blue cheese from the creamery. Again, you could also use a creamy blue cheese like Stichelton, Barkham Blue and of course Stilton, though this will have a more crumbly texture. Pears and blue cheese are a classic combination, but you need a relatively firm, yet ripe, flavoursome variety of pear, such as Williams or ripe Conference, which can stand up to being cooked and pickled.

The addition of chickpeas and quinoa lends a little contrasting texture. Remember you need to soak the chickpeas overnight before cooking.

250g chickpeas

250g quinoa

120g toasted hazelnuts

100g sunflower seeds, toasted in a dry pan

5 tablespoons extra virgin olive oil

juice and zest of ½ a lemon

1 small bunch of fresh flat-leaf parsley, roughly chopped

sea salt and freshly ground black pepper

150g blue cheese, such as Daylesford Blue, rind removed

For the pickled pears:

2 firm pears, peeled, but with stalks left on

2 tablespoons sugar

100ml white wine vinegar

½ a red chilli, split and seeds removed

Soak the chickpeas in water overnight, then rinse and drain. Half fill a medium pan with water, add the chickpeas and bring to the boil, then turn the heat down to a simmer and cook for 40 minutes, or until tender. Drain and transfer to a large bowl to cool.

Half fill a medium pan with water, bring to the boil, then add the quinoa and turn the heat down to a simmer. Cook for 5 minutes, then remove from the heat and leave to stand for 5 minutes. Drain and transfer to a separate bowl to cool.

While the pulses are cooking and cooling, put the pears
into a small pan with the sugar, vinegar, chilli and 800ml
of water – the liquid should cover the pears. Bring to
the boil, then turn down the heat and simmer gently for
around 20 minutes, until the pears are tender. Leave to
cool in their liquid, and once cool remove the stalks,
cut in half, and remove the cores. Cut each half into 8
lengthways, to give 16 wedges in total.

Add the quinoa to the bowl of chickpeas, along with the
pieces of poached pear, the nuts and seeds, olive oil, lemon
juice and zest, and parsley, and toss lightly.

Taste and season as necessary, then tumble on to a large
serving platter. Cut the cheese into rough cubes, dot over
the salad, then fold them in very lightly, taking care not
to break up the cheese too much, and serve.

Curried Cauliflower, Red Pepper and Nigella Seeds

An autumn-going-into winter salad, when the cauliflowers are good. Cauliflower is a vegetable that lends itself to a little heat, spice, and sweet and sour flavours – in this dish the sweetness comes from raisins. The key is to use a big and wide enough pan to allow the cauliflower space to sauté and take on a little colour, before adding some water and letting it soften. If you overcrowd the pan, you will bring the temperature of the oil down and the cauliflower will steam, rather than fry.

50ml sunflower oil

2 teaspoons medium curry powder

2 teaspoons ground turmeric

1 teaspoon mustard seeds

1 teaspoon cumin seeds

1 medium white onion, finely sliced

1.4kg cauliflower, cut into small florets

2 large red peppers, deseeded and cut into thin strips

1 hot red chilli, deseeded and very finely chopped

1 tablespoon nigella (black onion) seeds, lightly toasted in a dry pan

1 medium bunch of fresh coriander, leaves roughly chopped

85g raisins

½ a medium red onion, finely sliced

50g toasted flaked almonds

2 tablespoons olive oil

2 teaspoons lemon juice

2 teaspoons white wine vinegar

sea salt and freshly ground black pepper

Heat the sunflower oil in a large, wide, heavy-based sauté pan or shallow flame-proof casserole and gently heat the curry powder, turmeric, mustard and cumin seeds for a few seconds, until the mustard seeds begin to pop. Add the white onion and sauté until soft, stirring regularly.

Put the cauliflower, red peppers and chilli into the pan, making sure that the cauliflower is in a single layer, and cook over a medium heat for 5 minutes, until the cauliflower has lightly coloured, stirring regularly. Add 6 tablespoons of water and continue to cook for 5 more minutes, until the cauliflower has softened but still has a crunch to it (there should be no liquid remaining in the pan).

Remove the spiced vegetables from the heat, transfer to a large serving bowl and leave to cool. Then add the nigella seeds and all the rest of the ingredients, tumbling the salad lightly together and seasoning to taste.

Chestnut, Quinoa, Kale and Broccoli

A feel-good salad for the winter, full of greens and goodness, that we put on the menu in the lead up to Christmas, when we have the first chestnuts in the kitchen – the very best come in from Italy, we always like to highlight special European produce at certain times throughout the year, in addition to what is grown on the farm and locally. The salad can be made with florets of green broccoli until the first purple sprouting broccoli appears from around the end of February right through to early May. The easiest thing is to use vacuum-packed chestnuts, but if you want to roast your own, preheat the oven to 200°C/gas 6. Cut a cross through the shell on the top of each nut, put them into a roasting tin, and let them roast in the oven for about 30 minutes, or until the shells have opened out and the nuts inside are tender. Let them cool, then peel away both the outer shells and the inner bitter skins.

The key to this salad is to blanch the broccoli and kale very, very briefly, to retain their crunch, colour and nutrients.

200g jarred, vacuum-packed or freshly roasted and peeled chestnuts

sea salt

500g quinoa

250g purple sprouting broccoli tops

200g young curly kale leaves (rough stalks removed), shredded quite thickly

4 tablespoons hazelnut oil

4 tablespoons extra virgin olive oil

2 cloves of garlic, crushed

1 long red chilli, deseeded and finely chopped

zest and juice of 1 large orange

freshly ground black pepper

If using vacuum-packed or jarred chestnuts, preheat the oven to 200°C/gas 6.

Spread the nuts out evenly on a baking tray and bake for 10 minutes, then remove and leave to cool.

Half fill a medium pan with water, bring to the boil, then add the quinoa and turn the heat down to a simmer. Cook for 5 minutes, then remove from the heat and leave to stand for 5 minutes. Drain and transfer to a separate bowl to cool.

Half fill a large saucepan with water and bring to the boil. Put in the broccoli and return quickly to the boil, then immediately lift out with a slotted spoon (leaving the water in the pan). Transfer the broccoli to a colander and drain under plenty of running water until completely cold. Drain well and tip into the bowl with the quinoa.

Return the water to the boil, add the kale, bring back to the boil and cook for just 5 seconds. Drain in a colander under running water until completely cold. Drain well again and add to the broccoli and quinoa.

In a small bowl, mix the oils, garlic, chilli and orange juice, add a good pinch of salt and a couple of twists of freshly ground black pepper, then pour over the vegetables and quinoa, sprinkle with the orange zest, toss well together and serve.

Purple Sprouting Broccoli, Spelt, Crispy Garlic and Toasted Almonds

This is all about celebrating the arrival of purple sprouting broccoli around the end of February. The spelt adds a little texture, as do the garlic crisps and almonds – crisping the garlic also gives softer bursts of flavour, which complements the broccoli, rather than overpowering it.

sea salt and freshly ground black pepper	4 cloves of garlic, very finely sliced
125g pearled spelt	20g toasted flaked almonds
800g purple sprouting broccoli (about 500g after stalk removed)	zest and juice of 1 lemon
150ml olive oil	1 plump red chilli, deseeded and finely chopped

Half fill a medium saucepan with water, add ½ teaspoon of salt, and bring to the boil. Stir in the spelt and return to a simmer. Cook for about 20–30 minutes, or until the spelt is just tender, stirring occasionally, then drain and rinse under running water until cold. Drain well and tip into a large bowl.

While the spelt is cooking, half fill a large saucepan with water and bring to the boil. Add the broccoli and bring back to the boil, then take off the heat immediately, so that the broccoli stays crisp. Drain through a colander under running water until completely cold. Leave to drain for 10 minutes, then tip into the bowl with the spelt.

Heat 100ml of the oil in a small frying pan and fry the garlic slices gently for 2–3 minutes until evenly golden and crisp, taking care not to let them burn, or they will taste bitter. Remove from the heat, lift out with a slotted spoon and drain on kitchen paper.

Add the almonds, lemon zest and juice and chilli to the bowl of spelt and broccoli, along with the rest of the olive oil, a good pinch of salt and some freshly ground black pepper. Toss well, tip into a wide serving bowl or platter, sprinkle with the reserved crispy garlic slivers and serve.

Lentils, Tomato, Daylesford Blue and Red Onion

A good all-year-round salad in which the nuttiness of the lentils balances with the slight saltiness of the blue cheese. Alternatives to Daylesford Blue include Stichelton, Barkham Blue, or possibly Stilton, though this has less creaminess. The salad needs to be served at room temperature, so that the tomatoes can also show off their fullest flavour. Good varieties to use for this are Stupice early in the season, and Marmande later.

200g Puy lentils, rinsed and drained

2 large ripe tomatoes, finely chopped

1 medium red onion, finely chopped

150g blue cheese, rind removed

1 small handful of fresh dill, roughly chopped

1 small bunch of fresh chives, finely chopped

For the dressing:

1 tablespoon wholegrain mustard

1 teaspoon Dijon mustard

juice of ½ a lemon

1 clove of garlic, crushed

4 tablespoons olive oil

freshly ground black pepper

Half fill a medium pan with water and bring to the boil. Add the lentils to the pan, stir well and return to the boil. Cook for 18–20 minutes, or until just tender.

While the lentils are cooking, make the dressing. Put the mustards, lemon juice and garlic into a bowl and stir until combined. Whisk in the olive oil a little at a time until the dressing emulsifies. Season with black pepper.

Drain the lentils through a sieve and rinse under running water until cold. Drain well again and tip into a serving dish. Scatter the tomatoes and red onion over the top. Pour the dressing over, and toss well together.

To serve, cut the cheese into rough cubes and dot over the salad. Toss very lightly, so as not to break up the cheese too much, and scatter with the dill and chives.

Notes on leaves

Much as I love to build up a salad with sliced raw vegetables, sprouts and seeds, in addition to a base of leaves and herbs, sometimes I just want a bowl of great leaves and a simple dressing. The great thing about winter salads, in particular, is that they are relatively easy to grow at home and you can keep them going throughout the cold months from around November all the way through to March/April, under a cold frame or a small polytunnel. Just keep harvesting them cleanly with a sharp knife, from the outside of the plant, so that you leave behind the smaller leaves in the plant rosette, from which more will grow. I don't recommend kitchen windowsills though, as the environment can be a bit extreme, with sunshine, or heat from the cooker, and the plants are likely to get hot and stressed, and leggy where they reach out towards the light.

I don't think there is such a thing as too many different leaves in a salad, but the key is to get a good mix of colour, texture, and shape – and to put in something peppery and spicy, something bitter, and something with some juiciness and crunchiness, bulked out with more neutral leaves. Sometimes in the kitchens the chefs want to emphasise the pepperiness, or bitterness, depending on what dish they are serving the leaves with, but for a mixed salad, as a rule of thumb I would keep the really strong, peppery or bitter-tasting leaves to 50 per cent of your salad, and no more than 10 per cent of any one leaf – remember, once you dress your leaves, the flavour will calm down, but too much of any strong leaf and a salad can become more challenging than enjoyable.

I put together different combinations of leaf in summer and winter.

For winter: I would start with salad brassicas, such as mizuna, mispoona, tatsoi, Chinese cabbage hearts, young tender spinach, kale and bull's blood beetroot. Corn salad (or mâche) and winter purslane (claytonia) give a bit of juiciness. Any of the mustards: red giant mustard, green-in-the-snow mustard, red frills and golden frills mustard, as well as salad and wild rocket, and land cress, will give a hit of peppery spice. Some of these, like the land cress, can be really spicy and dominant, though, so you need some winter lettuce, such as oak leaf and broad leaf, to neutralise the spice. For bitterness I would put in endive or a radicchio – the red and white striped Treviso type.

For summer: I still have my pick of some of the salad brassicas for pepperiness, but there will be no tatsoi, Chinese cabbage, kale or green-in-the-snow mustard. I will include sorrel when it's at its leafy best in April and May. All the other mustards and rockets are still around too, and I like to use a lot of chard – when we have spinach and chard out in the fields in May and June, I will thin out the young tender leaves – nothing bigger than 6cm – for salads, as they add colour and juiciness.

The key difference, though, between a winter and a summer leaf salad is that in summer there is a much wider choice of lettuces. And you do want more of these in summer, as on a hot day, it is good to have a salad that is quite crunchy, juicy and refreshing: so look for little gems, cos, and variegated leaves like batavia – I prefer these to lollo rosso, which is a bit too frilly for my liking, and prone to damage when you harvest it. I use architectural-looking frizzy endives, for bitterness. Then around April/June I like to add pea shoots. The chefs love them, so we take the shoots from the mangetout growing in polytunnels until about May, and then we move on to those from the peas out in the fields, so there is a natural progression throughout the season.

Jez Taylor

Raw Beetroot, Kidney Beans and Mustard Leaf with Horseradish Dressing

A wintry, quite hearty salad, making good use of the later, bigger beetroot and peppery winter salad leaves. If you can't find mustard leaves, use baby spinach instead. Our head chef Gaven Fuller originally made this with slivers of cold roast beef – his favourite thing for a Monday lunchtime, using beef left over from a Sunday roast. Beef and horseradish, and horseradish and beetroot, are great combinations, so it makes sense to put all three together. If you have some cold, roast beef, you could either mix in some thin strips, or alternatively carve some slices and serve the salad on the side. Gaven says the salad would be just as good with a steak, too.

Though you could use tinned beans, it is always preferable to cook your own. If you want to do this, soak 200g dried kidney beans in a large bowl and cover with cold water. Leave in a cool place for at least 8 hours, or overnight. The next day, rinse the beans thoroughly. Half fill a large saucepan with cold water and add the beans, ensuring they are fully covered. Bring to the boil over a high heat for 10 minutes, then turn the heat down and cook very gently for 45–60 minutes, until tender – you really want the beans to be nice and soft for this; to test, take out one of the beans and press it with your thumb – it should give easily. Rinse in a colander under running water until cold, and drain before using.

6 small handfuls of mustard leaves or baby spinach leaves

300g raw beetroot

400g cooked red kidney beans, drained and rinsed

1 small bunch of fresh flat-leaf parsley, roughly chopped

For the horseradish dressing:

140g mayonnaise

100g hot horseradish sauce

125g natural yoghurt

sea salt and freshly ground black pepper

To make the dressing, mix the mayonnaise with the horseradish and yoghurt in a large bowl and season to taste.

Cut the larger leaves into thin strips. You can do this quickly by piling 4 or 5 leaves on top of each other and slicing them together. Trim and peel the beetroot, then grate coarsely, either by hand or using a food processor. Bearing in mind that the beetroot juice will stain, you may want to use latex gloves to protect your hands.

Add the grated beetroot to the bowl of dressing, along with the kidney beans, leaves and chopped parsley. Mix thoroughly, then taste and adjust the seasoning if necessary before serving.

Mushroom, Celeriac, Truffle Honey and Toasted Pine Nuts

This is an adaptation of a salad we made for the raw bar in Notting Hill, when the farmshop first opened there. Ceps and celeriac are around at the same time in the autumn, and are just sliced and marinated, then finished off with Jez's winter micro-cress, but you can use watercress.

You can usually buy truffle honey in good delis, but if you can't find it, mix 7 tablespoons of clear honey with 1 tablespoon of black truffle paste. And if you are able to treat yourself to some white truffle, then a little, grated over the salad at the end, will make it extra special.

Soak the pine nuts for the purée overnight or for around 4–6 hours, as this will soften them and result in a much smoother texture.

400g cep mushrooms, cleaned

400g chestnut mushrooms, cleaned

6 tablespoons white wine vinegar

5 tablespoons extra virgin olive oil

2 tablespoons chopped fresh flat-leaf parsley

1 large head of celeriac

3 tablespoons pine nuts, toasted in a dry pan

1 good handful of micro-cress or watercress

8 tablespoons truffle honey (see introduction, above)

5g white truffle (optional), to finish

For the pine nut purée:

200g pine nuts

4 tablespoons extra virgin olive oil

juice of ½ a lemon

freshly ground black pepper

Soak the pine nuts for the purée in water overnight, then drain and put into a blender with the olive oil, lemon juice and 5 tablespoons of water. Season with black pepper and blend, adding a little more water if necessary until you have a smooth purée consistency. Transfer to a bowl and put into the fridge while you prepare the rest of the salad.

Thinly slice the mushrooms on a mandoline, or with a sharp knife, and put them into a bowl with 2 tablespoons of the white wine vinegar, 4 tablespoons of the olive oil and the chopped parsley. Season and leave for about 20 minutes.

Peel the celeriac and cut it in half. To get a good mixture of shapes and textures, take one half and cut it into strips about 6cm long and 5mm wide. Slice the other half very thinly, using a mandoline or a sharp knife, then cut the slices into very thin spaghetti-like strips. Put all the celeriac into a separate bowl, mix with the remaining olive oil and vinegar, and season.

To serve, divide the pine nut purée between four plates. Lift the mushrooms and celeriac out of their marinades, and scatter over the top, followed by the toasted pine nuts and the cress. Drizzle with the truffle honey and finish with a fine shaving of fresh white truffle, if using.

Wild Rice, Red Cabbage, Apple and Toasted Cobnuts

From mid to late August through to September, we can gather cobnuts, the cultivated version of wild hazelnuts, from the trees around the farm – you have to be quick, though, to beat the squirrels. In season you should be able to find the nuts in shops, greengrocers and markets.

If you can't find cobnuts, you can use thinly sliced hazelnuts (though these have a slightly more intense flavour), or whole almonds, again thinly sliced.

Cobnuts and apples are ready for harvesting at the same time – and we make this salad with many different apple varieties throughout the season, including heritage ones, such as Blenheim Gold, a popular, old, local variety. You need apples with some sweetness and preferably some good streaks of red in the skin, to give a nice colour to the salad, so of the more readily available apple varieties, Jonagold is a good one to choose.

200g wild rice, rinsed in cold water	40g thinly sliced cobnuts, lightly toasted in a dry pan
150g red cabbage	juice of 1 lemon
½ a medium red onion, finely sliced	2 tablespoons extra virgin olive oil
2 red-tinged eating apples, such as Jonagold	1½ tablespoons good balsamic vinegar
25g watercress	1 teaspoon fine sea salt
5 tablespoons finely chopped fresh flat-leaf parsley	a few twists of freshly ground black pepper

Half fill a medium pan with water, bring to the boil, then add the wild rice and stir a couple of times. Bring up to a simmer and cook for 35–40 minutes, or until the rice is tender. Drain in a sieve under running water until the rice is cold, then drain well again, and tip into a mixing bowl.

Trim the cabbage of any damaged outer leaves, cut in half and remove the central core then slice the leaves very finely. Add to the rice, along with the red onion. Quarter and core the apples, grate coarsely then add to the bowl, with the rest of the ingredients, toss gently and serve.

Chicken Caesar

Caesar salad is one of those recipes that gets people worked up over the 'correct' ingredients. The original was dreamed up by American restaurateur Caesar Cardini in 1924, and was quite sparing: just crunchy lettuce, dressing, croutons and grated Parmesan; but over the centuries all kinds of variations have found their way on to menus – including anchovies in the dressing, which causes much controversy. Whatever ingredients are used, two things can let a Caesar salad down: the dressing can be just a creamy medium with no real flavour, and the croutons can be clumsily big and either tooth-breakingly crunchy, or so soft they soak up too much oil and become greasy.

We put capers in the dressing, which give it a lift, but with a little less pungency than anchovies, though you can also add a couple of these if you like, and, instead of croutons, we make our signature thin, baked toasts (which we also use to accompany smoked mackerel pâté, see page 36) using our seven-seed bread (see page 333). They give the essential crunch to the salad, but they are lighter, non-greasy and easy to eat.

3 boneless, skinless chicken breasts

sea salt and freshly ground black pepper

3 tablespoons olive oil

4 medium eggs

6 rashers of rindless smoked streaky bacon

6 very thin slices of multi-seed bread

6 little gem lettuces, separated into leaves

75g Parmesan cheese, shaved thinly

For the Caesar dressing:

40g Parmesan cheese, finely grated

1 tablespoon capers in vinegar, drained, plus 2 teaspoons of their vinegar

2 teaspoons fresh lemon juice

1 plump clove of garlic, roughly chopped

freshly ground black pepper

200g mayonnaise

Preheat the oven to 200°C/gas 6.

Place the chicken on a baking tray and season. Rub with 2 tablespoons of the oil and then roast for 15 minutes, until very lightly browned and cooked throughout (the juices should run clear if the chicken is pierced with the tip of a sharp knife). Transfer to a plate and leave to cool, but leave the oven on, turning down the heat to 180°C/gas 4.

While the chicken is cooking, half fill a medium pan with water and bring to the boil. Gently lower the eggs into the water and return it to the boil. Cook for 7 minutes, drain the eggs under running water until cold, then peel.

Put a large non-stick frying pan over a medium heat and add the bacon. Cook for about 3 minutes on each side until very crisp, then remove and drain on kitchen paper.

Arrange the bread on a baking tray, drizzle with the rest of the olive oil and season with a pinch of salt and freshly ground black pepper. Put into the oven and bake for 6–8 minutes, until very crisp and golden brown. Remove and leave to cool while you make the dressing.

For the dressing, put all the ingredients, except for the mayonnaise, into a food processor, season with ground black pepper, and blitz until as smooth as possible. You may need to remove the lid and push the mixture down with a rubber spatula once or twice. Transfer to a small bowl and stir in the mayonnaise.

To assemble, cut the chicken breasts into small chunks. Quarter the eggs. Scatter the lettuce over a serving dish or platter and arrange the chicken on top, then drizzle with the Caesar dressing. Break the crispy bacon and toasted bread into rough pieces and scatter over, finish with the eggs and sprinkle with the Parmesan.

VEGETABLES

Root vegetables, buttered, crushed and roasted
Spinach, vibrant with lemon zest, pine nuts
and sultanas
A shepherd's pie of mushrooms
Garden fresh risotto

Vegetables from the market garden are at the heart of all the savoury cooking we do at the farm, and we are always spoilt for choice; however, the recipes in this chapter show some of our favourite combinations for serving as accompaniments to meat or fish, while some can be served as main courses, such as the woodland mushroom shepherd's pie on page 136, the spiced pumpkin, butter bean and spinach casserole on page 143, and the beetroot, swede and potato bake on page 139, all of which make a tasty lunch or supper with a bowl of mixed leaf salad. Our vegetable risotti, some of which feature locally grown spelt and pearl barley, as an alternative to rice, are equally good served in smaller portions as starters or as substantial main courses.

Crushed New Potatoes with Olives, Capers and Herbs

This combination goes particularly well with fish, and is lovely when the new potatoes are in season, around May for Jersey Royals and June for other varieties, and the tender skins give this mixture a nice earthiness. Of course you could still make this at other times of the year with maincrop potatoes – peel them first, though.

650g new potatoes, such as Jersey Royals, skin on

sea salt and freshly ground black pepper

50g pitted Kalamata black olives, drained and chopped

4 tablespoons capers, drained

¼ of a small fennel bulb, trimmed and very finely grated

4 tablespoons finely chopped fresh parsley

5 tablespoons extra virgin olive oil

juice of 1 lemon

Put the potatoes into a pan of cold, lightly salted water and bring to the boil, then turn down the heat and simmer until tender. Drain, then return the potatoes to the pan, crushing them slightly with a fork, and add all the rest of the ingredients. Place over a low heat and warm through for 3–4 minutes, stirring regularly until hot throughout.

Smashed Broad Beans, Peas and Mint

A celebration of the height of summer: really fresh vibrant flavours that go well with lamb, chicken or fish.

250g fresh peas	2 handfuls of pea shoots
250g podded broad beans	50g butter
3 tablespoons chopped fresh mint	sea salt and freshly ground black pepper
3 tablespoons finely chopped fresh chives	

Have ready a bowl of iced water.

Half fill a large saucepan with water and bring to the boil. Add the peas first if fresh and cook for about 5 minutes, adding the beans for the last 30 seconds. If the peas are frozen, you can put them in together and bring back to the boil, then take off the heat after 30 seconds. Drain in a colander, then transfer to the bowl of iced water and leave for 5 minutes. Drain well again and slip off the skins from the broad beans.

Transfer the peas and beans to a bowl and crush with the back of a fork. Stir in the herbs and pea shoots and stir well.

Melt the butter in a large non-stick pan. Add the crushed bean and pea mixture and heat gently, stirring regularly, until warmed through. Season and serve.

Wilted Spinach with Toasted Pine Nuts, Sultanas and Lemon Zest

This has a Mediterranean feel, and goes well with roast chicken or slowly roasted lamb shoulder, along with the broad bean, bulgar wheat and herb salad (see page 79).

50g pine nuts

40g butter

1 medium onion, thinly sliced

2 cloves of garlic, finely chopped

50g sultanas

4 tablespoons white wine

360g baby spinach, washed and well dried

sea salt and freshly ground black pepper

zest of 1 lemon

Lightly toast the pine nuts in a dry pan over a low heat until just golden – take care not to let them burn.

In a medium-sized pan, melt the butter over a low heat, then add the onion and garlic and continue to cook for about 5 minutes, until the onion is soft, but not coloured. Add the sultanas and white wine and cook for a further 5 minutes, until all the liquid has gone. Add the toasted pine nuts and spinach and cook for a further minute, until the spinach has wilted.

Season and add the lemon zest. Stir well and serve.

Green Beans with Almonds, Parsley and Garlic Butter

This is good with fish or chicken. Fish and almonds are an especially fine marriage.

sea salt and freshly ground black pepper

500g green beans, tops removed

80g butter

60g flaked almonds

4 cloves of garlic, finely chopped

2 tablespoons roughly chopped fresh flat-leaf parsley

juice of ½ a lemon

Half fill a large pan with lightly salted water and bring to a rapid boil. Drop in the prepared green beans and cook over a high heat for about 8 minutes, until the beans are fully cooked but still have a little bite to them, then drain.

Heat the butter in a frying pan until it starts to foam, then cook for a couple more minutes until it becomes golden brown and takes on a nutty flavour – but take care not to let it burn.

Add the flaked almonds and continue to cook, stirring constantly, until the almonds are golden brown and toasted. Add the drained beans, garlic and parsley and season with salt and pepper.

Add the lemon juice, toss well and serve immediately.

Potato Wedges with Garlic and Rosemary Butter

The Daylesford alternative to chips. The key is to do as you would when boiling potatoes before roasting them – slightly roughen and break them up around the edges, so that when they go into the oven, you get nice crunchy crags and corners.

1.2kg baking potatoes, such as Sante, Cara, or the red Romano, well scrubbed

sea salt and freshly ground black pepper

1 tablespoon olive oil

25g butter, at room temperature

1 clove of garlic, finely crushed

1 tablespoon chopped fresh rosemary leaves

1 tablespoon finely chopped fresh flat-leaf parsley

Preheat the oven to 200°C/gas 6.

Cut the potatoes into wedges, put them into a pan of cold, lightly salted water and bring to the boil. Turn down the heat and simmer for about 5 minutes, or until tender, but not breaking apart. Drain in a colander and leave to steam for 5 minutes, shaking the colander gently to roughen the exposed surface of the potatoes.

Pat any remaining moisture from the potatoes with some kitchen paper and arrange them over a baking tray in a single layer. Drizzle with the olive oil and season. Toss lightly, put into the preheated oven and bake for 15–20 minutes, turning once, until golden brown.

Meanwhile, mix the butter with the garlic and rosemary until thoroughly combined.

Once the potatoes are golden, dot them with pieces of the garlic butter and return them to the oven until the butter has melted. Remove and season again, if necessary, then serve immediately, scattered with chopped parsley.

Crushed, Buttered Root Vegetables and Cabbage

This combination works really well alongside winter stews and casseroles that have big robust flavours. The crushed vegetables should look quite rustic, and the key is to chop them fairly small, not in great chunks, so that you can just crush them with a fork and retain a good texture and a little of their shape here and there – then the fine shreds of cabbage are just mixed through.

2 medium carrots, roughly chopped

½ a medium swede, roughly chopped

sea salt and freshly ground black pepper

½ a medium Savoy or white cabbage, tough core removed, finely shredded

40g butter

Put the carrots and swede into a pan of cold, lightly salted water and bring to the boil, then turn down the heat and simmer for 25–30 minutes, until tender. Lift out with a slotted spoon (leaving the water in the pan), transfer to a bowl and leave to cool.

Return the pan of vegetable water to the heat and put in the cabbage. Bring back to the boil and cook for 1 minute, then drain well in a sieve and pat dry.

When ready to serve, melt the butter in a large non-stick pan over a low heat. Add the carrot and swede and crush lightly with the back of a fork until they are roughly mashed, but still have some texture. Stir in the cabbage, season and cook for 3–5 minutes, stirring regularly, until hot throughout. Serve immediately.

Woodland Mushroom Shepherd's Pie

A vegetarian alternative to shepherd's pie for the autumn. When you cook the mushrooms, do so in batches, so that they sauté properly and become nice and golden. If you cram too many into the pan at the same time, you will reduce the heat and they will steam, rather than fry. If you can't find enough of the mushroom varieties suggested, you can add some chestnut mushrooms.

When you chop the vegetables they should be quite small – about 1cm.

500g mixed wild mushrooms, such as portabello, ceps, chanterelles and pied bleu

75g butter

4 tablespoons olive oil

3 medium white onions, finely chopped

2 sticks of celery, chopped

1 carrot, chopped

¼ of a swede, chopped

6 cloves of garlic, finely chopped

100ml sherry

200ml white wine

300ml double cream

1 teaspoon Dijon mustard

1 tablespoon Worcestershire sauce

a pinch of cayenne pepper

2 tablespoons chopped fresh flat-leaf parsley leaves

3 tablespoons Parmesan cheese, finely grated

For the mash:

5 large potatoes, peeled and quartered

70g butter

50ml milk

sea salt and freshly ground black pepper

First make the mash. Put the potatoes into a medium pan, cover with cold, lightly salted water and bring to the boil, then turn down the heat and simmer for around 20 minutes, until the potatoes are cooked through and easily fall away if pierced with the tip of a sharp knife. Drain in a colander and leave to steam briefly, then return them to the pan and mash well (alternatively put them through a potato ricer, then return them to the pan). Add the butter and milk and season. Leave the pan at the side of the stove while you prepare the mushrooms.

Divide the mushrooms into 4 equal mounds, as you want to fry them in batches. Also cut the butter into 5 equal pieces – set one aside to cook the onions and other vegetables in a moment. Heat one of the remaining 4 pieces of butter with a tablespoon of oil in a large non-stick frying pan. Add the first mound of mushrooms and fry for a couple of minutes, until golden brown, then remove. Put in the next piece of butter and another tablespoon of oil and when the butter has melted fry the next mound of mushrooms. Repeat twice more.

In a casserole (one that has a lid), melt the reserved piece of butter and add the chopped onions, celery, carrot, swede and garlic. Cook without a lid over a medium heat for 10 minutes, until the vegetables are starting to colour slightly and become soft.

Add the cooked mushrooms, together with the sherry and wine, and bring to the boil. Simmer for around 10 minutes, until nearly all the liquid has gone.

Add the cream, mustard, Worcestershire sauce, cayenne and chopped parsley, and season. Bring back to the boil, then take off the heat straight away, taste and season again if necessary.

Preheat the oven to 180°C/gas 4.

Spoon the mixture into a deep pie dish and either spoon or pipe the reserved mashed potatoes over the top. Sprinkle with the grated Parmesan.

Put into the preheated oven for about 45 minutes, until golden brown on top and hot all the way through.

Beetroot, Swede and Potato Bake

Beetroot and swede add extra flavours and colours to what is essentially potato dauphinoise. This is a nice autumnal dish that pairs well with venison.

450ml double cream

450ml milk

2 cloves of garlic, thinly sliced

1 large sprig of fresh thyme, leaves only

sea salt and freshly ground black pepper

2 large baking potatoes, peeled

3 large beetroot, peeled

2 medium swede, peeled

Preheat the oven to 170°C/gas 3.

Put the cream, milk, garlic and thyme leaves into a medium pan and bring to a simmer, then immediately remove from the heat, season and leave to stand, so that the flavours can infuse, while you prepare the vegetables.

With a mandoline or sharp knife, slice each of the vegetables very finely (about 2mm), keeping each type separate.

Now start to layer up the vegetables in a deep baking dish – each layer should be quite thin – starting with potato. Season, then spread with 3 tablespoons of the milk and cream mixture. Next put in a thin layer of beetroot, season and add 3 more tablespoons of milk and cream. Follow with a thin layer of swede, season and spoon over 3 more tablespoons of milk and cream. Continue until all the vegetables are used up, but keep back enough potato to make sure that you finish with this. Season again, then pour any remaining creamy liquid over the top.

Push the vegetables down gently with your fingers to ensure that all the layers are fully immersed in the liquid. Cover with a sheet of greaseproof paper and then some foil. With the tip of a sharp knife, prick a few holes through both the foil and the greaseproof, to allow some steam to escape during cooking.

Place the baking dish on a baking tray, as the cream will probably bubble over. Put into the preheated oven for 1 hour, then remove the foil and continue to bake for 10 more minutes, until golden brown on top.

Remove from the oven, leave to settle for 5 minutes, then serve.

Cider Baked Leeks

In autumn, cider makes a perfect partner for leeks. Serve this with pork and slices of apple, caramelised in a pan with a little butter and sugar, or with chicken.

4 leeks

40g butter

1 clove of garlic, thinly sliced

500ml dry cider

2 tablespoons cider vinegar

400ml good vegetable stock

1 sprig of fresh thyme, leaves only

200ml double cream

sea salt and freshly ground black pepper

For the Parmesan and herb crumbs:

55g breadcrumbs

2 tablespoons fresh flat-leaf parsley leaves

1 clove of garlic, finely chopped

½ teaspoon sea salt

freshly ground black pepper

2 tablespoons grated Parmesan cheese

Preheat the oven to 180°C/gas 4.

Trim the leeks, removing and discarding the outer layer. Cut off the green part of the leeks about 2.5cm into the white part, and then cut the green (and little bit of white) into 1cm slices. Wash well and drain in a colander. Cut the remaining white part of the leeks into 4 equal lengths, leaving these as whole cylinders. By cutting off the green parts quite low down, into the white area, you will have taken away the bits that need a good wash to remove soil that is trapped inside, so the tight white cylinders need only a rinse on the outside.

In a medium pan melt the butter and add the chopped green of leek, together with the garlic. Allow to soften for a few minutes over a medium heat, then add the cider and cider vinegar and bring to the boil. Cook for about 10 minutes on a high heat, until all the liquid has gone.

Add the stock and thyme leaves, then bring back to the boil and cook until only a quarter of the liquid remains.

Add the cream and again bring back to the boil, then remove from the heat straight away. Taste and season.

Lift the cooked green of leek out of the liquid and place in the bottom of a baking dish. Arrange the raw white cylinders of leek on top in rows. Spoon over the creamy liquid and season with a little more salt and pepper. Cover with foil and place in the preheated oven for 30 minutes.

Whilst the leeks are baking, put the breadcrumbs, parsley, garlic, salt and pepper into a blender or food processor and whiz until you have fine green crumbs, then add the grated Parmesan and continue to blend for 30 seconds more.

Remove the leeks from the oven, take off the foil and sprinkle the herby breadcrumbs over the top. Put back into the oven for a further 10 minutes, to brown slightly, then serve.

Spiced Pumpkin, Butter Bean and Spinach Casserole

If you prefer to cook your own butterbeans, use 100g, and see the method on page 229. 'I love pumpkin and spice, and this is a great alternative to a meat casserole,' says John Hardwick. 'Good with rice or couscous and a dollop of sour cream.'

2 tablespoons olive oil

400g pumpkin, peeled, deseeded and cut into chunks (about 3cm)

1 small onion, finely sliced

1 stick of celery, chopped

1 medium carrot, chopped

2 cloves of garlic, finely chopped

2.5cm piece of fresh root ginger, finely chopped

1 teaspoon ground cumin

1 teaspoon coriander seeds

½ teaspoon ground turmeric

½ a long red chilli, finely chopped

200g tomatoes, chopped

3 tablespoons honey

200g jarred or tinned butter beans, drained and rinsed

50g Puy lentils, rinsed

1½ teaspoons sea salt

50g young spinach leaves, sliced

1 small bunch of fresh basil, finely chopped

2 tablespoons finely chopped fresh coriander

freshly ground black pepper

Heat the oil in a large non-stick pan or flame-proof casserole. Add the pumpkin, onion, celery, carrot, garlic and ginger, and cook over a medium heat for 5 minutes, or until the vegetables are beginning to soften and are lightly browned, stirring constantly. Add the spices and chilli and cook for 3 minutes more, again stirring constantly, and being careful not to let them burn.

Next add the tomatoes, honey, beans, lentils, 1 litre of water and the salt and bring to a simmer. Cook for 25–30 minutes, stirring regularly, until the liquid is well reduced and the pumpkin has broken down and blended into it, so that the dish looks like a curry.

Stir in the spinach, basil and coriander and cook for 1–2 minutes more. Taste, adjust the seasoning and serve.

Five Risotti

The rice in a great risotto should retain a little bite to it, but at the same time the risotto should be quite loose and creamy – not soupy, but if you tap the underneath of the plate or dish in which you are serving it, the risotto should flatten out. Usually the creaminess is achieved by beating in plenty of butter, or a combination of butter and extra Parmesan, or even cream, before serving. We differ a little in that we add onion purée, which gives the risotto all the velvety texture and richness it needs, but without the addition of extra fat.

You can make up a big batch of the purée and keep it portioned up in bags in the freezer, then defrost it just before you want to use it.

The purée also makes a nice little sauce with roasted meat.

In a risotto, good stock is as vital as it is in soups, so either buy a good vegetable one, or preferably make your own (see page 416).

Onion Purée

Preheat the oven to 150°C/gas 2.

Put 1kg thinly sliced onions and 2 cloves of finely chopped garlic into a medium casserole (one that has a lid) with 300g butter, 2 tablespoons chopped fresh oregano, a sprig of fresh thyme (leaves only) and 500ml of water. Season with a little salt and pepper.

Cover and put into the preheated oven for 1½ hours, or until the onions have completely softened but there is still a little liquid in the bottom of the casserole. Take out of the oven, leave to cool a little then blend to a smooth purée. Divide into portions and freeze until ready to defrost and use in risotto – or to accompany roasted meat.

Broad Bean, Pea and Watercress Risotto

160g peas, fresh or frozen

160g podded broad beans

45g butter

1 tablespoon olive oil

1 small onion, finely chopped

1 clove of garlic, crushed to a paste

150g carnaroli or arborio risotto rice

50ml white wine

700ml good vegetable stock, hot (see page 416)

150g onion purée

1 tablespoon chopped fresh mint

4 tablespoons watercress and pumpkin seed pesto (see page 385)

60g Parmesan cheese, finely grated, plus 30g, shaved with a vegetable peeler, to finish

sea salt and freshly ground black pepper

1 handful of watercress, roughly chopped

2 tablespoons extra virgin olive oil

Half fill a large saucepan with water and bring to the boil. Add the peas first, if fresh, and cook for about 5 minutes, adding the broad beans for the last 30 seconds. If the peas are frozen, you can put the peas and beans in together and bring back to the boil, then take off the heat after 30 seconds. Drain in a colander under running water, then slip off the skins from the broad beans. Keep to one side.

Melt 15g of the butter with the oil in a heavy wide-based pan. Add the onion and garlic and soften gently without colouring.

Add the rice and cook for 5 minutes, stirring constantly, over a low heat.

Add the white wine, turn up the heat a little and let the liquid reduce until it has almost gone, then add the hot stock a ladleful at a time, stirring continually and only adding the next ladleful when the previous one has been absorbed. Keep going until all the stock has gone and you have a creamy, quite loose consistency – the rice should still have a little bite to it.

Stir in the onion purée, the rest of the butter and the reserved broad beans and peas, and let the vegetables warm through. Stir in the mint, pesto and grated Parmesan, and taste and season as necessary.

Divide the risotto between four warmed wide bowls, or deep plates, and garnish with the Parmesan shavings and chopped watercress. Drizzle with the extra virgin olive oil and serve immediately.

Jerusalem Artichoke Risotto with Garlic and Almond Breadcrumbs

45g butter

1 tablespoon olive oil

1 small onion, finely chopped

1 clove of garlic, crushed to a paste

150g carnaroli or arborio risotto rice

50ml white wine

700ml good vegetable stock, hot (see page 416)

60g Parmesan cheese, grated

sea salt and freshly ground black pepper

1 handful of micro- or baby salad leaves, to finish

2 teaspoons truffle oil, to finish

For the artichoke purée:

320g Jerusalem artichokes, peeled and roughly chopped

250ml milk

50g butter

1 tablespoon lemon juice

sea salt

For the breadcrumbs:

2 tablespoons olive oil

30g breadcrumbs

1 tablespoon chopped fresh rosemary leaves

1 teaspoon chopped fresh thyme leaves

½ a clove of garlic, crushed

15g flaked almonds

To make the artichoke purée, put the artichokes and milk into a pan with half the butter and 400ml of water. Bring to the boil, then reduce the heat and simmer until the artichokes are soft. Lift them out and transfer to a blender, adding just enough of the cooking liquid (about 4 tablespoons) to form a purée. Add the rest of the butter and the lemon juice and blend again. Taste and season with salt as necessary, then keep to one side.

For the risotto, melt 15g of the butter with the oil in a heavy wide-based pan. Add the onion and garlic and soften gently without colouring. Add the rice and cook for 5 minutes, stirring constantly, over a low heat.

Add the white wine, turn up the heat a little and let the liquid reduce until it has almost gone, then add the hot stock a ladleful at a time, stirring continually and only adding the next ladleful when the previous one has been absorbed. Keep going until all the stock has gone and you

have a creamy, quite loose consistency – the rice should still have a little bite to it.

Add the artichoke purée, the Parmesan and the rest of the butter, stir and take off the heat. Taste and season as necessary.

For the breadcrumbs, heat the oil in a pan and quickly fry the breadcrumbs with the herbs and garlic. Drain on kitchen paper, then combine with the almonds.

Divide the risotto between four warmed wide bowls, or deep plates, and garnish with the garlic breadcrumbs and the micro- or baby leaves. Drizzle with the truffle oil, finish with some freshly ground black pepper and serve immediately.

Leek and Wild Garlic Pesto Risotto

15g butter

1 tablespoon olive oil

1 small onion, finely chopped

1 clove of garlic, crushed to a paste

150g carnaroli or arborio risotto rice

50ml white wine

700ml good vegetable stock, hot (see page 416)

2 leeks, finely chopped

150g onion purée (see page 146)

50g Parmesan cheese, grated, plus an extra 30g, shaved with a vegetable peeler, to finish

60ml wild garlic and pumpkin seed pesto (see page 385)

1 small bunch of fresh chives, chopped

sea salt and freshly ground black pepper

1 handful of micro- or baby salad leaves

2 tablespoons olive oil

Melt 15g of the butter with the oil in a heavy wide-based pan. Add the onion and garlic and soften gently without colouring.

Add the rice and cook for 5 minutes, stirring constantly, over a low heat.

Add the white wine, turn up the heat a little and let the liquid reduce until it has almost gone, then add the hot stock a ladleful at a time, stirring continually and only adding the next ladleful when the previous one has been absorbed. Keep going until all the stock has gone and you have a creamy, quite loose consistency – the rice should still have a little bite to it.

Stir in the leeks and heat through, then stir in the onion purée and the grated Parmesan and after 30 seconds add the wild garlic pesto and the chives. Taste and season accordingly.

Divide the risotto between four warmed wide bowls, or deep plates, and garnish with the Parmesan shavings and the micro- or baby leaves. Drizzle with the olive oil and serve immediately.

Spelt, Garden Vegetable and Herb Risotto

120g podded broad beans

100g pearled spelt

75g butter

1 small summer squash, such as Crown Prince, peeled, deseeded and chopped (about 1cm)

2 leeks, finely chopped

1 tablespoon olive oil

1 small onion, finely chopped

1 clove of garlic, crushed to a paste

150g carnaroli or arborio risotto rice

50ml white wine

700ml good vegetable stock, hot (see page 416)

150g onion purée (see page 146)

2 courgettes, finely chopped

100g baby spinach

100g Parmesan cheese, finely grated

2 tablespoons chopped fresh herbs, such as parsley, sage and thyme

sea salt and freshly ground black pepper

1 handful of micro- or baby salad leaves

Half fill a large saucepan with water and bring to the boil. Add the beans, bring back to the boil, then take off the heat straight away. Drain through a colander under running water, then slip the skins from the beans (if you like). Keep to one side.

Put the spelt into a pan of cold water and bring to the boil. Turn down the heat to a simmer for 20 minutes, until the grains are just cooked, then drain and set aside.

Meanwhile, heat 60g of the butter in a frying pan and sauté the squash until it is just starting to soften. Stir in the leeks, continue to cook until they are just beginning to colour, then remove from the heat.

Melt the rest of the butter with the oil in a heavy wide-based pan, then add the onion and garlic and soften gently without colouring.

Add the rice and cook for 5 minutes, stirring constantly, over a low heat.

Add the white wine, turn up the heat a little and let the liquid reduce until it has almost gone, then add the hot stock a ladleful at a time, stirring continually and only adding the next ladleful when the previous one has been absorbed. Keep going until all the stock has gone and you have a creamy, quite loose consistency – the rice should still have a little bite to it.

Stir in the onion purée, cooked spelt, courgettes, spinach, reserved broad beans and the sautéd vegetables and let them heat through.

Add the Parmesan and herbs, taste and season accordingly. Divide the risotto between four warmed wide bowls, or deep plates, garnish with the leaves and serve immediately.

Pearl Barley, Asparagus and Pea Shoot Risotto

'I love this risotto', says Rosie Henderson, who has been helping to run the farmshop for nine years now. 'Jez grows the pea shoots lovingly in the market garden, and it is a real treat when they come into season.' As this is made with pearl barley, rather than rice, you can add the stock in one go, rather than ladleful by ladleful. This is because the barley cooks in a completely different way, absorbing the stock and softening. If you were to add all the stock at once when making a risotto with rice, the outside of each grain would soften, but the kernel in the centre would stay hard.

90g butter

1 medium onion, finely chopped

2 cloves of garlic, crushed

285g pearl barley

1.35 litres good vegetable stock, hot (see page 416)

150g slender asparagus, stalks thinly sliced, tips left whole

125g onion purée (see page 146)

2 teaspoons fresh lemon juice

60g young spinach (leaves only) and thinly sliced

4 spring onions, white parts only, thinly sliced

1 tablespoon finely chopped fresh mint leaves

75g Parmesan cheese, finely grated, plus an extra 65g, shaved with a vegetable peeler, to finish

sea salt and freshly ground black pepper

1 small handful of pea shoots

2 teaspoons extra virgin olive oil

Melt 50g of the butter in a large non-stick saucepan or flame-proof casserole and gently cook the onion and garlic until softened, stirring occasionally.

Rinse the barley in a sieve under running water and add to the pan. Stir in 950ml of the stock and bring to the boil, then turn down the heat and simmer for 25–30 minutes, or until the barley is swollen and tender and most of the liquid has evaporated. Take off the heat.

Heat the remaining vegetable stock in a small pan and blanch the asparagus tips for 3 minutes, until just cooked, then lift out with a slotted spoon, keep to one side, and add the stock to the pan of barley. Bring this back to a gentle simmer, stirring regularly, then add the onion purée, lemon juice, spinach, spring onions, sliced asparagus stalks, mint, grated Parmesan and the rest of the butter. Cook for 2 minutes, stirring constantly. Season with salt and pepper.

Divide the risotto between four warmed wide bowls, or deep plates, and garnish with the reserved asparagus tips, the Parmesan shavings and the pea shoots. Drizzle with a little extra virgin olive oil, and serve.

'The cheese is the boss . . .'
John Longman, The Cheese Room

Making cheese in the traditional way, by hand, is a lot like cooking. Half a dozen people can start with the same ingredients and follow the same recipe but the result will be surprisingly different; and you can't always put your finger on why, because it is the little things that are significant: the way an individual handles the cheese, but also the process itself. It isn't like mixing cement to a formula, you are dealing with something much more volatile. Also the protein and fat content in the milk can vary according to the season, or a sudden blip in the weather. Occasionally you might get an unusual, sometimes wonderful, and exciting flavour coming through, because the cows have eaten a particular herb or a weed in the meadows. But that is what is fascinating and challenging about artisan cheese-making. The differences and nuances are all part of the attraction, whereas in industrial-scale cheese-making it is all about consistency: every batch must look and taste the same.

Some cheese-makers use an analysis of the milk to decide how to make each batch of cheese in advance, but I prefer to take it as it comes, and judge it as I go along. Every style of cheese is made slightly differently, but once you add your culture to the milk and warm it up to start things off, the process can be quite quick or relatively slow, and the cheese is the boss. That's why we make one batch at a time. If you were to have more vats on the go, and one was behaving more slowly or quickly than the rest, you might end up with compromised cheese. With one batch you can be totally focused and either on your toes ready to stay with it, and not let it get ahead of you; or be patient and calm and wait and wait if it isn't ready, because the cheese won't be rushed. It might need a bit more temperature or time . . . it's no good being in a hurry to go off and do something else.

My background is Cheddar-making in Somerset. My family had a dairy farm and made Cheddar through the generations for over 100 years, so it is in my blood. However, we also began diversifying into other cheeses before I decided to go to Australia for a year in 2007 to work in a small artisan dairy in Queensland – a wild thing to do at nearly sixty – where we made nineteen different cheeses.

When I came back to England and to Daylesford, many of the farm cheeses had already been introduced, initially by Joe Schneider, who established the creamery and made the first Cheddar. His successor, James McCall, introduced an early version of the Double and Single Gloucester, as well as the Adlestrop, which I have since made my own. It is called after a local village, though most people recognise the name from the poem 'Adlestrop' by Edward Thomas. It's a delightful cheese, which is rind-washed and matured for ten weeks.

As a cheese-maker you can never arrive somewhere new and impose your ideas or think you know best; because I'm afraid you don't. Every dairy has its own conditions, and particular micro-flora of bacteria in the room, and the only thing to do is to feel your way and then gradually, over time, begin to develop the cheeses in your own style. I think now, if it were possible by some kind of time travel to taste some of my predecessors' cheese alongside mine in a blind-tasting, I would recognise mine straight away.

There are only a few farms that make Single Gloucester, as it now has Protected Designation of Origin status (PDO) and can only be made with the milk from a farm that has a registered herd of Gloucestershire cattle, a heritage breed, which Richard, the farm manager, introduced to Daylesford in 2006.

Single Gloucester dates back over two centuries. It was what was known as a kitchen cheese, as it was made with the partially skimmed milk left over from making Double Gloucester cheese and butter on small farms. Whereas Double Gloucester would be sold, the Single Gloucester was kept for the family and was rarely seen beyond a particular farm or village, let alone Gloucestershire county. It was a cheese that had been almost lost until relatively recently, and barely anyone remembers how the original was made, so the modern-day Single Gloucester has been reinvented and is made to a standardised recipe, using whole milk. As a result it is now acclaimed and sought after, rather than the lowly poor relation to Double Gloucester – and personally I prefer it.

The two cheeses are made quite differently, with different starters and maturing times. Single Gloucester is a nice, fresh, buttery-tasting young cheese that has quite a bit of character – you can really taste the flavour of the milk in it – and is best around six to eight weeks old. If you keep it too much longer, it can dry out. Double Gloucester is much closer to a Cheddar, but with a more mellow flavour, and is traditionally coloured with annatto, a natural vegetable dye, to give it its orangey appearance. It is also matured for much longer: three to six months.

Since I have been here we have also introduced Baywell, which is a soft, creamy, but quite mature-tasting cow's milk cheese, made in a heart-shape with an orangey-pink rind. It is an extension of the ripe, creamy-soft Penyston, named after Penyston Hastings, whose family owned Daylesford in the eighteenth century – a cheese we used to make, and may well revive one day. As often happens in artisan cheese-making, the Baywell came about almost by accident, when someone tried rind-washing

a troublesome batch of Penyston. The result: a new style of cheese. Penyston was also the starting point for the white-mould goat's cheese we call Penygoat. I decided to make an experimental batch of Penyston, but using goat's milk instead of cow's milk, and originally called it Penygoat as a joke – but everyone liked the cheese, and the name, so it has stuck.

We have also developed the soft Oddington goat's cheese, and the hard Trenchard – and I have ideas for a goat's cheese made to a Gouda recipe – and of course we make a cream cheese for the bakery to use, and a feta-style cheese for the kitchens. Then there are the blue cheeses. The latest are the Bledington Blue cheeses, which are small, creamy versions of Daylesford Blue, in which the curds are stirred for less time so they are softer, and stay in salt for slightly less time, then the cheese is matured for just four to nine weeks.

Although we make around a dozen different cheeses our production is still relatively small. We only make twenty tonnes a year of everything, whereas in a big industrial process you might make 190 tonnes a day! Our Cheddar is our biggest production, and it is still the cheese I love to make most: even after forty-five years. Sometimes people say to me, 'I couldn't just make Cheddar, day in day out.' Well, I could. It's never boring, because the art of it is always having to make those little adjustments here and there. I get quite protective about every batch – and I want to see it through from beginning to end.

Some people say that true Cheddar can only be made in Somerset, but it is the process that makes a Cheddar, really, although every dairy makes it slightly differently; some make it slightly wetter than others, and obviously everyone is starting with different milk – in our case the milk comes straight in from our own Friesian herd.

Once the coagulated milk is cut to separate the curds and whey, the whey is drained off, and the mass of curds come together in springy pillows which are layered up, left for around ten to twenty minutes, then turned and re-stacked – this is the 'cheddaring' process, which we repeat around five times over to press and drain the curd and let the acidity rise, then it is shredded and salted. At this point you can finally relax and let the pieces of curd sit and cool briefly before packing them into the moulds, which are lined with cotton muslin and then pressed. It's an extraordinary process really, achieving something solid out of soft curds. People think that the pressing is to get the moisture out – a bit like cider-making – but not at all; that has already happened, so the pressing is to shape the cheese and allow it to come together. Traditional clothbound Cheddar, being a hard cheese and one of the driest, needs more pressure than most. We still use the old wooden presses that work with ropes, pulleys and weights, which Joe Schneider brought over from Holland and are at their absolute limit for pressing big cheeses.

Finally the cheese is turned out, wrapped in new cloth and greased with our own rendered-down beef lard. Traditionally in Somerset, Cheddar was greased with pork lard, because smallholdings kept pigs, which ate the whey left over from the cheese-making – whereas here we have cattle herds, and it is all part of the way the various aspects of the farm work together, that the cattle provide the lard for the cheese. Finally the cheeses are labelled, dated and moved to the maturing shelves, where they have to be turned and checked as they develop.

We aim to mature the Cheddar for nine months plus. I actually think it is at its nicest between ten and twelve months. We do age some cheeses for eighteen months, and they can be wonderful, with a more nutty flavour, but as soon as you cut into an older cheese, it will start to dry out, so you can't keep it for long. Only cheeses of a certain character are suitable for longer ageing. You check each one at around nine months using a stainless steel cheese iron, which is pushed into the centre and pulls out a plug of cheese, so you can assess the aroma, body, texture and flavour – and if it has a good clean flavour, but is not over acidic, then it will be capable of ageing a bit longer. If there is already a big flavour there, keeping it longer might just make it stronger, rather than nicer.

In many big dairies they use a different culture and most of the cheese-making is done by machine, ending with the cheese being forced down a long tube and into its plastic wrapper. It can be very good cheese, but it tends to have a sweeter taste that isn't a true Cheddar flavour, and that people have got used to, so they are sometimes surprised when they taste a traditional hand-made cheese. It is a sweetness more allied to a Gruyère, which is a cheese I actually love – but Cheddar isn't Gruyère.

In a big factory production the whole process has to be planned, fine-tuned and backed up by laboratory statistics and a very high degree of expertise, because if something were to go wrong on a big scale you might not be able to rescue it in the way that you usually can with a single, hand-made batch, and a whole day's production could be lost, which would be very embarrassing. I am sure that getting it right is very satisfying for a cheese-maker in its own way, but in my view you can't cheat time. Industrial processes try to, but time is everything. Here at Daylesford the creamery is next door to the bakery, and we share the same philosophy: bread and cheese have always gone together, and they both need time and skill to make them well. You can churn out bread very fast in a factory, using the Chorleywood process, or you can make a sourdough slowly, giving it time to develop; just as you can produce tonnes of blocks of cheese in a day, or you can make single batches and nurture them all the way through the process. I am addicted to the lovely bread they make next door, especially the seven seed sourdough . . . even without cheese. But with a piece of Cheddar, it is beautiful. In fact the fruit bread goes well with Cheddar too, and I have also discovered, since being here, that the best bread to eat with blue cheese is rye: a perfect combination.

SAVOURY TARTS

& PIES

An open tart for every season
Goat's cheese and asparagus
Blue cheese and broccoli
Butternut squash and kale
Vivid heritage tomatoes on crispy,
flaky pastry
Tarte tatins of red onion
Hearty warming pies for winter

We constantly change the open tarts we make throughout the seasons, combining vegetables from the market garden with different cheeses from the creamery – packing the pastry cases quite full with whatever produce we are using, so that there is a high ratio of vegetables to creamy cheese mixture. Most are made with shortcrust pastry, with the exception of red onion tarte tatins, and tomato tarts, which we make to show off Jez's heritage red and yellow fruits, using crispy, light puff pastry.

In autumn, especially when local game comes into the kitchen and we move into much more slow casserole-style cooking, it is time to start making homely, comforting pies in deep dishes, the kind in which the pastry is held up by an old-fashioned pie prop which pops through the centre of the golden brown pastry. Lovely served with winter brassicas, or crushed, buttered root vegetables and cabbage (see page 135).

Savoury Pastry

This makes enough for two of the savoury tarts on the following pages (each one 20cm round and around 5–7cm deep); or one each of the Cheddar, potato and onion pie on page 184 and the Wootton Estate game pie on page 191. If you are only making one tart, the remaining pastry can be frozen and used up to two months later – and, of course, you can double the quantity and make a bigger batch in one go, then portion it and put it into the freezer for whenever you need it.

735g plain flour	530g butter
a pinch of salt	3 eggs (plus 1 egg, beaten, for brushing)

Sift the flour into a bowl and add the salt. Grate in the butter and mix lightly with the tips of your fingers until the mixture resembles breadcrumbs, ensuring there are no lumps of butter in the mix (alternatively you can do this using a food processor).

Crack the eggs into a measuring jug, beat lightly and top up with cold water until you have 280ml. Pour this slowly into the flour and butter, mixing for a few seconds until the mixture forms a dough. Don't overwork it, or the pastry will be tough. Divide into 2 roughly shaped balls, wrap in clingfilm and chill in the fridge for at least 30 minutes before using. (Or freeze until needed).

Preheat the oven to 160°C/gas 3.

Lightly flour your work surface and then, for each tart, roll out one of your balls of pastry into a circle big enough to line a 20cm x 5–7cm deep flan tin with a removable base, leaving enough pastry to overhang the sides. Wrap the pastry carefully around your rolling pin to lift it and drop it carefully into the flan tin, pushing it gently into the base and sides of the tin – don't trim the overhanging pastry. Put the tin on a baking tray – this makes it easier to move it around – then into the fridge to rest and chill for another 30 minutes (to help prevent the pastry shrinking during baking).

When ready to blind-bake, prick the base of the pastry case with a fork, line with greaseproof paper – crinkle it up first to soften it and avoid it denting the pastry – and fill with baking beans. Put into the preheated oven for about 30 minutes, until light golden brown, then take out, remove the paper and baking beans (you no longer need these), and brush all over the inside of the pastry case with the beaten egg, to seal up any little holes.

Put the tin back into the oven for a further 5–10 minutes, until the base is fully baked and golden brown. Don't be scared of taking the pastry to this point. The key to a good tart base is to hold your nerve, and colour and crisp the pastry to the stage at which you would like to eat it, as once you put in your filling and return it to the oven it won't colour any more, except maybe a little around the edges, and the base will stay crispy and flaky as the filling cooks. If you only lightly colour the pastry, and the base isn't fully baked, it will be soft and doughy, making the whole tart seem heavy.

Remove from the oven and, when cool, carefully trim off the overhanging pastry with a small, sharp, serrated knife. Keep to one side. Now you can make whichever filling you like, and bake your tart according to the instructions in each recipe.

Note: We bake the tarts at a very low temperature, so that the eggs don't expand and cause the filling to rise up, like a soufflé, as if this happens the mixture will drop again as the tart cools, and the surface will crack. Instead the more gentle baking allows the filling simply to set. Also, these are deep tarts, so if you use too high a temperature, the top will be brown before the mixture has cooked in the centre.

Adlestrop Cheese and Kale

Our Adlestrop cheese, which takes its name from a local village, is a washed-rind, quite pungent, semi-soft cheese, matured for 10 weeks. You could also use a cheese like Caerphilly.

For this tart we use a heritage variety of kale called Red Russian, which is green with a reddish tinge around the edges and is a little flatter and less frilly than the more usual varieties. Cavolo nero works well, too.

80g butter	2 eggs
2 small white onions, finely chopped	4 egg yolks
2 cloves of garlic, finely chopped	250g mascarpone
	100ml double cream
250g kale leaves, stalk removed and leaves shredded	250g Adlestrop or similar cheese, chopped (about 2cm)
sea salt and freshly ground black pepper	1 blind-baked 20cm x 5–7cm shortcrust tart case (see page 167)

Preheat the oven to 140°C/gas 1.

Melt the butter in a large pan, then put in the onions and garlic and cook over a low heat for 5 minutes, until the onions have softened but not coloured. Add the kale and cook for another 5 minutes, stirring constantly, until it has just slightly softened. Taste and season as necessary. Transfer to a bowl and leave to cool.

In a separate large bowl whisk the eggs, yolks, mascarpone and cream for a few seconds, then add the cheese. Squeeze the excess water from the kale and onions, and add to the mixture. Stir in lightly and spoon into the prepared pastry case, making sure the cheese is evenly distributed. Put into the preheated oven and bake for about 40 minutes, or until the top is golden and the mixture is fully cooked – to check, insert a metal skewer into the centre, and if it doesn't smear, the tart is done.

Oddington Goat's Cheese and Asparagus

We make this in spring and early summer, when English asparagus is in season, and it pairs well with our Oddington goat's cheese, which is semi-soft and creamy, not too fresh, and not too strong. You could also make it with a goat's cheese like Ragstone, Golden Cross or Crottin de Chèvre.

250g asparagus

2 eggs

4 egg yolks

250g mascarpone

100ml double cream

1 small bunch of chervil, chopped

sea salt and freshly ground black pepper

1 blind-baked 20cm x 5–7cm shortcrust tart case (see page 167)

230g fresh goat's cheese, such as Oddington

Preheat the oven to 140°C/gas 1.

Unless your asparagus is young and tender, take off the white woody bases and slice the spears very thinly crossways, leaving just the very tips intact.

In a large bowl, whisk the eggs, yolks, mascarpone and cream for a few seconds, then add the asparagus, chervil and seasoning, mix lightly and spoon into the prepared pastry case.

Crumble the goat's cheese and dot over the surface, so that some pieces stick out. Put into the preheated oven and bake for about 40 minutes, or until the top of the tart is golden and the mixture is fully cooked – to check, insert a metal skewer into the centre, and if it doesn't smear, the tart is done.

Bledington Blue Cheese and Broccoli

Bledington Blue is a softer-flavoured, less crumbly but slightly more creamy cheese than, say, a Stilton. Alternatives include Barkham Blue, Cambozola, or Stichelton, which is made by Joe Schneider, Daylesford's first ever cheese-maker, together with Randolph Hodgson of Neal's Yard Dairy, on the Welbeck Estate in Nottinghamshire.

2 heads of broccoli, separated into florets

2 eggs

4 egg yolks

250g mascarpone

100ml double cream

3 tablespoons chopped fresh chervil

sea salt and freshly ground black pepper

1 blind-baked 20cm x 5–7cm shortcrust tart case (see page 167)

150g blue cheese, such as Bledington

Preheat the oven to 140°C/gas 1.

Two-thirds fill a large pan with cold water and bring to a rapid boil. Add the broccoli and cook over a high heat for 2 minutes, then take off the heat and drain through a colander under cold running water until cold. Leave the broccoli to stand in the colander for 10 minutes, then pat dry with a clean tea towel or kitchen paper.

In a large bowl, whisk the eggs, yolks, mascarpone and cream for a few seconds, then add the cooked broccoli and chervil, season, mix lightly, and spoon into the prepared pastry case.

Crumble the blue cheese and dot over the surface, so that some pieces stick out. Put into the preheated oven and bake for about 40 minutes, or until the top is golden and the mixture is fully cooked – to check, insert a metal skewer into the centre, and if it doesn't smear, the tart is done.

Single Gloucester, Spinach and Smoked Bacon

Single Gloucester, with its distinctive yet quite light and subtle flavour, has its own PDO (Protected Designation of Origin), so we are one of only a handful of creameries who make it. Other cheeses that combine well with the spinach and smoked bacon include Adlestrop and Caerphilly.

The cooking of the bacon is important here: you just want to colour it, so you get a nice roasted, smoky flavour through the tart, but don't let it become crispy. Also, make sure that when you have washed your spinach, you dry it thoroughly, before adding it to the pan with the bacon and onions, and then, when it is wilted, drain it really well and squeeze it out so that it doesn't make the filling watery.

50g butter

150g smoked streaky bacon, cut into small pieces

1 onion, finely chopped

450g baby spinach

2 eggs

4 egg yolks

250g mascarpone

100ml double cream

150g Single Gloucester cheese, grated

sea salt and freshly ground black pepper

1 blind-baked 20cm x 5–7cm shortcrust tart case (see page 167)

Melt the butter in a large non-stick frying pan over a medium heat. Put in the bacon pieces and cook for about 5 minutes, until golden brown (but not crispy), stirring constantly, then lower the heat, add the onion and continue to cook for about 10 minutes, until the onion has softened but not coloured.

Add the spinach and continue to cook for 1 minute or until it just wilts, then take off the heat immediately, drain through a sieve and transfer to a bowl to cool.

In a separate large bowl whisk the eggs, yolks, mascarpone and cream for a few seconds, then add the cheese. Squeeze any remaining moisture from the spinach mixture and add to the bowl, season and mix lightly, then spoon into the prepared pastry case and smooth level with the back of the spoon.

Put into the preheated oven and bake for about 35 minutes, or until the top is golden and the mixture is fully cooked – to check, insert a metal skewer into the centre, and if it doesn't smear, the tart is done.

Butternut Squash and Kale

Another autumnal tart – you can use cavolo nero as a
change from kale if you prefer, or even spinach. As always,
the secret is to cook and drain the greens well, to remove
any moisture before adding to the filling.

80g butter	250g mascarpone
100g kale leaves, shredded	100ml double cream
1 medium butternut squash, peeled, halved, seeds removed, and flesh grated	70g Cheddar cheese, grated
	100g Parmesan cheese, finely grated
sea salt and freshly ground black pepper	1 blind-baked 20cm x 5–7cm shortcrust tart case (see page 167)
2 eggs	
4 egg yolks	

Preheat the oven to 140°C/ gas 1.

Melt the butter in a medium pan, add the kale and cook
for 2 minutes, stirring constantly. Increase the heat, add
the grated butternut squash and continue to cook for
2–3 minutes, until the vegetables are just slightly softened.
Taste and season accordingly, then take the pan from the
heat and turn the mixture into a bowl or on to a plate
to cool.

In a separate bowl whisk the eggs, yolks, mascarpone
and cream for a few seconds, then add the Cheddar and
Parmesan. Drain any excess moisture from the kale and
squash mixture, season again to taste, and mix lightly.
Spoon into the prepared pastry case and smooth level
with the back of the spoon.

Put into the preheated oven and bake for about 40
minutes, or until the top of the tart is golden and the
mixture is fully cooked – to check, insert a metal skewer
into the centre, and if it doesn't smear, the tart is done.

Jerusalem Artichoke and Cavolo Nero

This is a tart for winter, since Jerusalem artichokes are always sweeter and more flavourful after the first frost.

700g Jerusalem artichokes	2 eggs
3 tablespoons olive oil	4 egg yolks
sea salt and freshly ground black pepper	250g mascarpone
	100ml double cream
2 tablespoons butter	100g Parmesan cheese, finely grated
300g bunch of cavolo nero, stalks removed and leaves finely chopped	1 x blind-baked 20cm x 5–7cm shortcrust tart case (see page 167)

Preheat the oven to 180°C/gas 4.

Cut the top and bottoms off the artichokes and wash them well in a bowl of water, using a nail scrubbing brush to remove all the sand and dirt. Cut into quarters, put into a small bowl with the olive oil, and season with a little salt and pepper. Toss well to coat, then transfer to a baking tray and put into the preheated oven for about 12 minutes, until softened and golden brown. Remove from the oven and leave to cool. Turn the oven down to 140°C/gas 1.

Melt the butter in a medium pan, then put in the cavolo nero and cook for 5 minutes over a medium heat. Season and leave to cool, then drain off any buttery liquid, transfer to a board and chop a little more finely.

In a large bowl, whisk the eggs, yolks, mascarpone and cream for a few seconds, then add the Parmesan, chopped cavolo nero and roasted artichokes. Season and mix lightly, then spoon into the prepared pastry case and smooth level with the back of the spoon. Put into the preheated oven and bake for about 40 minutes, or until the top is golden and the mixture is fully cooked – to check, insert a metal skewer into the centre, and if it doesn't smear, the tart is done.

Three Tomato Tart

This is all about the quality of your tomatoes. You want a biggish, beefsteak red tomato for the sauce and for slicing. Around August Jez recommends Marmande, which are the rich, sweet, 'ribbed', bulbous-looking ones that have more flesh than seeds. Earlier in the year Stupice is one of the first tomatoes to ripen, and is a good, full-flavoured one to use for the sauce. Sweet, juicy Golden Cherry tomatoes are perfect for the finishing layer.

12 large ripe red vine tomatoes, preferably heritage (see introduction, above)

6 tablespoons extra virgin olive oil

1 medium red onion, thinly sliced

2 cloves of garlic, thinly sliced

1 teaspoon coriander seeds

1 teaspoon cumin seeds

1 teaspoon tomato paste

1 teaspoon chopped fresh red chilli

juice of ½ a lemon

1 good sprig of thyme, leaves only

sea salt and freshly ground black pepper

500g puff pastry

3 tablespoons freshly grated Parmesan cheese

20 yellow vine cherry tomatoes, preferably heritage (see introduction, above)

Preheat the oven to 180°C/gas 4.

Chop 6 of the large tomatoes.

Heat 3 tablespoons of the olive oil in a medium pan over a low heat, then add the onion, garlic and the coriander and cumin seeds and cook for about 10 minutes, until the onion softens, stirring constantly. Add the chopped tomatoes, tomato paste, chilli, lemon juice and half the thyme leaves and continue to cook for 5 minutes.

Add 200ml of water and bring to the boil, then cook over a medium heat for about 15 minutes, until the tomatoes have broken down and all the juice has evaporated. Taste

and season as necessary. Remove from the heat and leave to cool.

Roll out the puff pastry on a lightly floured surface to about 3–4mm thick, and cut around a small plate or use a large cutter (about 12cm in diameter) to cut out 6 discs. Line a baking tray with a sheet of greaseproof paper, place the discs on top and put into the fridge to rest for 20 minutes (this will help to stop the pastry shrinking in the oven).

When ready to cook, remove the pastry discs from the fridge and prick all over with a fork. Bake in the preheated oven for 15 minutes, until light golden and crisp.

Remove and leave to cool. Slice the remaining red tomatoes thinly (around 3mm).

Divide the cooked tomato mixture between the pastry discs, spreading it right to the edge. Arrange the slices of red tomato on top (approximately 6 slices on each). Sprinkle with the Parmesan and return the tarts to the oven for a further 10 minutes.

Meanwhile, cut the yellow cherry tomatoes into halves or quarters depending on their size, put into a bowl, combine with the rest of the olive oil and the remaining thyme leaves and season.

Remove the tarts from the oven, spoon some of the yellow tomatoes and their juices on to each tart and serve.

Red Onion Tarte Tatins with Baywell Cheese

These are individual tarts, which we make in 12cm blini pans that will transfer to the oven. Or you could use similar-sized individual tart tins.

Baywell is a development of the Penyston cheese we used to make, which took its name from an ancient ancestor who once owned the Daylesford farm. The Baywell is a rind-washed cheese, soft and creamy, but quite mature in flavour, which is just sliced and melted on top of the caramelised red onions. Cheeses of a similar style that you could use include Camembert, Brie, Adlestrop, or Crottin goat's cheese.

6 small red onions (try to choose onions all the same size), peeled and left whole

1 tablespoon olive oil

a couple of knobs of butter

1 tablespoon balsamic vinegar

20g sugar

3 tablespoons red wine

1 x 200g pack of puff pastry

1 Baywell cheese, cut into 8 slices, leaving the rind on

4 handfuls of mixed salad leaves, to serve

For the dressing:

3 tablespoons olive oil

2 tablespoons balsamic vinegar

sea salt and freshly ground black pepper

Slice each onion exactly in half through the root, to give two identical, intact halves from each onion – so you end up with 12 halves of the same size.

Preheat the oven to 180°C/gas 4.

Heat the oil and butter in a large, non-stick and ovenproof frying pan. When the butter is foaming, put in all the onions, cut side down, and cook gently until the cut sides are golden brown. Mix together the vinegar, sugar and red wine, then add to the pan and bring to the boil. Cover the pan with foil, transfer to the preheated oven and bake for 15 minutes, or until the onions are tender.

Meanwhile, lightly flour a work surface and roll out the pastry to about 3–4mm thickness. Cut 4 rounds slightly larger than your blini pans or tart tins and layer on a plate in the fridge until needed.

Remove the pan of onions from the oven and carefully lift out the onion halves. Divide the cooking liquor between each pan or tin, and then arrange 3 onion halves, cut side down on top.

Drape a chilled pastry top over each trio of onion halves, tucking in the pastry around the insides of the pan/tin. Put on a baking tray and bake in the oven for about 20–25 minutes, or until the pastry is well risen and golden brown.

Meanwhile, mix the olive oil and balsamic vinegar together for the dressing, season and toss through the mixed leaves.

Remove the tarts from the oven and turn out on to four plates – to do this, hold each plate firmly over the top of a pan/tin and flip both over together, so that the tart ends up on the plate with the onion side upwards. Top each one with 2 slices of cheese (this will melt) and serve with some of the dressed leaves.

Cheddar, Potato and Onion Pie

This is a meal in itself, good served with the green beans with almonds, parsley and garlic butter on page 132 or a simple mixed leaf salad.

If you like, you can add a handful of cooked smoked bacon or ham to the cheese and potato mixture just before you assemble the pie.

1 quantity of savoury pastry (see page 167)	2 medium onions, chopped
a little plain flour, for rolling out	600g Cheddar cheese, coarsely grated
500g (peeled weight) potatoes, cut into cubes (about 2cm)	3 medium eggs, beaten
	1 medium egg yolk, beaten

To make this you need a flan tin with a removable base, 25cm in diameter and around 5–7cm deep.

Lightly flour your work surface. Take around two-thirds of the pastry (wrap the rest in clingfilm and chill in the fridge), and roll out into a circle about 3mm thick and 5cm larger than the tin. Wrap the pastry carefully around your rolling pin to lift it, and drop it gently into the flan tin. Press the pastry into the base and sides of the tin, leaving a little excess overhanging the edge.

Put the tin on a baking tray and chill in the fridge while you prepare the filling.

Half fill a medium pan with lightly salted water and bring to the boil. Add the potatoes and return to the boil. Cook for 5 minutes, or until cooked but still slightly firm. Add the onions and return to the boil, then drain immediately in a colander. Tip into a large bowl and leave to cool.

When the vegetables are cold, stir in the cheese and beaten whole eggs until thoroughly combined.

Take the pastry case from the fridge and fill with the potato and cheese mixture.

Lightly flour your work surface again and roll out the remaining pastry into a circle around 3mm thick and big enough to cover the pastry case, leaving a little overhang. Brush the edges of the pastry case with the beaten egg yolk, then wrap the pastry circle over your rolling pin and carefully drape it over the top. Press to seal the edges, then trim off the excess pastry. Make a large hole in the centre of the pie and brush all over the pastry lid with the remaining egg yolk. Put back into the fridge on a baking tray for an hour to chill and set – this will help to prevent the pastry from shrinking in the oven.

Preheat the oven to 180°C/gas 4. To decorate the top, take a sharp knife, and with the tip gently score the pastry in gently curved lines from the centre to the sides of the pie, to resemble the spokes of a wheel.

Bake on the baking tray in the preheated oven for 45–60 minutes, until the pastry is nicely browned and the filling is hot throughout – you can check by inserting a skewer into the centre of the pie. It should be piping hot when you remove it.

Chicken, Leek and Bacon Pie

This dates back to the very first days of the café in the farmshop, and is based on the Scottish cock-a-leekie soup combination of chicken and leeks. We have added a little smoked bacon to give the dish a richer depth of flavour. This is best made with small, young, tender leeks.

2 potatoes, peeled and finely chopped

2 tablespoons sunflower oil

3 onions, finely chopped

2 sticks of celery, finely chopped

1 teaspoon chopped fresh thyme leaves

50g smoked bacon lardons

sea salt and freshly ground black pepper

1 teaspoon sugar

800g raw chicken, cut into bite-size pieces (use a mixture of thigh/leg and breast meat)

50g plain flour

1 tablespoon lemon juice

800ml good chicken stock

2 leeks, sliced

3 tablespoons crème fraîche

1 tablespoon chopped fresh flat-leaf parsley leaves

½ quantity of shortcrust pastry (see page 167)

1 beaten egg, for brushing the pastry

Preheat the oven to 200°C/gas 6.

Half fill a medium pan with lightly salted water and bring to the boil. Add the potatoes and return to the boil. Cook for about 10 minutes, or until tender but still holding their shape. Drain and set aside.

Heat the oil in a pan, put in the onions, celery, thyme and bacon, together with a pinch of salt and the sugar, and cook gently until the onions are soft but not coloured.

Add the chicken and again cook gently without colouring for about 10 minutes. Add the flour, then slowly stir in the lemon juice and chicken stock. Bring slowly to the boil, then turn down the heat and simmer until the sauce has thickened.

Add the leeks and continue cooking until they are tender, then gently stir in the cooked potatoes. Take off the heat and stir in the crème fraîche and chopped parsley.

Taste and season as necessary, then spoon into a round pie dish, roughly 20cm in diameter (or equivalent) and leave to cool. Put a pie prop in the middle.

Lightly flour your work surface and roll out the pastry to the shape of your pie dish, allowing enough for a good overhang all round.

Wrap the pastry over your rolling pin and carefully drape it over the top of the dish. Make a large hole in the centre of the pie above the prop and let it push through, then brush all over with the beaten egg.

Put into the preheated oven for 30–35 minutes, until the pastry is golden brown and the meat is piping hot.

Venison and Cranberry Pies

These are lovely, rich autumnal/winter pies, in which the tartness of the cranberries really lifts the flavour. You can quickly and easily cut out six tops from two sheets of good, ready-rolled puff pastry. However, if you prefer to make one big pie (approximately 25cm round, or 20cm x 30cm if you have an oblong-shaped dish) it is easier to buy a block of pastry and roll it out yourself on a floured surface to the size needed. A large pie will need a pie prop placed in the middle of the venison mixture before you drape your pastry over the top (make a hole in the centre for it to poke through) and about 45 minutes in the oven.

The pies can be made up to a few hours in advance of cooking – just keep them in the fridge until you're ready to bake. If you do this, however, bring them up to room temperature before cooking.

1 kg venison haunch or shoulder, cut into bite-size pieces

375ml red wine

2 medium carrots, chopped

2 medium onions, sliced

1 bay leaf

2 juniper berries

1 sprig of fresh thyme

50g butter, plus a little extra if needed

2 tablespoons olive oil

25g sugar

40g plain flour

1 tablespoon tomato purée

500ml good chicken stock

100g sun-dried cranberries

sea salt and freshly ground pepper

2 sheets of ready-made puff pastry (see introduction, above)

1 egg, beaten

Put the venison into a bowl with the red wine, carrots, onions, bay leaf, juniper berries and thyme and leave to marinate in the fridge for 24 hours.

When ready to make the pies, preheat the oven to 200°C/gas 6.

Remove the venison from the marinade and pat dry with kitchen paper. Strain the liquid into a bowl and keep to one side. Discard the juniper berries and thyme sprig, but keep back the carrots and onions.

Heat the butter and oil in a casserole. Put in the venison and sauté until golden brown all over, then lift out and reduce the heat. Add the reserved sliced onions and carrots from the marinade, together with the sugar, and soften the vegetables gently, adding a little more butter if needed.

Add the flour and tomato purée and cook for 1–2 minutes more, then add the marinade liquid a little at a time, stirring continually to prevent lumps from forming.

Return the browned meat to the pan, together with the stock, bring to the boil, then turn down the heat and simmer for about 2 hours, covered, until the venison is cooked and tender, and the sauce has thickened.

Stir in the cranberries, taste and season as necessary, then divide between six individual pie dishes.

Cut out 3 lids from each sheet of pastry – they should be big enough to overhang the dishes by at least 1cm. Drape over the top and brush with the beaten egg.

Put the dishes on a baking tray in the preheated oven for 30 minutes, or until the pastry is risen and golden brown.

Wootton Estate Game Pie

The two constants in this pie are venison and duck legs; as for the rest, you can vary the game birds. However, you really need to use the legs of birds such as pheasant or partridge, rather than the breasts, which tend to become dry if they are braised slowly. You could keep back the legs any time you buy a partridge or pheasant for roasting, since these tend to be nicer if you just roast the crown anyway (as the legs can be a bit tough). Put the legs into the freezer, then when you have enough, defrost them to make a pie. If you don't have rabbit legs, you can add a couple more game bird legs.

As for the duck, we use mallard, which comes from a nearby estate, as this is a smaller duck with a gamier flavour than the milder-tasting Gressingham or Barbary breeds – however, if you can only find these bigger duck legs, you can balance things up by using partridge legs in with them, as these have a little more gaminess than pheasant.

You need to allow time to make this, as the game meat needs to be marinated overnight, then cooked slowly for 4 hours, and allowed to cool and chill in the fridge for another 2 hours before you assemble the pie. This chilling of the meat might seem excessive, but it is important, because you will have lined your pie dish and rolled out your lid ready to go, then put these into the fridge to chill and relax and so avoid any shrinking in the oven. So if you were to put warm meat into the chilled pie casing it would melt the pastry.

If you are making your own stock, choose the roast chicken stock on page 417.

2 pheasant (or partridge) legs

2 duck legs

2 rabbit legs

500ml red wine

2 juniper berries

5 peppercorns

½ a head of garlic

5 sprigs of fresh thyme

sea salt and freshly ground black pepper

250g diced haunch of venison

2 tablespoons olive oil

1 onion, chopped

2 sticks of celery, chopped

2 carrots, chopped

2 litres good chicken stock

1 celeriac, chopped

75g dried cranberries

1 quantity of savoury pastry (see page 167)

1 egg, beaten, for brushing the pastry

Put the pheasant, duck and rabbit legs into a large bowl with the wine, juniper berries, peppercorns, garlic and one of the sprigs of thyme. Cover and put into the fridge to marinate overnight.

Next day, preheat the oven to 150°C/gas 2.

Lift out the legs from the marinade and pat the meat dry with kitchen paper. Strain the liquid into a bowl and keep to one side. Discard the juniper berries, peppercorns, garlic and thyme.

Season the legs and also the venison. Heat the olive oil in a casserole (one that has a lid), put in the legs and the venison and sauté until browned on all sides. Lift out and keep to one side. Add the onion, celery and carrots and gently soften until browned, stirring occasionally.

Add the marinade and bubble up, scraping all the bits from the bottom of the casserole, until the alcohol has burned off. Return the legs and the venison to the casserole and cover with the chicken stock. Add the rest of the thyme.

Put the lid on the casserole and transfer to the oven for about 4 hours, until the meat is completely tender and the leg meat is falling away from the bones.

When the meat is tender, remove the casserole from the oven. Lift out all the meat and put it into a bowl to chill slightly (leave the cooking liquor in the casserole). When cool enough to handle, strip the meat from the bones (discard the bones). Keep the meat to one side.

Put the casserole dish containing the cooking liquor on the hob over a medium heat and bubble up to reduce by half. Add the celeriac and cranberries and simmer for 10 minutes, until the cranberries have softened and the celeriac is tender. Then put back the reserved meat. Stir gently, remove from the heat and leave to cool down, then put into the fridge to chill for 2 hours.

While the meat is chilling, line your pie dish. You need a dish of around 20cm in diameter (or equivalent). Lightly flour your work surface. Take around two-thirds of the pastry (wrap the rest in clingfilm and chill in the fridge), and roll out into the shape of your pie dish, but around 5cm larger. It needs to be about 4mm thick. Wrap the pastry carefully around your rolling pin to lift it, then drop it gently into the dish. Press into the base and sides, leaving a little excess overhanging the edge. Put the dish on a baking tray and chill in the fridge until ready to bake.

For the lid of the pie, lightly flour your work surface again and roll out the remaining pastry into the shape of your dish, but big enough to leave a little overhang – again it should be around 4mm thick. Lay this on a plate or tray and put into the fridge to chill.

When ready to bake, preheat the oven again to 180°C/gas 4. Take the pastry-lined dish from the fridge and spoon in the chilled meat mixture. Place a pie prop in the middle.

Brush the edges of the pastry in the dish with the beaten egg yolk, then wrap the chilled pastry for the lid over your rolling pin and carefully drape it over the top. Press to seal the edges, then trim off the excess pastry. Make a hole in the centre of the pie above the prop and let it push through, then brush all over the pastry lid with the remaining egg yolk.

Put the pie into the oven and bake for 1 hour, or until the pastry is golden brown and the filling is piping hot.

FISH

Mackerel with earthy lentils and beetroot
Halibut and Morecambe Bay shrimps
Elegant crab linguine
Homely fishcakes and pillowy potato-topped pie

Visitors to the farmshop and kitchen always like to buy and eat fish that they can trust to be sustainably sourced. But of course we are in the middle of the Gloucestershire countryside, and farming livestock and growing fruit and vegetables is what we do – not fishing. So we bring in our fish from trusted suppliers around the coast, mainly Cornwall, who know to supply us only with a catch that meets the stringent guidelines drawn up by Tim Field, our environmental scientist, who is also a dedicated wild food hunter and forager. In fact, says Tim, in the River Evenlode, which runs alongside the wetland area he has created for the farm, 'there is a lovely little population of wild brown trout, and I am sure they would taste beautiful, but they are all about five inches long: not even big enough for breakfast.'

There are crayfish in the Evenlode too, but as in most British rivers they are the rampant American red claw or 'Signal' species, which are quite territorial and aggressive and have largely driven out the population of white-clawed British crayfish. They also carry a disease which doesn't affect them, but wipes out the natives. 'It is a bit like the grey and red squirrel situation,' says Tim. 'Catching crayfish is a wonderful experience. I was brought up locally and my brother and I used to catch them virtually with a jam jar, bare hands and lightning reflexes, but these days you can only fish crayfish under licence. It's to keep tabs on the populations, and also to try and prevent the intruders and their disease spreading. So lovely as it is to catch the odd crayfish, it would be terrible to think we were contributing to the further demise of the white-clawed ones.'

'Trying to fish sustainably is a very complex, constantly changing subject,' he admits, 'since the sea is a dynamic environment, and fish move around a great deal from warm to cold seas and rivers at different times of the year. So you have to look at the seasons in terms of breeding and migrating, as well as the method of fishing, to avoid damage to the seabed habitat, sea birds, juvenile fish and non-targeted species caught as by-catch.

'Our wild fish comes primarily from small dayboats and members of the Responsible Fishing Scheme, so we know the stocks are healthy, and we can be confident we are not damaging either the fish populations themselves or the ocean environment. The simple way to choose wisely is to check the Marine Conservation Society's Good Fish Guide (www.goodfishguide.co.uk) and Fishonline (www.fishonline.org).' Because of the issues involved, we put relatively few fish dishes on the menu. These, however, are some of the favourites.

Grilled Mackerel with Roasted Beetroot and Spiced Lentils

This is a lovely healthy dish, one of head chef Gaven Fuller's favourites. Crispy-skinned mackerel paired with earthy, sweet beetroot has become something of a British classic, but this recipe also reflects the influence of chefs of different nationalities who have worked in the Daylesford kitchens over the years, with the hint of chilli, ginger, sesame and soy sauce in the creamy lentils, and the fresh citrus, mint and coriander flavours in the yoghurt dressing.

Because oily, omega-3-rich mackerel is so good for you, and we have all been urged to eat more of it, there are some fisheries which have been put on the Fish to Avoid list; however, all our mackerel is sustainably fished from dayboats using hand lines off the Cornish or Devon coast. Ask your fishmonger to pin-bone the fish for you.

The pomegranate vinegar that we use to dress the beetroots is a bit special – you can really taste the pomegranate, which gives a little edge of bitterness. But aged red wine vinegar is fine – you just want a touch of acidity to balance the sweetness of the beetroot, so don't use balsamic vinegar.

Although we use sea salt mostly in our cooking, as it dissolves quickly, for the yoghurt dressing we use rock salt, as it is harder and crushes better with the spices.

8 fillets of mackerel, pin-boned

2 tablespoons olive oil, plus a little extra virgin olive oil to finish

sea salt and freshly ground black pepper

For the spiced lentils:

230g dried green lentils

1 large red chilli, finely chopped

3cm piece of fresh root ginger, peeled and finely chopped

3 tablespoons olive oil

3 tablespoons sesame oil

2 tablespoons soy sauce

2 tablespoons white wine vinegar

2 tablespoons chopped fresh coriander

sea salt and freshly ground black pepper

For the roasted beetroot:

500g beetroot, unpeeled but washed

2 tablespoons olive oil

2 tablespoons pomegranate vinegar or aged red wine vinegar

For the dressing:

1 teaspoon coriander seeds

1 teaspoon cumin seeds

½ teaspoon rock salt

150g natural yoghurt

50g crème fraîche

zest of ½ a lemon

zest of ½ an orange

1 tablespoon chopped fresh mint

1 tablespoon chopped fresh coriander

First prepare the lentils. Rinse them carefully, then cover with 750ml of cold water. Add the chilli and ginger, bring to the boil, then turn down the heat and simmer until the water is absorbed and the lentils are tender, but still retain a little bite. Leave to cool, then add the olive oil, sesame oil, soy sauce, vinegar and coriander. Season well and keep to one side.

While the lentils are cooking, put the beetroot into a medium-sized pan and cover with cold water. Bring to the boil, then turn down the heat and simmer for about 45 minutes, until tender. Drain, peel and roughly chop into bite-size chunks. Mix with 1 tablespoon of the olive oil, season and spread on a baking tray.

Preheat the oven to 170°C/gas 3. Put the beetroot into the oven for 10 minutes, so that the pieces roast a little and their flavour will be concentrated, then tip into a small bowl and add the vinegar and the rest of the oil. Toss together lightly.

To make the dressing, lightly toast the seeds in a small dry pan, just enough to release their aroma, then transfer them to a pestle and mortar, add the rock salt and crush to a fine powder. In a bowl mix the yoghurt, crème fraîche, lemon and orange zest and chopped herbs, then add the crushed seeds and salt and stir. Taste and add a little more salt if necessary.

Preheat the grill to hot. Brush the mackerel with the olive oil, season, then place under the grill, skin side up, and cook for about 5 minutes, until the skin is golden brown and the flesh is cooked through (it will turn opaque) but is still moist. Serve with the lentils and roasted beetroot and drizzle with some extra virgin olive oil and a good dollop of yoghurt dressing.

Pan-roasted Pollock with Crushed Potatoes and Watercress Mayonnaise

Cooking with pollock is easier on fish stocks than buying cod (unless this comes from a sustainable fishery), and it is very similar in texture and appearance, though it has a slightly less pronounced taste – however, the zingy flavours in the crushed potatoes and the pepperiness of the watercress mayonnaise combine to make this a really vibrant dish.

Ask your fishmonger to pin-bone the fish for you.

2 tablespoons rapeseed oil

4 x 150g pieces of pollock, skin on and pin-boned

1 tablespoon butter

juice of ½ a lemon, plus 4 lemon wedges

2 tablespoons finely shredded fresh basil

2 tablespoons finely shredded fresh mint

zest of 1 lemon

sea salt and freshly ground black pepper

For the crushed potatoes:

400g salad potatoes, peeled and cut into bite-size pieces

2 tablespoons olive oil

125g podded fresh peas (or frozen peas, defrosted)

4 spring onions, finely sliced

For the watercress mayonnaise:

1 bunch of watercress, large stalks removed

100g mayonnaise

zest of 1 lemon and the juice of ½ a lemon

Preheat the oven to 200°C/gas 6.

For the crushed potatoes, put the potatoes into a pan of cold, lightly salted water and bring to the boil, then turn down the heat and simmer for 10 minutes, until tender. Drain in a colander and return them to the pan, crush slightly with a back of a spoon, then mix in the olive oil, peas, spring onions, herbs and lemon zest. Season to taste.

While the potatoes are cooking, make the watercress mayonnaise. Have ready a bowl of iced water. Bring a pan of water to the boil, then dip in the watercress to blanch it for 5 seconds only, lift out with a slotted spoon or sieve, and put into the iced water to cool. Squeeze out the water, then chop and mix with the mayonnaise, lemon zest and juice. Season to taste.

To cook the pollock, heat the oil in a non-stick frying pan that will transfer to the oven. Season the fish and put into the pan, skin side down. Cook over a medium heat until the skin is crisp and golden, then turn over and put into the oven for about 6 minutes, until just cooked (it should be opaque all the way through).

Remove the pan from the oven, add the butter and lemon juice, let the butter melt, then spoon over the fish. Divide the slices of fish, with the buttery juices, between four plates, and add a lemon wedge to each, together with some of the crushed potatoes and a good dollop of watercress mayonnaise.

Salmon and Smoked Haddock Fishcakes

The flavours of smoked haddock and salmon combine really well together. Also, smoked fish has a different texture to fresh, so combining the two gives an interesting dimension to the fishcakes (the same principle applies to fish pie, see page 207).

We don't believe in cooking the fish before mixing it with the mash, because the cakes still have to be fried and then finished in the oven – if the fish is cooked first, by the time the cakes come out of the oven the fish will be dry, whereas if you start with it raw, the cakes will be nice and crunchy on the outside, but the fish will still be moist inside.

Of course you can buy a good tartare sauce to go with the fishcakes – or serve them on their own – but it is quick and easy to make.

1kg potatoes, peeled and cut into chunks

350g salmon, skinned, boned and chopped (about 1cm)

100g smoked haddock, skinned, boned and chopped (about 1cm)

2 tablespoons capers, chopped

2 tablespoons chopped fresh flat-leaf parsley

zest and juice of 1 lemon

sea salt and freshly ground black pepper

4 tablespoons plain flour

2 eggs, beaten

about 200g dried white breadcrumbs

sunflower oil, for frying

rocket leaves (optional), for garnish, dressed with French dressing (see page 381)

lemon wedges, to serve

For the tartare sauce:

2 tablespoons capers

2 tablespoons gherkins, finely chopped

300g mayonnaise

2 tablespoons chopped fresh flat-leaf parsley

freshly ground black pepper

Put the potatoes into a pan of cold, lightly salted water and bring to the boil, then turn down the heat and simmer until the potatoes are tender if pierced with the tip of a sharp knife, but not falling apart. Drain through a colander, put into a bowl, allow to cool slightly, then lightly mash.

Add the chopped fish, capers, parsley, lemon juice and zest, season, and mix well. Divide the mixture evenly into 12 balls, then flatten them and shape them into round cakes. Put them into the fridge to chill for at least 1 hour to firm up.

Meanwhile, if you are making the tartare sauce, combine the capers, gherkins, mayonnaise and parsley and season with pepper. Put into the fridge until you are ready to fry the fishcakes.

Preheat the oven to 180°C/gas 4.

Have ready the flour, beaten egg and breadcrumbs in separate shallow bowls. Dip the chilled fishcakes first into the flour, shaking off the excess, then into the egg, and then finally into the breadcrumbs, pressing them in lightly all over.

Heat the oil in a frying pan, put in the fishcakes and gently fry over a medium heat, in batches, until golden brown on both sides. As they cook, transfer them to a baking tray, and once they are all ready place them in the preheated oven for 8 minutes, until hot in the centre.

Arrange 2 fishcakes per person on each plate, with a wedge of lemon; garnish, if you like, with rocket, and serve with the tartare sauce.

Traditional Fish Pie

This is always a winner in the café, and good served with steamed beans with almond, parsley and garlic butter (see page 132).

As with the fishcakes on page 205, the key is to keep the fish moist in its sauce, and not to swamp it with too much potato, otherwise the pie will feel quite stodgy. The ratio should be three-quarters fish and sauce, to a quarter potato. You don't want to cook the fish too much, or let the sauce become too thick before you assemble the pie – the temptation is to think of it as being the way you want to eat it, but remember that the pie still has to go into the oven for about half an hour, and the fish and sauce will dry out some more.

You can mix and match the fish as you like, adding different sustainable fresh white and smoked varieties (the smokiness gives an extra layer of flavour), or you could add some prawns.

The capers are there to add a bit of texture and a vinegary sharpness and saltiness that works classically with fish: just think fish and chips.

200g smoked haddock, skinned and boned

250g salmon, skinned and boned

250g pollock, skinned and boned

200g leeks, sliced

3 eggs

1.5kg potatoes, peeled and cut into four

150g butter

sea salt and freshly ground black pepper

200ml white wine

1 bay leaf

50g plain flour

100ml double cream

1 tablespoon Dijon mustard

1 tablespoon capers

1 tablespoon chopped fresh flat-leaf parsley

Preheat the oven to 180°C/gas 4.

Cut all the fish into bite-size pieces.

Blanch the sliced leeks in boiling water for 30 seconds.

Remove to a colander with a slotted spoon, then drain under the cold tap and keep to one side.

Put the eggs into a pan and cover with cold water. Bring to the boil and cook for 10 minutes. Take off the heat, rinse the eggs immediately in cold water to prevent discolouring, then peel, and grate or roughly chop.

Put the potatoes into a separate pan of cold, lightly salted water, bring to the boil, then turn down the heat and simmer until the potatoes are tender if pierced with the tip of a sharp knife, but not falling apart. Drain in a colander, then put into a bowl and mash well (alternatively put them through a potato ricer). Stir in 50g of the butter and season with salt and pepper.

Pour the wine into a pan, add 500ml of water, and bring to the boil. Add the chopped fish and the bay leaf. Simmer for about 2 minutes, until the fish is cooked (it will turn opaque), then take the pan off the heat, lift out the fish and leave to cool, reserving the poaching liquid.

Melt the rest of the butter in a separate pan and whisk in the flour until smooth. Gradually add the reserved poaching liquid from the fish, then the cream, stirring constantly until thickened – but not too thick (see introduction, above). Season and add the mustard. Gently stir in the cooked leeks, capers, parsley and reserved cooked fish.

Spoon the mixture into an ovenproof dish, top with the grated egg, spoon over the mashed potato (or pipe it, if you prefer) and put into the preheated oven for about 30 minutes, until golden brown and piping hot.

Cod with Lemon, Parsley and Tomato Butter

Much has been written about the depletion of cod stocks, but we buy our cod only from fisheries that are well managed and sustainable. Choose nice fat pieces of fillet that have been cut from a big fish. Serve this with mashed potato.

4 large red vine tomatoes, or 20 cherry tomatoes

4 x 160g pieces of thick cod fillet (scales and pin-bones removed)

sea salt and freshly ground black pepper

3 tablespoons olive oil

4 lemons

6 tablespoons butter

4 tablespoons capers

½ a bunch of fresh flat-leaf parsley, leaves roughly chopped

4 bunches of watercress to serve (optional)

Preheat the oven to 180°C/gas 4.

Remove the cores from the tomatoes (if large) and cut the flesh into rough cubes of about 2cm (if using cherry tomatoes, just cut them in half). Set them aside.

Make sure the skin of the cod is nice and dry and season on both sides.

Place a large non-stick frying pan (one that will transfer to the oven) over a medium heat, add the oil and wait until it just starts to smoke. Carefully put in the cod, skin side down, and leave it alone until the skin is lightly golden brown. Transfer the pan to the oven and continue to cook for about 8–10 minutes, depending on the thickness of your cod – it should be just opaque.

While the cod is in the oven, heat the grill or a griddle pan. Cut 2 of the lemons in half and grill them (cut side up) or griddle (cut side down) until charred.

Remove the cod from the oven and transfer to four warm plates, skin side up. Put the pan on the hob and add the

butter. Season with a little salt and pepper, and when the
butter starts to foam and turn a golden nut-brown colour
(you can see this more clearly if you scoop a little up with
a teaspoon), add the tomatoes and cook for 2 minutes, to
let them soften slightly.

Add the juice of the remaining 2 lemons, capers and
parsley and spoon over the cod. Serve with the grilled
lemon halves and the watercress, if using.

Halibut with Morecambe Bay Shrimp Butter Sauce

Tiny, brown, quite sweet-tasting shrimps have been caught in Morecambe Bay on the Lancashire coast since the eighteenth century, using tractors, which drag long nets behind them through the shallow waters of the bay (up to the fifties the nets were still drawn by horses). As the sandy water is disturbed, the shrimps jump into the nets. They are boiled up straight away, then peeled. Most of them go to be potted in the traditional way (cooked, then sealed in butter with a little warm spice), but you can also buy them peeled to cook yourself. In this dish we keep to the spirit of potted shrimps, adding them to a butter sauce, flavoured with nutmeg and herbs, to serve with the halibut. We source Scottish farmed halibut, as it is the most sustainable option from British waters.

100g butter

1 large shallot, finely chopped

1 clove of garlic, finely chopped

200ml white wine

2 tablespoons double cream

juice of ½ a lemon

100g peeled Morecambe Bay brown shrimps

½ teaspoon ground nutmeg

1 tablespoon chopped fresh chives

1 tablespoon chopped fresh chervil

1 tablespoon chopped fresh flat-leaf parsley

400g purple sprouting broccoli, stalks removed

2 tablespoons olive oil

4 x 200g halibut steaks

sea salt and freshly ground black pepper

Melt 1 tablespoon of the butter in a small pan, add the shallot and garlic and cook over a low heat for 10 minutes, until the shallot has softened but not coloured. Add the white wine, bring to a simmer and let the liquid reduce by two-thirds. Add the cream and bring back to a gentle simmer, then turn down the heat to low and, whisking swiftly, add all but a knob of the butter a little bit at a time, making sure the sauce doesn't boil, or the butter will split and the sauce will curdle. Once the butter is added and the sauce is thick and silky, add half the

lemon juice, along with the shrimps, nutmeg and herbs. Take off the heat and keep warm at the side of the hob.

Meanwhile steam the purple sprouting broccoli until just tender (3–4 minutes).

Heat the olive oil in a large non-stick frying pan over a medium heat. Season the halibut with salt and pepper and put it into the pan. Cook for 3–4 minutes on each side, until golden brown and just opaque in the centre. Squeeze the rest of the lemon juice over the fish, add the remaining knob of butter, and spoon the juices from the pan over the fish.

Arrange the halibut on warmed plates, with the steamed broccoli. Spoon the shrimp sauce over the fish and serve.

Clam Linguine

This is a favourite of Carole Bamford: a classic Italian pasta vongole, really. The character of the wine is key – you want something not too overpoweringly fruity, a little drier, with a good edge of acidity and sharpness to the fruit, like a Sauvignon Blanc or Muscadet.

1.5kg fresh clams, in their shells

200g butter

2 small white onions, finely chopped

4 cloves of garlic, finely chopped

1 fresh red chilli, very thinly sliced

400ml white wine

200ml double cream

400g good-quality linguine (fresh or dried)

sea salt and freshly ground black pepper

juice of 1 lemon

1 small bunch of fresh tarragon, chopped

1 small bunch of fresh flat-leaf parsley, chopped

Wash the clam shells well under cold running water and discard any that are open, or that won't close if you tap them.

In a large wide pan (big enough to take the pasta once it is cooked), melt 2 tablespoons of the butter. Add the onions and garlic and cook over a low heat for 10 minutes, until the onion has softened but is not coloured. Add the chilli, the clams and the white wine and bring to a rapid boil. As soon as the clams open, remove them from the pan with a slotted spoon and put them into a bowl. Remove the shells from half of them and discard these – so you have a mix of clams in and out of shells, which will make the finished dish look more interesting. Bubble up the remaining liquid in the pan to reduce by half, then add the cream and bring back to a simmer.

Meanwhile, bring a large pan of salted water to a rapid boil and drop in the linguine. Stir it around with a fork to make sure it is all under the water and to stop the strands sticking together, and cook at a rolling boil until just al

dente (if using fresh pasta, this will probably be less than 2 minutes). Drain very briefly, then add to the pan of sauce, along with the reserved clams.

Toss the pasta lightly with the sauce, adding the remaining butter a knob at a time. When it is all absorbed and the sauce is thick and silky, add the lemon juice and herbs. Taste and season as necessary, and serve immediately.

Baked Salmon, Spinach and Smoked Haddock Kedgeree

This is a bit of a twist on the more traditional kedgeree, in that we cook the fish in its spicy, creamy sauce separately to the rice, in individual ovenproof dishes or skillets. We serve each skillet alongside a bowl of rice on a wooden board, so people can mix everything together as they like. You can cook the fish and sauce in one big dish if you prefer – just put it into the oven for around 25 minutes, until the top is coloured and bubbling – and serve with a big bowl of rice.

4 eggs

sea salt

300ml good vegetable stock

1 large (300g) fillet of smoked haddock, skinned and boned

400g brown rice

2 tablespoons butter

1 medium onion, finely sliced

1 clove of garlic, finely chopped

4 tablespoons medium curry powder

1 tablespoon onion seeds

2 tablespoons finely chopped fresh ginger

1 large medium-hot red chilli, seeds removed, very thinly sliced

200ml double cream

4 tablespoons natural yoghurt

2 tablespoons chopped fresh parsley

2 tablespoons chopped fresh coriander

1 handful of spinach leaves

1 x 350g fillet of salmon, skinned and boned, and cut into bite-size pieces

2 tablespoons dried breadcrumbs

Have the eggs at room temperature. Bring a medium pan of water to the boil and add a pinch of sea salt (this will make the eggs easier to peel). Gently lower in the eggs and simmer for exactly 7 minutes. Take off the heat and rinse them immediately in cold water to prevent discolouring, then peel the eggs.

Preheat the oven to 180°C/gas 4.

Pour the stock into a pan, bring to a simmer and drop in the fillet of haddock. Simmer for 5 minutes, then remove the pan from the heat and allow to cool slightly. Lift out the haddock and flake it, then strain the stock into a bowl and keep to one side.

Put the brown rice into a large pan with plenty of cold salted water, bring to a simmer, and cook, covered, for about 25–30 minutes, until it is soft and tender. Strain through a colander, then put the rice back into the pan with a knob of butter, season it, stir, put the lid back on and leave it to steam (off the heat) until you need it.

Meanwhile, melt the butter in a large pan (one that has a lid) and add the onion and garlic. Cook over a medium heat for 5 minutes, until the onion is soft, but not coloured. Add the curry powder, onion seeds and chopped ginger, cover and continue to cook for a further 10 minutes, stirring occasionally. Add the chilli and reserved stock, then bring to a simmer and cook until the liquid has reduced down and thickened enough to coat the back of a spoon.

Add the cream, yoghurt and flaked haddock, bring back to a simmer again, then add the parsley and coriander. Taste and season as necessary.

Divide the spinach leaves between four individual dishes or cast iron skillets (around 10cm in diameter and 4cm deep). Spoon 4 tablespoons of the haddock in its sauce on top.

Cut each boiled egg into quarters and arrange on top, with the pieces of salmon in between. Season, then spoon the remaining sauce over the top. Finish each dish with a sprinkling of breadcrumbs.

Put into the preheated oven for 15 minutes, until the sauce is bubbling and the top is golden brown – but make sure you don't overcook it, or the salmon will become dry.

Serve with the brown rice.

'It's about animals in closed herds and flocks, thriving on a home-grown, diverse, forage-based diet.'
Richard Smith, The Livestock

I ache all over to try to get people to understand that farming can't carry on the way it is going. Intensive monocultures don't work; agriculture has to have diversity in order to be sustainable. Yes, we have more and more mouths to feed, but surely the way forward is to eat a little less meat, but of better quality, produced locally, from animals that are raised slowly and naturally on grass, in sustainable systems, without the artificial fertilisers and pesticides that release greenhouse gases, so the environment is being nurtured, rather than destroyed.

The way I feel about farming has evolved over many, many years, since I first knew – without question – that I wanted to be a farmer, when I was ten years old. I've seen and worked in lots of different systems, but I think British agriculture at its finest is the most diverse – and the best in the world.

There are a lot of farmers out there, who say, 'Bloody organic . . . can't do this, can't do that.' That's rubbish. The reality is that we are only two generations on from a time when most farming was organic anyway. My view is that if you go back to the absolute basics of agriculture – raising animal welfare standards, concentrating on the right breeds for the environment you want to raise them in, managing the production of great grass for grazing, great crops for silage, great hay, and the conservation of feed for winter – then the end result is you can produce food of superb quality, without chemicals in the soil and routine medicine for the animals.

I prefer the word sustainable to organic, which has been hi-jacked somewhat, but what organic certification gives people is an assurance of specific standards, levels of animal welfare and traceability. Much of the food and farming industry has carried on behind closed doors, and people haven't always known what they were buying; haven't even really wanted to think about it. Cheap food has been far too easy to come by, and good food hasn't been respected enough, which is why we waste so much. But now more and more people do want to know, and do care, and the guts of it is that what we stand for here at Daylesford is the honest and transparent production of food, and we are more than happy for people to visit and see what we do.

We have a lot of requests from students and also farming groups to come and look around. Often their background is in quite intensive systems, and I can see in their eyes that they are expecting me to be a tree-hugging, woolly, home-spun sort of fellow, and they are going to see a less efficient, less productive standard of agriculture. I put them on a trailer and take them round the farm, talk to them about crop rotations, properly costed-out systems, and show them our flocks and herds that are not reliant on cereals and high-energy proteins forced down their throats, but thrive on a home-grown, diverse, forage-based diet. Suddenly people are listening intently, because they realise we really are on to something, and they are mobbing me for information.

I have always lived on a farm. My dad worked on a large mixed farming estate in Northamptonshire and as soon as I was old enough I was pestering him and the neighbouring farmers to let me help out. My biggest farming role model was my grandfather, a proper no-nonsense, incredibly knowledgeable character from Northumberland, who came to the Midlands to work as a shepherd in the 1950s. My uncle is also a tenant farmer on a hill farm in the Cheviot Hills in Northumberland, a very passionate, specialist sheep breeder, so after I left school I went to live with him for six months of each year for five years, then came home for the harvest, hay-making and autumn cultivations. I loved all of it, but what really drove me was the livestock.

When I was twenty-four, I spent two years managing a farm in Cornwall, specialising in beef cattle and sheep – I loved the place and the people, but it was very intensive and fertilisers were used heavily. Afterwards I worked briefly in Kent, managing one of the largest beef herds in the country, and I can honestly say it was the most unhappy I have ever been in my farming life: I hated the whole intensive system. So it was with great relief that, after I met and married my wife, Claire, who came from New Zealand, and we moved there for seven years, I was lucky enough to be offered a share-farming agreement near Wellington, after having spent a year working on a large sheep and beef station in the Hawkes Bay area. It was a huge break for me and a very special time. I farmed about 2,500 local breed grass-fed Romney sheep, venison and Aberdeen Angus cattle.

When Claire died suddenly I came back to England in 1999, and was fortunate enough to be offered a job at the Oxford University Farm, where they research and develop sustainable farming systems built around animal welfare and care of the environment – not far from Daylesford. So, if you believe in divine intervention, I was destined to meet Carole Bamford in 2005. What excited me was that she very genuinely wanted to do something to shout about in agriculture. I knew immediately that this was where I wanted to be, and what an opportunity we had to raise the bar for British farming, to help to make organic, sustainable agriculture credible and respected.

Eight years on we now farm 2,350 acres in Gloucestershire, and a further 3,000 on the Wootton Estate in Staffordshire, and I want us to be as self-sustaining as possible, so we are constantly planting new acres of silage crops, and pastures for grazing. Sheep and cattle are ruminants that have evolved to make the most of forage-based diets, to walk around the countryside, eating different things at different times, and their stomachs are designed for that, so the more diverse and species-rich you can make those pastures, with a mixture of grasses, herbs, legumes and clovers, the better. Something will be happening all year round: plants flowering, coming into leaf, forming seed heads . . . and foraging on them is what helps to keep an animal healthy. Stockmen have always understood that – that is what the system of transhumance is all about in mountainous regions of Europe, moving herds up and down the mountains and from pasture to pasture, according to season, so that the animals have variation in their diet.

One of the challenges of organic sheep farming is to keep the flocks free of internal parasites, which they can suffer badly from. In modern, more intensive farming, everyone is taught how to use 'anthelmintic' drugs to worm sheep, but we use a faecal egg counting system called FECPAK, to monitor problem areas, and because the farm has such a diversity of pasture, I always have clean grassland to move the flocks on to.

———

Sustainable farming depends on the right breeds of animal in the right place, and over the years we have been building our own carefully selected closed herds, so that every generation is more suited to the environment I am asking it to live in. Take sheep: I could talk all day about farming sheep. We have breeds in Britain that have evolved and been cross-bred over hundreds of years to suit the particular terrain and environment in different parts of this island that we live on. You can go all over Europe and see genuine old breeds of animals, but they are not performing in the way ours do. We are the kings of sheep farming and breeding. The Cotswolds, in particular, were built on sheep: the old English word 'cot' refers to the compounds where sheep are kept, and 'wold' means rolling hills, and so it seems only natural that we have a flock of native Cotswold sheep – one of four heritage breeds we now have on the farm.

If you take two animals of pure blood and cross them, the progeny they produce will inherit traits from both the maternal and paternal lines. This is what is known as 'hybrid vigour'. For instance, generations of farmers in the north of England and the Scottish Borders have specialised in breeding sheep that are wonderfully adapted to the local terrain, crossing ewes from naturally hardy hill breeds, such as Scottish Black Face and Swaledale, with more prolific, faster-growing animals, such as Border Leicesters and Blue Face Leicesters, and their progeny are known as 'Mules'. The hardy hill breeds have coarse fibrous wool, so they can survive tough winters, and a metabolism that helps them run on brackens and poor-quality grasses up on the hills; while the less hardy, high-performance breeds, with their fine wool and Roman noses, need easier, higher-quality grazing – but bring the two together and you have a sheep that has the hardiness of its mother and also the growth rate, prolificacy and improved conformation of its father.

These Mules can be further crossed with 'terminal sires' of breeds such as Texels, Suffolk and Charollais which are chosen for their excellent conformation and quality of meat – the name 'terminal sire' comes from the fact that all their lambs will go to market – and this whole process is known as 'sheep stratification'.

A few years ago, we were bringing down north-country Mules, like most farms, but now we are breeding our own Lleyn sheep to do the same job. They are a Welsh breed developed on the Lleyn peninsula in North Wales, about two thirds of the size of a north-country Mule, but they produce a wonderful amount of meat. By closing off the flocks in this way, and keeping the bloodlines as pure as possible, we have complete control of the breeding and health status of our flocks.

We also have a flock of Ryelands, one of the oldest of British breeds – apparently Queen Elizabeth I insisted on her stockings being made only from Ryeland wool – and our newest arrivals are a pedigree flock of Kerry Hills, a very old breed from the English/Welsh borders: very striking-looking – the lambs in particular have endearingly funny faces, with black noses, panda eyes and pricked black ears, but they produce beautiful, succulent, full-flavoured meat.

The skill in rearing grass and forage crop lamb is to consistently produce the same size of carcass and quality of meat fifty-two weeks of the year and to know when an animal is at its prime and ready for slaughter. When you have graded as many lambs as I have you can tell just by looking at them, and running your hands over their backs.

People go mad for 'spring lamb' for Easter, but grass-fed lambs are naturally *born* at Easter – so young lamb that is for sale at Easter comes from animals that were born in November and reared on concentrated diets. I understand it is a top-dollar market, but I hate it: I don't want my lambs born when there is likely to be snow on the ground, and they may never go outside. All our lambing is in spring, and the animals graze on pasture throughout the summer, so the lamb we sell at Easter comes from hoggets – lambs that are born late in May, and are nearly a year old.

One of the questions visitors to the farm usually ask, is 'What do you do if you have a sick animal?' Well, open any guide to organic farming, and animal health and welfare is at the top of the agenda. Of course if an animal is unwell, you treat it, but you simply have to record everything carefully, and withdraw the milk or meat for a specific period of time.

The welfare of our animals is a priority, even if that means that we can produce less meat or milk or eggs than in intensive systems. Our chickens and hens forage where they like, as do our traditional bronze turkeys, which are funny things: on a bright sunny day they won't come out of their houses, because they think a predator is going to dive out of the sky and attack them, unless they have trees to range under. So we planted trees all around their pastures, which they rush to when the sun comes out, and then they are happy, because they feel protected.

Probably the animals that live closest to the way they would in the wild are the deer, which are all farmed on the Wootton estate in Staffordshire. There have been herds there for thousands of years, but they have only been farmed seriously since the 1980s. Organic deer farming is all very natural and the animals are true foragers with a real free spirit and a strong will to live. They can live for twelve to sixteen years, they have a fantastic life, and when their time comes to be slaughtered it is completely stress-free, in their natural habitat, carried out by our own marksman, with a vet in attendance.

One of the animals that can really suffer from stress in intensive systems is the dairy cow. We have Friesians, fed on a home-grown diet, and they produce an average of 7,000 litres per lactation, in comparison to the 10–12,000 litres that you would expect from the Holstein breed – which is the dairy equivalent of a Formula One racing car. The vast majority of milk in this country, throughout Europe and large areas of the world, comes from Holstein cattle – but you can't put a racing car on a country lane, and likewise, you can't let a high-producing Holstein milk machine just forage on grass. It has to be fed around 4 tonnes of high-energy, compound feed. The higher the protein, the higher the fuel, and the higher you are going to get your Formula One cow to perform. Farmers have been pushed into this corner, because they have had to become more and more efficient, and are expected to get more and more from each animal and every acre of land, but often the result is that the cow's metabolism is stressed, and its reproductive system upset, and of course if a cow can't reproduce, then it can't calve, and enter a new lactation.

Thirty-forty years ago the British dairy industry was the backbone of the British beef industry, because the male calves, which obviously couldn't produce milk, would be reared for their meat. It's a well-known fact in farming that beef from dairy animals, raised on grass, is always good to eat, but these days most farmers can't afford to keep them for beef, as ultimately they don't yield enough meat to make them profitable in comparison with pure beef cattle.

In the big dairies if a calf is a female it will be reared for the milk chain, but if it is male, it is often considered to be of no further use, and statistics show that at least 100,000 male calves are shot at birth every year. Here, though, our male Friesian calves are raised on grass, either for rose veal, or we allow them to grow to become mature beef.

2006 was a big year for us, because we also established our herd of Gloucester cattle. The Gloucester breed can be traced back to the thirteenth century – they are one of the original 'dual purpose' breeds, and a family would have kept one in the byre to provide them with both milk and beef. Until recently there were very few left in the world, but we stumbled upon a herd that was in poor health and built it up with the help of a beautiful champion cow with a lovely nature, called Peglards Lola, and a handsome bull, called Ambrosia Hethelpit Cross. Now we have seventy registered animals, which I believe is the biggest herd in the world. The Gloucesters have become a minority breed in terms of dairy farming for a reason: they can't keep up with the pressures of modern expectations and don't give a huge quantity of milk, but what you do get is of lovely quality. And having the herd means that we can also make Single Gloucester cheese. Above all, they produce meat of superb quality: the marbling, or fat content, texture and taste is just beautiful, and so every so often we are able to release a limited amount of it to the farmshop.

Occasionally we hold suppers at the farm to show off particular produce, and not so long ago we invited people to taste the Gloucester beef. Before they tucked in I told everyone, 'What you have in front of you is part of our living heritage: 700 years in the making, and no else else in the world will be eating what you are eating tonight.' When you can produce food that special, with chefs on the farm to cook it beautifully, that is satisfaction.

Carole Bamford is a natural 'stockman', with an eye for classy stock at a country show or a bull sale – it was she who researched and first suggested adding a herd of South Devon cattle to the Gloucesters and the Aberdeen Angus. Another old breed, they are also known as Orange Elephants, because of the colour of their coats, and their size: a full-grown bull can weigh one and a half tonnes. They are magnificent, strong, but gentle creatures, which were well known in England in the eighteenth and nineteenth centuries, when they had a triple purpose: producing milk, beef, and working as draught animals that would have pulled ploughs and carts.

I had initially favoured a herd of Herefords, but Carole and I went to see both breeds at a show, and there was a butcher there, so she bought a rib joint and sirloin steaks from each to take back to the farm for a taste test. While the butcher was wrapping the meat, Carole asked him which breed he thought had the best flavour and quality. I was standing behind her mouthing: 'Hereford, Hereford,' but he told her: 'South Devon.' We took the meat back to Daylesford, cooked it and tasted it, and everyone – including me – agreed that the South Devons were the right choice.

The idea is that we will grow the herd, and cross a percentage of them with our Aberdeen Angus herd, which has been in the Bamford family for many years, but which is now 100 per cent pedigree. The way forward, as with all our livestock, is to continue to breed animals that, through the generations, become more and more suited to this land on which we farm.

MEAT

Slow-cooked casseroles of lamb and beans
Roast rib of beef
Spicy, fruity chicken
Slow-cooked beef with ale and barley
Venison and cavolo nero layered in a lasagne

The recipes in this chapter focus on beef, lamb and venison, as well as chicken – these are the meats we produce from our heritage herds, flocks and colonies, and the dishes make good use of different cuts, from prime ones for roasting, to the cheaper cuts, such as shin and shoulder, which are packed with flavour, but need long, slow cooking.

When you buy beef, look for meat that has been well hung and will look a rich ruby red colour, rather than crimson. There is a tendency to see bright red meat and think it looks fresher, but meat that hasn't been hung will be less mature in flavour, and likely to be less tender when cooked. The purpose of hanging beef is to relax it and concentrate the depth of its flavour, and all ours is hung for twenty-eight days. Lamb, too, benefits from hanging, but for a shorter time: just a week or two, while our venison is only hung for a week, otherwise its flavour can become too gamey.

Lamb and Butter Bean Casserole with Tomatoes, Caperberries and Olives

This is a lovely warming winter dish, especially with mashed potatoes. In contrast to some of the more British lamb casseroles we make, this has a touch of the Mediterranean about it, with tomatoes, olives, the caperberries and a little spice in the sauce.

You can use good jarred or tinned beans, if you are pushed for time, but we always cook butter beans from scratch, as they absorb the juices and flavours in the casserole better, and they are very simple to do. You just need to soak the dried beans overnight first. We cook them separately from the casserole, and only combine the two at the end, otherwise you can compromise either the meat or the beans, if one or the other isn't ready.

If you want to cook your own beans, as a rule of thumb all pulses (and rice) will double in size once cooked. So if a recipe calls for 450g of cooked butter beans, as this one does, start with 225g of dried beans.

Put them into a bowl and add enough cold water to cover them by about a centimetre. Leave to soak overnight, then drain the beans, rinse, transfer to a large pan, and again, add enough cold water to cover by a centimetre. Don't add any salt, as this will harden the skins of the beans. The key to cooking any pulses is not to boil them rapidly (except for the initial cooking of kidney beans), as they will break up; so bring them to a simmer, then turn the heat right down, so that there is virtually no movement in the water, and cook them for 45 minutes to 1 hour, until the beans are perfectly soft and creamy, but still intact.

1.5kg lamb neck fillet, cut into cubes of around 4cm

sea salt and freshly ground black pepper

3 teaspoons ground coriander

100ml olive oil

2 red onions, thinly sliced

½ a red chilli, finely chopped

1 heaped tablespoon tomato purée

250ml white wine

1 litre good chicken stock

450g cooked butter beans (see introduction, above)

zest of 1 large lemon

1 clove of garlic, thinly sliced

300g cherry tomatoes

50g black Kalamata olives, pitted

70g caperberries, stalks removed, halved

2 tablespoons chopped fresh flat-leaf parsley

Preheat the oven to 160°C/gas 3.

Season the lamb with salt, pepper and the coriander. Heat the oil in an ovenproof casserole (one that has a lid), then add the lamb and brown it all over.

Lower the heat and add the onions, chilli and tomato purée. Continue to cook for 2–3 minutes, until the onions have softened slightly, then add the white wine and bubble up until reduced by half.

Add the stock and bring to the boil, then put the lid on the casserole and transfer it to the preheated oven.

Cook for about 2 hours, until the meat is soft and tender and the gravy has thickened, then take the casserole out of the oven, put it back on the hob and bring to a simmer. If you need to thicken the gravy a little, let it bubble up and reduce for a few minutes before adding the beans. If not, add them straight away, along with the lemon zest, garlic, tomatoes, olives, caperberries and chopped parsley. Bring back to a simmer, then take off the heat and serve.

Slow-cooked Lamb Shoulder with White Beans and Salsa Verde Mayonnaise

This is a favourite of head chef Gaven Fuller: 'A lovely, rustic, slow-cooked and warming stew that really showcases the lamb. It does involve a little time, as the meat needs to go into the oven first, so that the fat melts through it and it becomes incredibly tender, then its cooking liquid is used to simmer the beans, so that they soak up all its flavour – but it's well worth it. Sometimes people think of shoulder of lamb as a "man's dish", quite heavy and butch, but this is quite light, the salsa verde mayonnaise gives it a real zing – and it seems to be popular with everyone.'

4 tablespoons olive oil, plus a little extra to finish

6 cloves of garlic, chopped

1 teaspoon fresh thyme leaves

sea salt and freshly ground black pepper

1.5kg shoulder of lamb, boned and rolled

2 carrots, roughly chopped

1 large onion, chopped

1 leek, chopped

1 heaped tablespoon tomato purée

125ml red wine

1 litre good chicken stock

salsa verde mayonnaise (see page 382), to serve

For the beans:

150g dried white beans

25g butter

1 small onion, finely chopped

1 clove of garlic, crushed

1 carrot, finely chopped (about 5mm)

2 tablespoons chopped fresh flat-leaf parsley

1 tablespoon chopped fresh tarragon

1 tablespoon chopped fresh mint

150g baby spinach leaves, roughly shredded

sea salt and freshly ground black pepper

Mix 2 tablespoons of the oil with the garlic, thyme and salt and pepper and then rub all over the lamb. Leave to marinate overnight in the fridge.

Soak the beans in cold water overnight, too, then drain.

The next day, preheat the oven to 160°C/gas 3.

Heat the rest of the oil in a casserole (one that has a lid), put in the lamb and brown on all sides, then lift out and keep to one side. Add the carrots, onion and leek and cook over a low heat for 5 minutes, until the vegetables have softened but are not coloured.

Add the tomato purée and the red wine and bubble up to reduce the liquid by half. Return the lamb to the casserole, add the stock, and pour in enough water to cover the meat. Bring to a simmer, cover and put into the preheated oven for about 3 hours, until the lamb is very tender.

Lift out the lamb from the casserole and keep to one side (reserving the cooking liquid).

To cook the beans, heat the butter in a large heavy-based saucepan. When it's foaming, add the onion and garlic and cook gently for 5 minutes or until the onion is translucent. Add the carrot and the drained white beans and strain in the reserved cooking liquid from the lamb. Bring to the boil, then turn down to a simmer for 30–40 minutes, stirring occasionally, until the beans are tender (you may need to top up with a little water).

Remove from the heat and stir in the herbs and chopped spinach. Taste and season as necessary.

Return the cooked lamb to the pan over a low heat until heated through.

To serve, lift out the lamb and slice into 4. Spoon the beans and sauce into a warmed, shallow serving dish or platter. Arrange the lamb on top and drizzle with a little olive oil. Serve with a bowl of salsa verde mayonnaise.

Pressed Lamb

A great thing to do when you have invited friends round is to slow-cook the lamb as in the previous recipe, but then press, slice and pan-fry it, so that the slices are crispy on the outside and meltingly soft in the middle – it is really beautiful this way. You do all the major cooking in advance, then shred the meat with some of the sauce and form it into a sausage shape, which can be chilling in the fridge, along with a bowl of minted aioli (see page 386), while you relax and enjoy yourself. Then you only have to slice the lamb, pan-fry it and serve it with the aioli. It goes especially well with smashed broad beans and peas (see page 129), which can be made really quickly while the lamb slices are in the pan.

You will probably have a little more sauce than you need, so any left over can be kept in the fridge for four to five days or the freezer. If you are making a Sunday roast, just add it to your pan of meat juices and loosen with some boiling water to make a great gravy.

To make the pressed lamb, follow the previous recipe, but omit the beans. After the lamb has been in the oven for about 3 hours, or is very tender, lift out the meat with a slotted spoon and leave it to cool.

Strain the cooking liquid through a fine sieve into a medium pan, bubble it up to reduce it to a thick sauce, the consistency of ketchup, then take off the heat.

When the lamb has cooled, flake it into a bowl, discarding the fat and gristle, and stir in 4 tablespoons of the reduced sauce.

Taste the meat mixture and season as necessary, then stir in a tablespoon each of chopped mint, tarragon and parsley.

Cut 2 squares of clingfilm about 30cm x 30cm and lay one on top of the other. Spoon the mixture on to the clingfilm,

form into a fat cylinder shape (about 7–8cm in diameter), then roll up tightly, twisting and tying the ends. Wrap a layer of foil around the outside and again twist the ends, so that the roll looks like a Christmas cracker.

Put into the fridge to chill for at least 2 hours. When ready to serve, cut the lamb into 8 slices. Heat a little olive oil in a pan and fry the slices until they are golden on each side and hot in the middle. Serve with smashed broad beans and peas, and minted aioli.

Notes on casseroles

The dishes that we make in the Black Barn for sale in the farmshop are all done in small batches, in exactly the same way as you would make a casserole at home, and an enormous amount of love and pride – and chopping of onions – goes into each one. You can follow a recipe over and over again, but every time you make a dish it will have its own identity and individuality; that is what makes cooking so enjoyable.

Everything is done slowly, and for me that is the key to a good casserole: you have to nurture it all the way through. You can't rush it; you need to build up the layers: sealing the meat, adding the onions and the other vegetables, then the stock, and finally let it cook really gently – long and slow.

Generally the cheaper the cut, the more flavour you get out of it. A shoulder of lamb, for example, will give you a more tender, melting meat in a casserole than a leg, because the fat content is higher, and fat, as we always say, is flavour.

A classic lamb or beef casserole, for me, follows the same basic stages, no matter what the flavourings. I always start by sealing the meat in oil in a nice hot pan, to get a good colour on it, then I add finely chopped onions, carrots and usually celery, season and turn the heat down so that they sweat and soften slowly until the vegetables turn a lightly golden brown colour, around the sealed meat – as the onions cook slowly their natural sugars come out and they sweeten up. Then I turn the heat right down and add tomato purée, which will give a rich colour and shine to the finished sauce. The important thing is to let the purée cook for a few minutes, but take care not to let it catch and burn or it will make the sauce bitter.

Then I sprinkle in the flour and stir it around a little, so that it can mop up all the fat and residue from the meat, and let it cook for a few minutes so that it is well worked into the meat and vegetables – that way when I add the liquid, it won't be lumpy.

If I am adding wine, I do this next, turning up the heat a bit to burn off and evaporate the alcohol, then I add the stock, slowly, stirring it in constantly until it is all absorbed into the flour, and gradually bringing it up to the boil.

Then I transfer the casserole to the oven at a low temperature – around 170°C/gas 3. A long time ago a chef in one of the kitchens where I worked told me to think of the casserole dish in the same way as the engine of a car: you want it to just tick over, not rev like mad.

I cover the dish and cook for at least 1–1½ hours, and often much longer, depending on the cut, until the meat is tender.

I prefer to put casseroles into the oven rather than cook them on the hob, as in the oven the heat comes from all around the dish, enveloping it, and you can put it in and forget about it – except to pull it out of the oven and give it a stir about halfway through the cooking time. Whereas if your casserole is on the hob, the heat is all coming from below, and there is always a tendency for the sauce to catch and stick on the bottom of the pan.

If I am adding pieces of root vegetables, such as parsnip or swede, I put these in when the dish goes into the oven. Potatoes would go in half an hour before the end of cooking; and if the dish contains beans, I always cook these separately, then add them towards the end, for just long enough to soak up the flavours.

Andy Wheeler

Chicken Casserole with a Splash of Brandy

This is a version of the Belgian dish Chicken Waterzooi. 'The children loved it when they were growing up,' says Carole Bamford. 'It is lovely and light, yet comforting. Real family food, there is nothing like it, especially when you're tired.' The casserole is good served with simple boiled potatoes.

90g butter

sea salt and freshly ground black pepper

1 free-range chicken

2 tablespoons brandy

1 bay leaf

500ml good chicken stock

2 carrots, sliced

2 large leeks, white part only, sliced

4 sticks of celery, sliced

250g small mushrooms, sliced

4 tablespoons chopped fresh flat-leaf parsley

3 egg yolks, beaten

100ml double cream

Preheat the oven to 160°C/gas 3.

Heat a third of the butter in a large flameproof casserole (one that has a lid). Season the chicken, and when the butter is foaming put it into the casserole and brown on all sides. Add the brandy and allow the alcohol to burn off, then put in the bay leaf, stock and enough water to just cover the chicken and bring to the boil.

In another pan heat half the remaining butter and put in the carrots, leeks and celery. Season, sauté until golden brown, then add to the casserole.

Heat the remaining butter in the same pan and put in the mushrooms. Season, and once again sauté until golden brown. Add to the casserole with half the parsley, cover with the lid and put into the preheated oven for 1 hour, or until the chicken is cooked (pierce the thigh with a skewer and the juices should run clear).

Lift out the chicken and put it on a board for carving. Lift out the vegetables with a slotted spoon and transfer to a large warm shallow serving dish.

Strain the cooking liquid into a bowl, then pour it back into the casserole and bubble up on the hob until it has reduced by three-quarters and is thick enough to coat the back of a spoon.

While the sauce is reducing, joint and carve the chicken and arrange the pieces on top of the vegetables.

Turn off the heat under the sauce and stir in the remaining parsley, egg yolks and cream, making sure the sauce doesn't boil or the eggs will scramble. Pour over the chicken and vegetables and serve immediately.

Chicken and Apricot Curry

The squash and apricots give this autumnal curry a gentle sweetness. For the best flavour, use a mixture of breast and thigh chicken meat, and cook it gently in its sauce, in order to keep the meat relaxed and tender. We serve this with brown rice.

sea salt and freshly ground black pepper

1.2kg chicken meat, cut into bite-size pieces

about 2 tablespoons sunflower oil

1 large onion, finely chopped

2.5cm piece of fresh root ginger, finely grated

2 cloves of garlic, finely chopped

1 red chilli, finely chopped

1 teaspoon cumin seeds

1 tablespoon curry powder

1 tablespoon chilli powder

1 tablespoon ground turmeric

2 large ripe red tomatoes, roughly chopped

150g squash, peeled and chopped

1 large baking potato, chopped (about 2cm)

½ a medium leek, sliced

100g apricots, roughly chopped

500ml good chicken stock

100ml coconut milk

Season the chicken. Heat 2 tablespoons of sunflower oil in a large casserole and brown the chicken in batches, removing each batch to a bowl.

Lower the heat and add the onion, ginger, garlic and chilli, together with a little more oil if needed, and cook gently until the onion is softened and golden. Stir in the cumin seeds, curry powder, chilli powder and turmeric and cook for a further 5 minutes, to release the flavour of the spices.

Return the chicken to the pan, together with the tomatoes, squash, potato, leek and apricots, and combine thoroughly.

Add the stock and the coconut milk and bring to a simmer. Cover and cook gently for about 30 minutes, until the chicken is cooked through and the vegetables are tender.

Taste and season as necessary. Leave to stand for 20 minutes before serving to allow all the flavours to merge, then reheat gently – make sure the chicken is hot all the way through – and serve.

Notes on roasts

One of the finest ways to showcase wonderful meat is in a classic, timeless roast. However, roasting meat isn't an exact science, because every chicken and every joint of beef is different, as is every oven, so it is better to get into the swing of using your eyes, sense of smell and touch to gauge when the meat is ready, rather than relying on charts. Remember, when you are cooking beef or lamb, fat is flavour. An ultra-lean cut will never be as succulent and tasty as a cut that has a fine marbling of fat running through it – which is why when you buy a piece of silverside or topside beef, a butcher will often tie a piece of fat on to it for you.

These are my guidelines:

Rib of Beef: Choose a well-hung piece of meat, with a fine marbling of fat. Preheat the oven to 190°C/gas 5. Tie the joint, or have your butcher do this, so that it keeps its shape. If you have kept any beef fat from a previous roasting, heat this in a roasting pan on the hob, or alternatively heat some vegetable oil. Season the beef at the last minute with sea salt and black pepper, put it into the pan and colour it all over, then transfer to the oven and turn the heat down to 180°C/gas 4. As the meat roasts, baste it with the juices and let it cook until the point where, once rested, it will be medium-rare. To test for this, use the skewer test. Run a cold tap over a metal skewer, so that it is very cold, insert it into the centre of the meat, leave it there for 5 seconds, then quickly remove it and put it carefully to the back of your hand. If the skewer still feels cold, the meat isn't ready. If the chill has just gone off the skewer, it is just right; and if it's about to burn your hand, it means that the meat is already well done, and becoming dry. Take the meat out and let it rest for about 15–20 minutes, covered with foil, to allow the meat to relax and for the heat to finish transferring through to the centre and, provided it passed the skewer test, it will be perfectly medium-rare.

Lamb Leg: For me, roast lamb leg needs to be medium, not as pink as, say, grilled chops, because the longer cooking allows all the fat to melt into the meat, flavouring and tenderising it. I would cook it in the same way as beef, above, but this time when you do the skewer test, make sure the skewer comes out hot, but not burning, which will mean that the meat will be medium by the time it has rested.

Chicken: Remember that organic chickens have a good life, running around in the open air, but that means they develop a lot more muscle than birds that

rarely leave their chicken-houses, so their flesh will be firmer, and resting will be important after cooking to relax the meat.

Start with the oven at 190°C/gas 5. Cut a lemon in half, squeeze some of the juice inside the cavity of the chicken, and also season it with sea salt inside. Smear the skin with softened butter or a little olive or vegetable oil, squeeze the rest of the lemon juice over, and rub in plenty of sea salt and freshly ground black pepper. The lemon will add to the seasoning and also help keep the chicken moist.

Put the chicken into a roasting tray and put into the oven for 15 minutes, then turn the oven down to 180°C/gas 4 and turn the chicken over so that it is resting breast side down for another 20 minutes. Then turn it back again, so that it is breast side upwards again for another 20 minutes. Now turn the oven back up to 190–200°/gas 5–6, and cook until the skin has become crisp and golden (this should only take about 10 minutes) and, if you insert the tip of a knife into the thickest part of the thigh, the juices run clear.

Christmas Turkey: Richard Smith, our farm manager, reckons he gets more favourable feedback on our turkeys than practically anything else on the farm. People love them because they are so moist. The secret is that they are finished on oats, which are an oil-based cereal, and so, not only do the turkeys go mad for them, but they give the finished meat a superb quality.

With turkeys, because they are so big, I break with my advice about not being too guided by charts. It is important to weigh the bird, as you don't want to have everyone sitting around the table, and the rest of the meal ruining, because you have seriously miscalculated the cooking time.

Preheat the oven to 200°C/Gas 6. I prefer to cook stuffing separately, as I think stuffing the cavity benefits the turkey more than the stuffing, and I like my stuffing with a bit of crispiness on the outside, which you can't achieve if it is cooked inside the bird. Smear the turkey with olive oil and butter, and also grease the roasting tin with a little oil, too. Season the skin with sea salt and pepper and rub it in well. Put the turkey in the oven and cook for 40 minutes (skin side down), then turn down the heat to 180°C/gas 4 and cook for 35 minutes per kg. Keep basting as the turkey cooks, and as the juices start to form in the roasting pan, add about 300ml of water to them, and top this up every so often, to create moisture, and also good juices for your gravy.

After about 2 hours, carefully turn the bird back over, so the breasts are facing upwards, and finish cooking. If the breasts start to colour too much, cover in foil. To check that the bird is ready insert a skewer into the thickest part of the thigh, and the juices should run clear. Take out of the oven, cover with foil, and allow to rest for 30 minutes before serving.

Roast Potatoes: I like to roast potatoes around a joint. I boil them first in lightly salted water to the point where they are about to break up, then drain them through a colander over the pan in which they have been cooked, so that they steam and dry out – shake the colander a little to roughen up the edges, then, once your meat is up to speed and sizzling gently, add them to the roasting pan. Don't put them in until the meat has got going, or you will bring the temperature down and slow the whole process. Once your meat is out of the oven and resting, turn the oven up to 200°C/gas 6 to get a good golden colour all over – you can add a knob of butter for extra richness, if you like. Once the potatoes start to crisp up, keep turning them over in the oil (it is important to wait until they crisp up, otherwise they will break). If you want to add some slivers of garlic and some rosemary leaves, do this a few minutes before serving, to stop them burning and becoming bitter, and preserve the green colour and fragrance of the rosemary.

John Hardwick

Roast Rib of Beef with Dijon Mustard and Balsamic Sauce

Head chef Gaven Fuller wanted to put an alternative to steak and chips on the menu, which could be served with a sauce other than the classic béarnaise, so he came up with this quite punchy, sweet-sharp sauce made with balsamic vinegar and mustard. A rib of beef is perfect for two people. In the café, we carve it for people at their table.

If you are making your own stock, choose the roasted chicken stock on page 417.

1 x 700g–1kg beef single rib on the bone	1 tablespoon balsamic vinegar
1 tablespoon butter	a little olive oil
100ml extra virgin olive oil	1 sprig of fresh thyme, leaves only
1 small onion, finely chopped	
2 cloves of garlic, finely chopped	sea salt and freshly ground black pepper
100ml red wine	To serve:
250ml good chicken stock	1 small bunch of watercress
2½ tablespoons Dijon mustard	potato wedges (see page 134)

Preheat the oven to 180°C/gas 4.

Take the rib of beef out of the fridge to allow it to come to room temperature.

In a small pan melt the butter and 1 tablespoon of the olive oil. Add the onion and garlic and cook over a low heat for 10 minutes, stirring often, until the onion is softened but not coloured. Add the wine, then bring to a simmer and let it reduce by three-quarters.

Add the stock, bring back to a simmer and reduce again by three-quarters. Take off the heat and whisk in the mustard and balsamic vinegar. Continue to whisk rapidly whilst very gradually adding the rest of the oil – don't rush this,

or the sauce won't emulsify properly and will be greasy. Keep by the hob.

Rub the beef with a little olive oil and the thyme leaves and season with plenty of salt and pepper. Get a griddle pan or frying pan (one that will transfer to the oven) smoking hot and put in the beef, cooking it on both sides, until well marked if you are using a griddle pan.

Transfer to the oven and cook for about 15 minutes for medium rare meat, or longer, depending on how well done you like your beef (see page 245). Remove from the oven and leave to stand for 15 minutes before serving.

Serve with the warm sauce, watercress and potato wedges.

Notes on cooking steak

Sometimes you just want to cook a succulent piece of steak and serve it as it is, perhaps with a leaf salad. But there is a skill to getting it just right.

First of all, bring your meat to room temperature. Take it out of the fridge for about an hour before you want to cook it, to allow it to relax.

Every chef has their own opinion on whether to season the meat before or after it goes in the pan. The one thing everyone agrees on, though, is that you don't want to add salt too early, or it will draw the moisture out of the meat, making it tougher. Personally I believe in adding plenty of salt and pepper just before the meat goes into the pan, so that the seasoning cooks into it.

Of course you can barbecue, griddle or grill a steak, but I like to cook it in a pan in butter and oil – one-third oil to two-thirds butter. The oil is only there to stop the butter burning.

Choose a vegetable oil, or an ordinary olive oil – not extra virgin. All oils have different smoking points, which means they break down at different stages of heat, and their character and goodness can alter. Extra virgin olive oil has a very low smoking point and so should be used for finishing off dishes, and for salads, but not for frying. Most oils that have high smoking points, and so can be used for deep-frying, also have a neutral flavour. Rapeseed oil is the one that bucks the trend, as it has one of the highest smoking points of all, but also a very strong and particular flavour – which people either like, or don't. Personally I think a more neutral oil is better for cooking steak, as it won't compete with the flavour of the meat.

Heat the oil in your pan first, without the butter – until it is on the verge of smoking. Season your steaks on both sides and put them in, cook until they start to colour slightly, then add the butter. The temperature at which you cook your steak is very important: you need to get a good colour and caramelisation going on the outside, which really enhances the flavour, but be careful not to burn the meat. What you are listening for is a nice gentle sizzling sound as the steak cooks. As the butter foams, spoon it over the top from time to time. Give each steak 2–3 minutes without moving it, until it seals and turns golden brown underneath, then turn it over.

I think a steak should always be served medium-rare, so that the fat can break down and flavour the meat during cooking. How long it takes to get it to this stage depends on the size and thickness of your meat, but when you cook steaks regularly, you learn to gauge it by touch.

If you press the meat with your thumb before it goes into the pan, you will get the feel of it when it is raw: it will be very firm. As it cooks, keep testing with your thumb, and when it gets to the rare stage, it will be really bouncy, and if you take it off the heat at this point, lift it out and let it rest, by the time the heat has spread through the meat as it relaxes, it will be a perfect medium-rare. If you let the steak continue to cook, and keep pressing it, you will feel that it gradually has less and less give, until it has no give at all, at which point it will be well done. Once you have tried this a few times, you will be able to recognise the stages, and tell just by the feel of it when the steak is done to your liking.

There is another, pretty foolproof, way to tell when the steak is ready to come off the heat if you want it to be medium-rare, which works for roast meat too (see page 245). Run a cold tap over a metal skewer, so that it is very cold, insert it into the centre of the steak, leave it there for 5 seconds, quickly remove it and put it carefully to the back of your hand. If the skewer still feels cold, the meat isn't ready. If the chill has just gone off the skewer, then it is just right; and if it is about to burn your hand, it is overcooked.

Finally, it is really important to let the meat rest. The rule is to rest it for as long as you cook it. If you serve the steak straight from the pan, with no resting, when you cut into it you will see the outside looking quite caramelised and brown, and underneath it a line of greyish cooked meat, which will give way to pinkness, and then, in the centre, it will be red-raw. If you let it rest, however, this relaxes the fibres of the meat, which have been subjected to quite aggressive heat, and, as I mentioned, it also allows the heat to carry on penetrating throughout the meat, so that it is uniformly tender and juicy all the way through.

John Hardwick

Featherblade of Beef with Creamed Wild Mushrooms

Featherblade is a great, much-overlooked cut of beef from behind the shoulder and is full of flavour, but because the muscle works very hard it needs slow cooking. After a couple of hours in a low oven it becomes meltingly tender, and is even better if you chill it to firm it up, then slice it into steaks and pan-fry them before serving – then the meat will just fall apart when you put your fork into it. If you want to do this, take the cooked beef from the oven, keeping back the cooking liquor, and roll up the beef tightly in clingfilm. Put it into the fridge for at least 2 hours, to chill and firm up.

When you are ready to serve, take the chilled meat from the fridge and cut it into 6 slices. Heat about 2 tablespoons of olive oil with a couple of good knobs of butter (each about the size of a tablespoon) in a large frying pan, and when the butter is foaming, put in the slices of beef and sauté for 4–5 minutes on each side, until golden brown and hot all the way through. Make the sauce as in the method below, while the slices of beef are sautéing.

Serve with some steamed and buttered brassicas, such as kale.

1 beef featherblade (about 1.5kg)

4 cloves of garlic, chopped

1 red onion, chopped

1 stick of celery, chopped

1 carrot, chopped

1 large sprig of fresh thyme

450ml full-bodied red wine, such as Merlot

sea salt and freshly ground black pepper

about 3 tablespoons olive oil

2 tablespoons tomato purée

1 litre good chicken stock

3 handfuls of mixed wild mushrooms (about 100g), cleaned and stalks removed

5 tablespoons double cream

1 tablespoon chopped fresh flat-leaf parsley

Put the piece of beef into a bowl with the garlic, vegetables, thyme and red wine, and leave in the fridge to marinate for 24 hours.

Preheat the oven to 160°C/gas 3.

Lift the meat out of the marinade, pat dry with kitchen paper and season. Strain the marinade into a bowl, keeping the vegetables.

Heat the olive oil in a casserole (one that has a lid), put in the piece of beef and brown on all sides, then lift out and keep on one side. Put in the reserved vegetables from the marinade, adding a little more oil if necessary, then add the tomato purée and cook for a few more minutes. Add the marinade and let it bubble up, at the same time scraping the caramelised bits from the bottom of the pan. Add the stock, bring to a simmer, then turn off the heat.

Return the beef to the casserole, cover and put into the preheated oven for around 2½ hours, until tender, then remove from the oven, lift out the beef, and leave it to rest, covered with some foil, while you make the sauce.

Strain the cooking liquid from the beef into a medium pan, bring to the boil, then turn down the heat and reduce until you have a sauce-like consistency. Drop in the wild mushrooms, add the cream, and simmer for a further minute or two, until the mushrooms are tender. Taste and season as necessary, then finish with the chopped parsley.

Serve a slice of beef on each of six warmed plates, and spoon over the sauce. Serve with buttered brassicas.

Smoky Slow-cooked Shin of Beef Chilli

This is a big favourite with Andy Wheeler, who makes batches of it in the Black Barn for people to buy in the farmshop and heat up at home (see page 238 for his thoughts on casseroles). You could use tinned kidney beans for this, but if, like Andy, you want to cook your own, start off with 100g and follow the method on page 114. Serve with rice – or even mashed potato.

The touch of coffee just adds a richness and depth of flavour and colour.

1 teaspoon dried oregano

1 teaspoon ground coriander

3 teaspoons smoked paprika

2 teaspoons hot chilli powder

3 tablespoons sunflower oil

780g beef shin, trimmed and cut into cubes (about 2cm)

40g beef marrow, chopped small

2 red onions, each cut into eight

sea salt

2 cloves of garlic, finely chopped

1 red pepper, chopped (about 2cm)

600ml good chicken stock

8 red vine tomatoes, roughly chopped (or 600g tinned chopped tomatoes)

2 teaspoons sugar

6 brown chestnut mushrooms, quartered

200g cooked kidney beans

1 small green chilli, thinly sliced (keep the seeds)

juice of 1 lime

1 teaspoon instant coffee

Preheat the oven to 150°C/gas 2.

Put the oregano and spices into a dry frying pan over a low flame and toast for a couple of minutes, until they release their aroma – take care not to let them burn. Take off the heat.

Heat the sunflower oil in a large casserole (one that has a lid), put in the cubed beef and sauté over a high heat until golden brown on all sides, then remove from the pan and keep to one side. Add the beef marrow, along with the onions, season with salt, then lower the heat and cook with the lid on for 5 minutes, until the onions start to soften. Add the garlic and toasted spices, stir, and cook for another 2 minutes.

Put back the beef, along with the rest of the ingredients. Bring to a simmer, then transfer to the oven and cook with the lid on for 3 hours. Take out and test a piece of meat – it should be soft and tender and easily broken with the back of a fork. If it is not tender enough, put it back into the oven for a bit longer. When it passes the tenderness test, taste and season if necessary and serve.

Braised Brisket with Lentils

The key to brisket is the thick layer of fat that melts while cooking, so don't trim it first.

5 tablespoons olive oil

sea salt and freshly ground black pepper

1.5kg boned rolled brisket

2 large onions, chopped

1 large carrot, chopped

2 sticks of celery, chopped

3 cloves of garlic, roughly chopped

½ a red chilli

1 tablespoon tomato purée

2 sprigs of fresh thyme

4 sprigs of fresh parsley, plus 2 tablespoons chopped fresh parsley to garnish

125ml red wine

2 litres good chicken stock

1 tablespoon Worcestershire sauce

125g Puy lentils

Preheat the oven to 170°C/gas 3.

Heat the olive oil in a large casserole (one that has a lid). Season the brisket, put it into the pan and sauté gently until golden brown all over, then lift out and keep to one side. Lower the heat, add the onions, carrot, celery and garlic and continue to cook until they are golden brown. Add the chilli, tomato purée and sprigs of thyme and parsley and continue cooking for a further minute.

Add the red wine and bubble up until the liquid has reduced by half, then put in the brisket, stock and Worcestershire sauce. Bring to the boil, then turn down to a simmer and skim the fat from the surface, cover with a lid and transfer to the preheated oven for 3 hours.

Remove the pan from the oven, lift out the meat and wrap it in foil to keep warm. Strain the cooking liquid into a pan and add the lentils. Bring to the boil, then turn down the heat and simmer until they are tender, but still retain some bite, and the gravy has thickened and coats the back of a spoon. Add the chopped parsley. Cut the brisket into 6 slices, and serve with the lentil gravy spooned over the top.

Corned Beef

Like salt beef, corned beef involves the meat being soaked in a brine, before cooking. The salt solution soaks through to the centre of the meat over the course of 8–10 days and gives it its distinctive flavour and pink appearance, which it keeps even after cooking. You can either slice it after cooking, to serve in traditional fashion with cabbage and potatoes, or allow it to cool and slice it for sandwiches. Alternatively, what we do is flake it, mix it with the thickened cooking liquor, then put it into the fridge so that the natural gelatine in the beef will allow it to thicken and set, and you have a consistency more like tinned corned beef or rillettes. Done this way it is good with sourdough bread and piccalilli (or cornichons), or fried up to make corned beef hash (see page 34).

250g sea salt

60g sugar

1 boned and rolled brisket of beef, about 1.7kg

2 tablespoons olive oil

1 carrot, chopped

2 onions, chopped

1 stick of celery, chopped

1 whole bulb of garlic, sliced horizontally

¼ of a fresh red chilli, deseeded and chopped

1 tablespoon tomato purée

1 small bunch of fresh parsley stalks

1 sprig of fresh thyme

100ml red wine

2 litres good chicken stock

1 tablespoon Worcestershire sauce

sea salt and freshly ground black pepper

To make the brine, put the salt, sugar and 2 litres of water into a large pan and bring to the boil, then take off the heat and leave to cool. Put the beef into a large casserole (one that has a lid), pour the brine over it, making sure it covers the meat, then cover and put into the fridge for 8–10 days.

Remove the beef from the brine (discarding this) and pat it dry with kitchen paper.

Preheat the oven to 170°C/gas 3.

Wash out and dry the casserole, put it back on the hob and heat the olive oil in it. Put in the beef and sear it on all sides until golden brown.

Add the carrot, onions, celery and garlic and continue to colour. When the vegetables are slightly golden, add the chilli, tomato purée, parsley stalks and thyme and cook for a further minute, then add the red wine. Bring to a simmer and continue to cook until the volume of liquid has reduced by half. Add the chicken stock and Worcestershire sauce and bring to the boil. Turn down to a simmer and skim off any scum from the surface, cover, and put into the preheated oven for 3 hours.

If serving it hot, make an accompanying sauce by straining the cooking liquor through a fine sieve into a clean pan, putting it back on the hob and bringing it to a rapid boil, until it has thickened to a coating consistency.

Alternatively, let the beef cool down in the cooking liquor, then lift it out (but retain the liquor), put the meat into a bowl and flake it into small pieces, removing any gristle, but keeping the fat. Mix vigorously with a fork to allow the pieces of meat and fat to break up. As above, strain the cooking liquor through a fine sieve into a clean pan, put it back on the hob and bring it to a rapid boil, until it has thickened to a coating consistency, then add to the bowl of flaked beef and mix well. Taste and adjust the seasoning as necessary, then transfer the mixture to a loaf tin, smooth the top and put into the fridge for about
2 hours to chill and set.

It will keep for up to a week, in the fridge, so you can slice it as required, or turn it into corned beef hash.

Beef, Ale and Barley Casserole

Ale and barley work really well with beef – we add the
ale in two stages: most of it goes in with the stock, which
adds flavour and depth to the casserole, then we add an
extra hit of it just before serving, so you get a real, more
identifiable sense of the ale.

4 tablespoons sunflower oil

800g stewing beef, cut into
cubes (about 2cm)

3 large onions, sliced

2 carrots, sliced

1 medium swede, chopped

2 cloves of garlic, crushed

2 tablespoons tomato purée

2 tablespoons plain flour

1 litre good chicken stock

90ml pale ale

1 teaspoon chopped fresh
thyme leaves

4 tablespoons pearl barley,
rinsed in cold water

sea salt and freshly ground
black pepper

Preheat the oven to 170°C/gas 3.

Heat the sunflower oil in a large casserole (one that has a
lid), put in the cubed beef and sauté over a high heat until
golden brown on all sides, then remove from the pan and
keep to one side – do this in batches if necessary, so as not
to overcrowd the pan and bring the heat down, or the beef
will steam rather than sauté.

Add the onions, carrots, swede and garlic, lower the heat
and cook until lightly coloured. Put in the tomato purée
and cook for a few minutes, then sprinkle in the flour. Stir
in, then gradually add the stock and two-thirds of the pale
ale, stirring constantly to stop the liquid becoming lumpy.

Put back the meat, and add the thyme and soaked barley.
Bring slowly to the boil, then take off the heat and transfer
to the oven. Cook with the lid on for 2–3 hours, until the
meat will easily fall apart when pressed with the back of
a fork. Stir in the rest of the pale ale, adjust the seasoning
and serve.

Venison and Cavolo Nero Lasagne

This is an autumnal twist on the usual beef lasagne, which we came up with to make good use of our venison during the game season. Cavolo nero is ready in the market garden at the end of autumn and lasts all through the winter, so it is around at the same time, and by adding a layer of it actually inside the lasagne, rather than serving it alongside, you make the dish into a complete meal. Fresh lasagne is always best, but you could also use the dried sheets that need no pre-soaking.

5 tablespoons light olive oil

sea salt and freshly ground black pepper

1kg minced venison

2 red onions, sliced

3 cloves of garlic, chopped

2 tablespoons tomato purée

300ml red wine

200g tinned chopped tomatoes

1.2 litres good chicken stock

30g butter

240g cavolo nero, roughly shredded

about 12 sheets of lasagne (see introduction, above)

20g Parmesan cheese, grated

For the béchamel sauce:

1 litre milk

2 cloves

30g onions, finely chopped

125g butter

125g plain flour

200g Cheddar cheese, grated

1 tablespoon English mustard

Heat 2 tablespoons of the oil in a large pan. Season the mince well and brown it in batches until golden, then keep to one side.

Add another 2 tablespoons of the oil to the pan, put in the red onions and garlic and cook gently for 5 minutes until softened, but not coloured.

Add the tomato purée and red wine and bubble up to reduce the liquid by half. Add the tomatoes, and return the mince to the pan. Add the stock, bring to the boil, skim off any fat from the surface, then lower the heat and cook

over a moderate heat for about 45 minutes. Taste and adjust the seasoning accordingly.

Meanwhile heat the rest of the oil and the butter in a pan, add the cavolo nero and cook briefly over a medium heat just until it wilts. Season well and keep to one side.

Preheat the oven to 180°C/gas 4.

When ready to assemble, make the béchamel sauce by first warming the milk in a small pan with the cloves and onions. Take it off the heat before it reaches a simmer and leave to infuse for 20 minutes. In another pan, melt the butter, then whisk in the flour and cook for 5 minutes over a low heat, stirring constantly. Strain in the milk and continue to cook gently, whisking constantly, for a further 3 minutes until you have a smooth sauce. Stir in the grated cheese and mustard and season well, then take off the heat.

Spoon one-third of the mince into an ovenproof dish (about 25cm x 15cm, and 6cm deep), and cover with a third of the lasagne sheets. Repeat using half the remaining mince and half the remaining lasagne sheets. Finally spoon in the rest of the mince, followed by the cavolo nero. Cover with the remaining pasta sheets, then pour over the béchamel sauce and sprinkle with the Parmesan cheese.

Put into the preheated oven for about 40–45 minutes, until golden brown and hot throughout.

Venison Cottage Pie with Beetroot and Apple Salad

A very traditional cottage pie, but, as in the case of the lasagne on page 265, made with venison rather than beef. The autumnal feel is accentuated by serving it with a salad made with apples from the orchard, paired with beetroot. It is also good with just a mixed leaf salad, for a lighter meal.

Mince, whether it is beef or venison, cooks quite quickly; however, as with any cheap cut of meat, if you want it to become nice and soft and tender, it is best to do it slowly over time, which is why we let the mince simmer gently in its sauce for 2 hours.

2 tablespoons olive oil

sea salt and freshly ground pepper

1.6kg minced venison

40g butter

1 large onion, chopped

2 large carrots, chopped

4 cloves of garlic, chopped

3 tablespoons tomato purée

500ml red wine

1.5 litres good chicken stock

For the mashed potatoes:

2kg potatoes, peeled and cut into quarters

200ml milk

75g butter

For the beetroot and apple salad:

2 large raw beetroots, peeled and finely shredded

2 apples, cored and finely shredded (with the peel left on)

2 bunches of watercress

2 tablespoons roughly chopped fresh flat-leaf parsley

2 tablespoons sun-dried cranberries, chopped

4 tablespoons French dressing

juice of ½ a lemon

Heat the olive oil in a large casserole. Season the mince, then put into the casserole and sauté until golden brown. Remove from the pan, lower the heat and add the butter, onions, carrots and garlic and cook gently until the vegetables have softened. Add the tomato purée and the red wine and bubble up to reduce the liquid by half.

Return the mince to the pan, together with the stock, bring back to a simmer, and cook over a low heat for about 2 hours, until the sauce has thickened. Take off the heat and leave to cool slightly.

Preheat the oven to 190°C/gas 5.

While the mince is cooking, put the potatoes into a pan and cover with cold, slightly salted water. Bring to the boil, then turn down the heat to a simmer for around 20 minutes, until the potatoes are cooked through and easily fall away if pierced with the tip of a sharp knife. Drain in a colander, put into a bowl and mash well (alternatively put through a potato ricer).

Put the milk and butter into a pan and heat until the butter has melted, season and then mix into the mashed potato.

Divide the mince between six individual oven dishes or one large one, then either spoon on the potato and run the prongs of a fork over it, creating little peaks, or pipe it, if you prefer. Put into the preheated oven and bake for 20 to 25 minutes for individual pies, or 45 minutes for a large one, until golden brown.

Combine all the salad ingredients in a mixing bowl, gently tossing the dressing and lemon juice throughout. Serve with the cottage pie or pies.

PUDDINGS

A burst of fruit
Winter compotes
Crunchy crumbles
Salted treacle
Swirls of meringue

Our puddings are never elaborate, and we don't deviate too far from the English classics – maybe a twist here and there, or a lighter touch visited on an old favourite, but nothing that detracts from simple, clear flavours. Most of the recipes are built around our own fruit from the gardens, helped along with oranges in winter, and so the pudding menu in the kitchens meanders through the seasons. At the height of summer we like to serve fruit as simply as possible: bowls of ripe red berries, just as they are with only a sprinkling of caster sugar and pouring cream, or we might serve the best Italian juicy peaches, thinly sliced and drizzled with a little sugar syrup (see page 41) and scattered with lemon zest and mint leaves.

Gooseberry Fool with Shortbread

Head chef Gaven loves old-fashioned puddings, but
with a contemporary feel, either in the flavours or in
the presentation. A few years ago he suggested putting
a proper, classic fool on the menu, like his mum used to
make, but rippled, so that you can really see the different
layers of gooseberry and creamy custard – and it is very
popular.

The best gooseberries are usually mid-season, when
they are not hard and mouth-puckeringly acidic as the
first ones tend to be, but also not as soft and sugary as the
last ones, which will make this pudding too sweet. Pop a
couple of berries into your mouth: what you are looking
for is something nice, firm and tart, but not overly so.

400g gooseberries, washed
and stalks removed

220g caster sugar

4 egg yolks

60g plain flour

450ml milk

1 vanilla pod, split

350ml double cream

To serve:

6 sprigs of fresh mint
(optional)

6 shortbread biscuits

Put the gooseberries into a pan with 100g of the sugar and
2 tablespoons of water and bring slowly to the boil, then
turn down the heat and simmer for 5 minutes, or until the
liquid has evaporated. Take off the heat and leave to cool.

Whisk the egg yolks, flour and remaining sugar in a bowl.

Put the milk and vanilla pod into a heavy-bottomed pan
and heat slowly, taking off the heat just before it comes
to a simmer. Add slowly to the egg yolk mixture, stirring
constantly, then return to the pan and continue to stir over
a low heat until you have quite a thick custard. Strain into
a clean bowl and leave to cool, stirring occasionally, then
cover with clingfilm to stop a skin forming.

Whip the cream until stiff and gently fold into the cooled
custard. Finally fold in the gooseberries very lightly – don't
mix them in completely, as you want a 'ripple' effect.

Either serve in bowls or if you want to make the pudding
look smarter spoon carefully into six glasses. Put into the
fridge until ready to serve. Garnish each glass with a sprig
of mint, if you like, and serve with a shortbread biscuit.

Notes on jelly

Fresh fruit jellies are a lovely, refreshing way to finish a meal, whether on their own, or as a layer in a trifle, or underneath a crumble topping.

The secret to a good jelly is not to use too much gelatine, or you end up with a very bouncy texture.

It used to be that only powdered gelatine was available, but leaf gelatine is easy to find and much better, as it is transparent, and has no flavour or aroma, so it just disappears into your liquid, turning it to jelly. Our rule of thumb is 1 leaf of gelatine to 100ml of liquid. However, when you are dealing with fruit it is never an exact science, since some fruit – blackcurrants, for example – are high in pectin, the naturally occurring substance which, when heated with sugar, helps jams and jellies to set. So you might find that some fruits will make a jelly that is a little firmer than others.

Soak your gelatine in ice-cold water, then squeeze it out – if the water is warm it will dissolve the leaf, and you don't want it to dissolve until you have put it into your warm juice.

John Hardwick

Orange-poached Rhubarb Jelly

1.5kg rhubarb, washed and cut into strips

150g caster sugar

zest and juice of 3 oranges

about 3 gelatine leaves

Put the rhubarb into an ovenproof dish with the sugar, orange zest and juice, and leave to marinate in the fridge for 8 hours.

Preheat the oven to 160°C/gas 3.

Cover the dish of rhubarb with foil and put into the preheated oven for 30 minutes, or until the rhubarb is just tender but still holding its shape.

Strain through a fine sieve placed over a bowl to catch the juice. Pour this juice into a measuring jug – you just need 300ml of liquid, so discard any excess. Keep back the rhubarb and arrange it in a serving dish.

Soak the gelatine in ice-cold water (the water must be cold or the gelatine will dissolve) and when soft squeeze out the water.

Pour the rhubarb juice into a pan and heat gently, then add the gelatine and stir until completely melted – but don't boil. Take off the heat, pour over the rhubarb and put into the fridge until set – this will probably take about 3 hours.

Mulled Wine and Orange Trifle

This is another recipe that Gaven, our head chef, came up with – they had been making mulled wine with oranges and spices in the Black Barn to sell in the farmshop, and we had some in the kitchen – he thought the warm, rich flavours would work really well with pieces of orange in a jelly for a trifle, and it is a really nice, quirky combination for winter. If you happen to have made the lemon drizzle cake on page 353, a few chunks of it in place of plain sponge cake make the trifle extra interesting.

2 oranges

12 small pieces/cubes of sponge cake or lemon drizzle cake

2 tablespoons brandy

180g double cream

4 tablespoons flaked almonds, lightly toasted in a dry pan

icing sugar for dusting

For the mulled wine jelly:

½ an orange

150ml red wine

a pinch of ground nutmeg

½ a cinnamon stick

a pinch of ground allspice

5 whole cloves

2 tablespoons caster sugar

1 sprig of fresh mint

1 tablespoon brandy

1 tablespoon whisky

3 tablespoons orange juice

2 gelatine leaves

First make the jelly. Peel the skin from the orange and put into a pan. Cut the flesh into rough pieces and add to the pan with the rest of the jelly ingredients, except for the gelatine. Bring to a simmer for 4–5 minutes, then turn off the heat and leave to infuse for 2 hours.

Strain the juice into a bowl through a fine sieve to remove the orange pieces and spices (throw all these away), then return the juice to the pan and warm very gently.

Soak the gelatine leaves in a bowl of ice-cold water until soft (the water must be cold or the gelatine will dissolve), then take out, squeeze and add to the pan of warm juice,

stirring until the gelatine dissolves. Take off the heat and keep to one side.

Finely grate the zest from one of the 2 oranges and keep on a saucer (you will be stirring it into the cream later), then peel and segment both. Divide the segments between four tumblers or small bowls and pour the slightly warm jelly over them. Put into the fridge to set for about 3 hours, until firm.

Arrange the cubes of sponge cake over the top of the jelly and drizzle with the brandy. Whip the cream with the reserved orange zest until it just falls from a spoon – in kitchens this is called the 'soft flop' – and spoon over the sponge. Put back into the fridge for 30 minutes, then top with the flaked almonds, finish with a dusting of icing sugar and serve.

Poached Apple and Pear Jelly with Crumble Topping and Prune Cream

An autumnal pudding that we have been making for many years, because it makes good use of the apples from the orchard at a time of year when there is not too much home-grown fruit to choose from. Setting the apple and prunes in a jelly just makes it a little lighter than a more traditional crumble.

We source our organic, unfiltered apple and prune juice from France, where it is a speciality in the apple-growing region of Nantes – however, you can make your own in a ratio of 80 per cent apple juice to 20 per cent prune juice.

For the fruit jelly:

2 small apples, peeled, cored and finely chopped

1 large pear, peeled, cored and finely chopped

375ml apple and prune juice (see introduction, above)

30g caster sugar

5 gelatine leaves

For the crumble:

100g plain flour

100g butter, chilled and chopped

75g light brown sugar

½ teaspoon ground cinnamon

100g oats

For the prune cream:

75g prunes, pitted

30g caster sugar

½ vanilla pod, split

150ml double cream

To make the jelly, put the apples and pear into a pan with the apple and prune juice, sugar and 100ml of water. Bring to the boil, then turn down the heat to a simmer until the pear is tender. Take off the heat.

Meanwhile put the gelatine leaves into a bowl of ice-cold water until soft (the water must be cold or the gelatine will dissolve). Take out, squeeze, and add to the hot liquid, stirring until dissolved. Divide between four large ramekins or glass jars, allow to cool, then put into the fridge for around 4 hours, to set.

Preheat the oven to 180°C/gas 4.

To make the prune cream, put the prunes into a pan with the sugar, vanilla pod and 125ml of water. Bring to a simmer for 5 minutes, then take off the heat and either whiz in a blender, or use a hand-held one, until smooth (leave the vanilla pod in, so that it is dispersed through the cream). Leave to cool.

To make the crumble topping, put the flour into a bowl and rub in the butter until the mixture resembles breadcrumbs, then stir in the sugar, cinnamon and oats. Spread the mixture over a baking tray and put into the preheated oven for 12 minutes, until golden brown and toasted.

To finish the prune cream, whip the double cream in a bowl, just until it forms soft peaks, then gently fold into the cooled prune mixture. Do this as lightly as possible so as not to split the cream.

Take the pots of jelly from the fridge and top each one with an equal quantity of the toasted crumble mixture. Serve with a good dollop of prune cream.

Coffee Jelly with Brown Bread Ice Cream

This is a real Bamford family favourite, going back years and years. 'At the start of every summer holidays we would think, "What shall we have for pudding?"' says Carole. 'The first thing that would come to mind was coffee jelly. And we still love it. It sounds like it is going to be heavy, but it is really light, and refreshing, and gives you a lift at the end of a meal.'

The jelly contains a lot more gelatine than the other jelly recipes, because there is no fruit, and therefore no pectin to help set it naturally.

For the coffee jelly:

12 leaves gelatine

2 tablespoons instant coffee

4 tablespoons caster sugar

For the brown bread ice cream:

55g unsalted butter

85g wholemeal breadcrumbs

170g caster sugar

8 egg yolks

1 vanilla pod, split

570ml single cream

2 tablespoons Madeira

Soak the gelatine leaves in a bowl of ice-cold water until soft (the water must be cold or the gelatine will dissolve), then take out and squeeze.

Put the coffee and sugar in a pan with 1 litre of water, bring to the boil and stir until the coffee and sugar have dissolved. Add the gelatine and stir until dissolved. Remove from the heat and leave to cool slightly, then pour into a jelly mould or flan ring and leave in the fridge to set for at least 4 hours, or overnight.

Heat the butter in a frying pan, put in the breadcrumbs and fry until crisp. Add half of the caster sugar and let the mixture caramelise and turn golden brown. Pour into a tray in a shallow layer and leave to set, then bash with a rolling pin, to break it up into fine crumbs.

In a large bowl, beat together the egg yolks and remaining sugar until thick and creamy (this is easiest with an electric hand mixer).

Put the vanilla pod and cream in a heavy-based pan and bring to the boil. Take the pan from the heat and remove the vanilla pod, then pour onto the beaten egg and sugar mixture, whisking all the time.

Pour this mixture into a heatproof bowl, set over a pan of simmering water (make sure that the base doesn't touch the water) and stir all the time until it thickens enough to coat the back of a wooden spoon. Leave to cool, then stir in the Madeira.

Churn in an ice cream maker until starting to set, then stir in the caramelised breadcrumbs and finish. Alternatively, place in a freezer container, put into the freezer and take out and stir at 30-minute intervals until half frozen.

Again, when the ice cream is starting to set, stir through the caramelised breadcrumbs and continue freezing.

Serve the ice cream with the coffee jelly.

Rhubarb Queen of Puddings

This is a real winner in the café. Again, we have our traditionalist head chef Gaven Fuller to thank for the idea. It is a marriage of two of his childhood favourites: Queen of Puddings, which is classically made with custard, spread with jam and a meringue topping; and rhubarb with custard and brown sugar, baked under the grill.

The meringue used in this recipe is Swiss meringue – which executive chef John Hardwick insists is the easiest and best to make. 'French meringue – the more usual kind in which you whisk the egg whites and then fold in the sugar – always has the potential to drop, and for the sugar and whites to separate,' he says. 'On the other hand Italian meringue, while it is more stable, is trickier to make, as you have to add boiling sugar syrup to whisked egg whites, and the sugar can stick to the sides of the bowl and not incorporate into the egg whites properly. Whereas this, Swiss meringue, holds as well as Italian meringue and never fails. Once you have made it you will never make French or Italian meringue again. You just need a sugar thermometer – a cheap investment that makes working with sugar much easier.'

3 egg yolks

210ml double cream

225ml milk

zest of 1 lemon

30g caster sugar

20g butter

90g fresh white breadcrumbs

For the rhubarb compote:

375g rhubarb, cut into small chunks

zest and juice of 1 orange

175g sugar

For the meringue:

3 egg whites

180g caster sugar

a pinch of salt

Preheat the oven to 160°C/gas 3.

Have the egg yolks ready in a bowl. Put the cream, milk, lemon zest and sugar into a pan and heat slowly until the sugar has dissolved, then pour over the egg yolks, stirring constantly. When all is mixed in, stir in the butter and breadcrumbs. Divide this custard between four ovenproof dishes and put these into a roasting pan.

Pour in enough boiling water around the dishes to come halfway up the outsides, and cook for 12–15 minutes, or until the custard is just set. Take out of the oven (but leave it on) and leave the dishes of custard to cool.

Put the rhubarb into an ovenproof dish with the orange zest, juice and sugar. Cover with foil and place in the oven for 30 minutes. Remove the rhubarb with a slotted spoon on to a plate, pour the juice into a pan and bubble up to reduce until very thick, then take off the heat and mix back the reserved rhubarb. Allow to cool.

When both the custard and the rhubarb are cool, put the egg whites into a heatproof bowl. Add the sugar and salt and place the bowl over a pan of simmering water, whisking until the temperature reaches 60°C on a sugar thermometer, then remove from the heat and whisk until cold, using an electric whisk. The mixture will double in size, form stiff peaks and be smooth and glossy.

Spread some of the rhubarb compote over the custard in the dishes, and spoon (or pipe) the meringue over the top.

Put into the oven for about 10 minutes, until the meringue is straw-coloured.

Vanilla Rice Pudding with Apple and Blackberry Compote

You will probably think this method of making rice pudding looks difficult because it is done in a bain-marie – i.e. in a bowl over a pan of simmering water – but in fact it is much easier than on a hob, as you barely have to stir it, and you don't have to watch it to make sure it isn't catching during the slow cooking over nearly 2 hours (this gentle cooking is what makes the pudding so soft and creamy). All you need to do is check now and then that the water in the pan below the bowl isn't boiling away.

We started making this with risotto rice, as it was impossible to find organic pudding rice – and it makes a perfect pudding. Of course you can make it at any time of the year, and serve it on its own, or with whatever fruit you like, but it is particularly good with apples and blackberries in the autumn.

150g risotto rice

75g sugar

500ml milk

10g butter

1 vanilla pod, split in half and seeds scraped out

1 teaspoon ground nutmeg

300ml double cream

For the compote:

2 small cooking apples, peeled, cored and chopped

60g sugar

juice of ½ a lemon

150g blackberries

Put the rice, sugar, milk, butter, vanilla and nutmeg into a large ovenproof bowl, cover with clingfilm and place over a pan of gently simmering water – make sure the base of the bowl isn't touching the water. Cook for about 1¾–2 hours, stirring occasionally and making sure that the water in the pan doesn't evaporate away – top it up as necessary. It is ready when most of the liquid has been absorbed, the rice is soft and the pudding has thickened. Take off the heat, stir in the double cream, and remove the vanilla pod.

While the rice is cooking, make the compote: put the apples, sugar and lemon juice into a small pan with

3 tablespoons of water, cover and bring to the boil, stirring occasionally until the apples soften. Stir in the blackberries, cook for a few more minutes until the berries 'bleed', then take off the heat.

Serve the rice pudding in individual bowls, with a spoonful of compote on top.

Three Sweet Tarts

Just as we make savoury tarts all year round, highlighting different cheeses and produce from the garden, we make different sweet tarts throughout the seasons, usually with fruit set in frangipane, or scattered with a crumble topping – though when the weather gets cold, one of our favourites is the salted ginger treacle tart on page 296.

Sweet Pastry

This makes enough for one 20cm tart case, 3-4 cm deep.

150g plain flour

a pinch of salt

80g caster sugar

100g butter

1 whole egg, beaten

1 egg yolk, for brushing the pastry

Sift the flour into a bowl and add the salt and the sugar. Grate in the butter and mix lightly with the tips of your fingers until the mixture resembles breadcrumbs, ensuring there are no lumps of butter in the mix (alternatively you can do this using a food processor). Add the egg and mix until you have a dough – taking care not to overwork it. Form into a ball, wrap in clingfilm, and chill in the fridge for at least 30 minutes before using.

Preheat the oven to 160°C/gas 3.

Lightly flour your work surface and roll out your ball of pastry into a circle big enough to line a 20cm x 4cm deep flan tin with a removable base, leaving enough pastry to overhang the sides. Wrap the pastry carefully around your rolling pin to lift it and drop it carefully into the flan tin, pushing it gently into the base and sides of the tin – don't trim the overhanging pastry. Put the tin on a baking tray – this makes it easier to move it around – then into the fridge to rest and chill for another 30 minutes (to help prevent the pastry shrinking during baking).

When ready to blind-bake, prick the base of the pastry case with a fork, line with greaseproof paper – crinkle it up first to soften it and avoid it denting the pastry – and fill with baking beans. Put into the preheated oven for about 30 minutes, until light golden brown, then take out, remove the paper and baking beans (you no longer need these), and brush all over the inside of the pastry case with the beaten egg, to seal up any little holes.

Put the tin back into the oven for a further 5–10 minutes, until the base is fully baked and golden brown. Don't be scared of taking the pastry to this point. The key to a good tart base is to hold your nerve, and colour and crisp the pastry to the stage at which you would like to eat it, as once you put in your filling and return it to the oven it won't colour any more, except maybe a little around the edges, and the base will stay crispy and flaky as the filling cooks. If you only lightly colour the pastry, and the base isn't fully baked, it will be soft and doughy, making the whole tart seem heavy.

Remove from the oven and, when cool, carefully trim off the overhanging pastry with a small, sharp, serrated knife. Now you can make whichever filling you like, and bake your tart according to the instructions in each recipe.

Blackberry and Apple Crumble Tart

Serve this with either custard or cream.

1 blind-baked 20cm x 4cm
sweet pastry tart case (see
page 293)

For the crumble:

110g flour

40g brown sugar

90g butter

55g hazelnuts, chopped

40g rolled oats

For the apple and blackberry
filling:

40g butter

400g Bramley apples, peeled
and cored

juice of 1 lemon

50g sugar

300g blackberries

Preheat the oven to 160°C/gas 3.

To make the crumble, put all the ingredients except the
oats into a blender, and blitz to a crumbly dough. Then stir
in the oats.

Spread the mixture over a baking sheet and put into the
preheated oven for 20 minutes, or until golden brown.
Take out, and when cool enough to handle, break up the
mix with your hands until it resembles breadcrumbs and
keep to one side.

Meanwhile, make the filling. Put the butter into a small
pan and heat gently until foaming, then add the apples,
lemon juice and sugar and stir well. When the apples start
to soften, add the blackberries and take the pan from the
heat.

To assemble, fill the tart case with the apple and
blackberry mixture, sprinkle the crumble topping all over
and put into the oven for about 20 minutes, or until the
topping turns golden brown.

Salted Ginger Treacle Tart

As in salted caramels, the combination of treacle and sea salt is a classic one. The cornflakes just add an interesting crunch and texture. This is good served with crème fraîche, which adds a little fresh, sharp touch to balance out the sweetness.

1 blind-baked 20cm x 4cm sweet pastry tart case (see page 293)

1 egg, plus 1 yolk

50g double cream

1 teaspoon sea salt

60g butter

540g golden syrup

1½ teaspoons ground ginger

2 tablespoons chopped stem ginger

70g fresh brown breadcrumbs

70g cornflakes, lightly crushed

Preheat the oven to 150°C/gas 2.

In a small mixing bowl, beat the egg, yolk, cream and salt until well combined.

Put the butter into a medium pan and melt over a medium heat until golden brown and nutty. Add the golden syrup, ground and stem ginger and warm slightly, then remove from the heat and stir into the egg mixture.

Mix in the breadcrumbs and cornflakes. Spoon into the pastry case, filling it right to the rim.

Put into the preheated oven and bake for 50 minutes, until golden brown on top – the filling should no longer wobble if you shake the tart gently. Remove from the oven and leave to cool. Serve warm.

Apricot and Almond Tart

This combines apricots with a classic almond cream (frangipane), but we also use the same recipe with whatever stone fruits, such as plums or cherries, are prolific in the market garden. You can even make the tart with soft fruits like figs, or raspberries, which won't look quite as spectacular as fruit that holds its shape, but will taste equally good. In autumn we sometimes use apples or pears, but these harder fruits need to be poached first in a little sugar and water to soften them.

Serve with vanilla ice cream or a bowl of whipped cream.

1 blind-baked 20cm x 4cm sweet pastry tart case (see page 293)

7–10 fresh ripe apricots

2 tablespoons apricot jam

For the frangipane:

100g butter

100g caster sugar

1 egg, plus 1 egg yolk

80g ground almonds

20g plain flour

First make the frangipane. Cream the butter and sugar together in a mixing bowl until light, creamy and pale in colour, then add the egg and yolk gradually (you can also do this in a mixer). When all the egg is combined, stir in the ground almonds and the flour. Put into the fridge to chill for 1–2 hours, for the mixture to firm up, then spoon into the tart base, using the back of a spoon moistened with a little water to smooth the surface.

Preheat the oven to 170°C/gas 3.

Cut the apricots in half, discarding the stones, then, depending on the size of the fruit, cut each half into two or three wedges. Starting at the outside of the tart, evenly space the apricots in a circular fashion, pushing each wedge halfway into the almond cream, and letting the other half protrude and point upwards. Repeat with more

circles, working towards the centre, until all the apricots have been used up.

Place the tart tin on a baking tray and put into the preheated oven for about 30 minutes, until the frangipane is golden brown, the apricots are nice and caramelised and a skewer inserted into the centre comes out clean.

Take out of the oven and leave in the tin. Meanwhile, put the apricot jam into a small pan with 2 tablespoons of water and bubble up until you have a syrup. Brush the top of the tart with the syrup. Allow to cool slightly, then remove the tart from the tin and serve while still warm.

Blood Orange and Polenta Cake with Orange Whipped Cream

We experimented with many different versions of polenta cake and orange before settling on this one, which is quite light, and adds a handsome splash of colour to the pudding menu at a time when there is not much in the fruit garden apart from apples and pears.

In an ideal world the cake mixture would use an equal number of egg yolks and whites, to keep things neat, but whereas in most savoury cooking an extra dash of this or that is all part of the interpretation of a dish, with cakes it is all about chemistry, and you have to be precise: so 2 egg yolks and 3 egg whites it is.

85g butter, softened

130g caster sugar, plus 1 tablespoon

1 teaspoon vanilla extract

2 egg yolks

120g plain flour

30g fine polenta

2 teaspoons baking powder

a pinch of salt

90ml milk

3 egg whites

sprigs of mint, to garnish (optional)

For the oranges in caramel:

2 blood oranges

180g sugar

For the orange cream:

240g double cream

75g caster sugar

juice and zest of 1 orange

Preheat the oven to 180°C/gas 4. Grease a 20cm loose-bottomed cake tin and line with baking parchment.

For the oranges in caramel, remove the skin and the pith with a small sharp knife, keeping the curve of the orange. Turn each orange on its side, then cut into slices about 4mm thick. Put the sugar into a small heavy-bottomed pan with 100ml of water and heat, stirring, until the sugar has dissolved, then continue to cook without stirring until the syrup changes from a light amber to a dark caramel. As soon as it reaches this point, take the pan off the heat and carefully pour the caramel evenly into the base of the prepared tin.

Pat the orange slices dry on kitchen paper and arrange in overlapping circles on top of the caramel (this will be the top of the cake, so try to do this as neatly as possible).

To make the cake, put the butter, 130g of sugar and vanilla extract in a bowl and cream together until light and fluffy, then mix in the egg yolks, a little at a time, until well combined. Fold in the flour, polenta flour, baking powder and salt, mix well, then add the milk gradually until you have a smooth batter.

Whisk the egg whites until they reach soft peaks, then add the tablespoon of caster sugar and whisk again to form stiff peaks. Gently fold a third of this meringue into the batter to begin with, to loosen it, then carefully fold in the rest as lightly as possible (you want to keep as much air in it as possible to keep the cake nice and light).

Spoon the batter over the layer of caramel and oranges in the cake tin and smooth gently.

Put into the preheated oven and bake for about 35–40 minutes, or until a skewer inserted into the middle comes out clean (the cake will become quite dark in colour). Take out of the oven and place the tin on a cooling rack for 10 minutes.

Meanwhile, make the orange cream by whipping the double cream and sugar together until it just holds its shape and then folding in the orange zest and juice.

To turn out the cake, place a flat plate over the top of the tin, then, holding both tightly, turn them over together so that the cake tin is sitting, base side up, on the plate. Carefully remove the tin and base. Slice the cake and serve slightly warm with the orange cream. Garnish, if you like, with a sprig of mint.

Christmas Pudding

This is Carole Bamford's family recipe.

120g suet

60g self-raising flour, sifted

120g white breadcrumbs

240g demerara sugar

120g sultanas

120g raisins

120g currants

1 apple, grated

grated zest of 1 orange
and 1 lemon

1 tablespoon candied
orange peel

1 tablespoon candied
lemon peel

1 teaspoon mixed spice

1 teaspoon ground nutmeg

1 teaspoon ground
cinnamon

30g chopped almonds

2 eggs

50ml rum

70ml white wine

70ml stout

In a large bowl mix together the suet, flour, breadcrumbs
and sugar, add the dried fruits, grated apple, zests, peel,
spices and almonds.

Beat the eggs with the rum, wine and stout in a separate
bowl, then pour in and mix thoroughly to give a thick
batter. Cover the bowl with clingfilm and leave overnight
in the fridge. The next day take out and stir.

Grease a 1.1 litre ovenproof pudding basin with butter, fill
the basin with the pudding mixture and smooth the top.
Cover the basin with a double layer of greaseproof paper,
make a pleat in the centre and then follow with a sheet
of foil. Tie a piece of string around the basin to secure
the foil and paper in place. Place on a trivet inside a large
pan. Pour in enough boiling water to come halfway up the
outside of the bowl, then cover the pan and keep the water
simmering for 8 hours, topping up with boiling water
from a kettle from time to time.

The pudding can either be eaten straight away, or cooled,
rewrapped and stored for up to a year. Re-steam in the
same way for 2½ hours before serving.

Cheese and . . .

At the end of a meal, or when you just want cheese, consider pairing a particular style with fruit, chutney, good bread or biscuits. These are some of the combinations we especially like:

Cheddar – mature cheese complemented beautifully by red tomato chilli jam.

Single Gloucester – fresh and subtle, great with a mound of dried cranberries and crackers.

Double Gloucester – good with apple and chilli chutney, crackers and celery.

Bledington Blue – this small and creamy cow's milk cheese marries well with pears, cobnuts, honey and seven seeds sourdough.

Daylesford Blue – larger and slightly drier in texture than Bledington Blue, the cheese is good with warm fruit bread and celery.

Baywell – a soft, heart-shaped cow's milk cheese that goes well with truffled honey on rye bread.

Adlestrop – the semi-soft cow's milk cheese pairs well with fresh apricots and butternut squash chutney.

Penygoat and Trenchard – both goat's cheeses, the white-mould Penygoat and hard Trenchard also go well with truffled honey – and walnuts.

Oddington – quince jelly is good with this soft goat's cheese, along with fresh figs and digestive biscuits.

Greek-style cheese – serve with minted crème fraîche and green leaf salad.

'Four ingredients: flour, yeast, salt and water – that is all it takes to make bread, but every time something different happens.'
Eric Duhamel, The Bakery

The holistic view of artisan food production is something I have long believed in. We have to have a more sustainable, less wasteful way to feed people and look after our planet, otherwise we are heading to the wall.

There is a terrible statistic from the Department for Environment, Food and Rural Affairs that in Britain 32 per cent of bread that is bought finishes in the bin, which represents nearly 700,000 tonnes per year. It is frustrating for me, being French, that there is often little respect for bread in the UK. It is just something that holds together other food in a sandwich, or that goes into the toaster. But for me, good bread should be on the side of every plate, at every meal. I'm not saying that in France everything is rosy. There, too, bakery knowledge needs a good renewal – and probably only about 20 per cent of bakeries produce really good bread these days – but the advantage in France is in the background, the value of bread, and the place it has on the table at every mealtime. Whereas in Britain, so often, people buy a big sliced loaf, eat ten slices, and after three days, when it starts to get mouldy, they throw it away.

When I was offered the chance to come to Daylesford five years ago, I wasn't at all sure I wanted to come to England, because my only experience of the UK was London – and I don't like the craziness of city life – and of terrible bread. At the time I was taking time off with my family in our home in Aveyron, near Roquefort, one of the most gorgeous places in France, to wind down after spending six months in an organic bakery in Paris. Working in the city was a shock after my previous positions in a gastronomic restaurant, La Villa Madie, in Cassis, in Provence, where I developed all the breads, and in Australia, in an artisan bakery, with wide open spaces all around me. There we made all our breads with natural leaven, and I was able to develop a new recipe for croissants and design a brioche made exclusively with sourdough, which is very unusual.

But when I arrived here, the countryside reminded me of Aveyron, and I realised that we had the chance to do something special, making breads using all the traditional skills of long, slow fermentation, time and patience, and with the luxury of only organic ingredients.

A well-made loaf is a beautiful and healthy thing, but fast industrially made bread is damaging people's health. There have never been so many people who either have, or think they have, an intolerance to gluten, because of the Chorleywood process, which was developed in 1961 to produce cheap, soft, springy bread and which is all about high speed, volume and profit margins. The dough is mixed at very high speed with a lot of yeast, and with the help of 'improvers': industrial mixes of enzymes and emulsifiers and other agents that are designed to 'condition' and 'improve' the texture and structure of fast-produced bread, so that the loaves expand massively and look fresh for as long as possible; but what you are being sold is water, instead of bread.

The process gives you nothing in terms of the organoleptic qualities of bread, and it is not properly digestible, because the structure of the gluten is developed really quickly, like scaffolding, reinforced by the improvers. As a result the gluten in the finished bread is extremely strong and resistant to the chemical aggression of our digestive juices. Because the bread has no real texture, what happens is that when you eat it, it shrinks in on itself and so you have a ball of paste and gluten just sitting in your stomach, and it is hard for your gastric juices to attack and break it down. And when it goes through your bowels, it is less degraded than it should be – so that is why people feel bloated and uncomfortable and think they have an intolerance to gluten, when in fact they have an intolerance to the bread-making method.

What is sad is that it is perfectly possible to produce very good bread on an industrial scale – and not just rustic-looking loaves, which are still made with the same process. It is not the equipment, it is the method, and if there is the will it can be done, but the will is not there. When you hear industrial bakers talking about their bread, it is almost as if they are not describing food. The words they use are all to do with speed and efficiency, softness, moisture and shelf life.

Even smaller bakeries that are making more rustic-looking bread on a slower scale are often still using improvers, because they give you consistency. An improver cheats for you: it is like playing with ten aces in your pack. But it degrades the quality, you lose flavour and colour and the crust on the bread is thinner.

Also, many bakers, myself included, develop allergies (and asthma) from the flour dust that you breathe in every day in a commercial bakery, and it is now known that one of the triggers is the enzyme alpha amylase, which is used to 'improve' doughs. I always knew that I wanted to work in an artisan bakery, with organic ingredients, but when I started out, it was in a conventional bakery that used these additives, and I am convinced this is what started off my allergy, which over the years has developed into a reaction to all flour, so I can't work without a special mask. Many bakers who suffer from 'baker's allergy' give up, but baking is what I love to do, so I keep going.

What bread needs is time, not speed. When you allow your dough to go through a slow fermentation, especially sourdough, the micro-organisms go to work and by the time the bread is baked it is perfectly digestible. Typically in our bakery at Daylesford, our doughs take twenty-four hours from beginning to end.

People often ask me if I am bringing French techniques to the making of the bread; well partly, yes, but also, what is interesting is that if you go back in time and look at the way people made the typical crusty, rustic cottage and cob loaves, which are first mentioned back in the seventh and eighth centuries, you can see that the methods are very, very similar to those used in French bread-making.

This kind of bread, just as in Europe, would have lasted a week. You would slice only what you needed, and when the bread began to be stale, there would be recipes, like bread pudding, for using it up. It didn't go in the bin.

On one level bread is one of the simplest and most basic of foods, involving just four ingredients: flour, yeast, salt and water – that is all it takes to make bread, but if you do it in the artisan way, every time you bake, something different happens. Thousands and thousands of pages of books and papers have been devoted to the science, the technique, the flour, the yeast, because we are dealing with something that is alive and complex, that takes a great deal of understanding.

The weather, the humidity, the exact temperature of your water, the length of time you leave the dough to prove, the way you shape it . . . everything has an effect. Even in the same room, if you have three different people shaping the same dough, you will get three subtly different batches of loaves. Especially when you are making a sourdough-style bread, built on a leaven (natural yeasts), an artisan baker has to go back to the old-fashioned skills and principles of bread-making, and understand and feel and control a complex population of micro-organisms, which, one day, might be in good shape, and another might be tired, just like human beings. About three years ago, we even had a situation where the leaven just died one day. Completely! Luckily I always keep a batch in the fridge that I have been feeding over many years, and so we could re-start.

People say you can't bake bread without strong white flour, and that the gluten isn't strong enough in other wheats. Not true. That is a myth promoted by Canadian and American millers. I have made beautiful baguettes with plain flour. You just have to use a long fermentation and fold the dough during the proving, which strengthens the gluten, and in the end you get a great result. Plain flour has a better flavour, and because it is lower in gluten it is more digestible, and I know that this can work for other breads too, so with the millers I want to develop a special flour for us, that is a little higher in gluten than the plain flour that you use in cakes (which is about 9 per cent) but much lower than in American and Canadian flour: around 11 per cent gluten I think is perfect.

It is a step-by-step process. When I arrived here, for example, we were using a particular flour, very high in gluten, designed for croissants; the next stage was to change this for strong white Canadian flour, and now, we are working with half strong flour and half plain flour, and the benefit is you have a dough that is easier for us to work with, and gives you a crispier croissant that tastes more buttery, but without extra butter. So everybody wins.

At the same time, we want to start introducing more interesting, different, old and heritage varieties of wheats from the UK and Europe into the flour. It used to be that farmers were much more diverse in their planting, and would have different varieties of wheat planted in the same field, so when the grains were milled, you would have an interesting, quite complex flour. But now, monoculture has taken over and it is rarely done any more.

Also, the way the grains are milled is important. It is possible to mill flour just as well, using cylinders in the modern way, as it is in traditional stone-ground mills, provided that you keep the temperature low and don't overheat the grains. Often millers strip out the germs of the grain before milling, because, if these are crushed, their oils go into the flour, so it has a shorter shelf-life, as the oils can turn it rancid after about three months. Whereas if you remove the germ, the bags of flour will last for a year. But the germ is what also gives the flour individuality. If you mill the whole grains, slowly and gently, at a lower temperature, you keep all the goodness and individual flavours of the grains intact.

One of the grains that I like to use is spelt, because it gives such a good flavour, but it can be tricky to work with when you are not used to it, because the gluten is more delicate, and so the dough is more fragile, and needs to be kneaded less, but strengthened by folding during a long fermentation.

The fact that spelt has a fragile gluten is mainly because it was a forgotten grain since the nineteenth century, which has only been rediscovered relatively recently, so it hasn't been developed in the way of modern wheats, grown for the bread industry with high levels of strong gluten as a priority. Sadly, though, I fear for its future, as growers pick up on its fashionability and start developing new, stronger strains.

For all my love of spelt and experimenting with different flours, I would say when you start out making bread, it is best to start with strong flour, which is why I have specified it in the recipes that follow. Once you get used to the technique of slow bread-making, and really understand the process of using natural leaven and only small quantities of yeast, then you can begin experimenting with more interesting flours, and perhaps introducing some plain flour into the mix. Do it, as we do at the bakery, step by step, seeing what happens, and adapting and developing your recipes, making them your own.

It has taken me years to build my team in the bakery, and everyone cares so much about what they do, and they are really proud of our breads, which is a great luxury for me, so we are continually creating new and interesting breads, incorporating cheeses from the creamery, or root vegetables, such as swedes, turnips, carrots and beetroot, or whatever Jez suggests might be good from the market garden. I like to develop ideas where the focus is on flavour and understanding, not only on show and cleverness, which might get you noticed, but has little to do with everyday bread that sustains life. When you make something that tastes beautiful and is based on correct technique and proper knowledge, only then can you start to be a bit fancy and have fun with your presentation.

And actually, when all is said and done, my favourite bread is still a beautifully made, plain sourdough, that tastes clean, refined and refreshing – and I would eat it with every meal.

BREADS

Slow, slow sourdoughs
Breads baked in flowerpots
Herbs and honey
Chilli and Cheddar
Dark pumpernickel

When you bake your own bread, not only do you have a real sense of pride in your achievement, but you have the simple satisfaction of knowing exactly what goes into it.

In the bakery Eric Duhamel and his team are constantly developing new breads, and the range changes frequently, but the recipes in this chapter are some of those that remain constant, because they are so popular. 'One of the characteristics of our bread,' says Eric, 'is that we either use our own leaven, which we have nurtured for many years, and which is the natural fermentation of wild yeasts, or, if we use commercial yeast, we use very little, in comparison with most British bakeries. There is a long tradition of using a high quantity of yeast in British baking, that goes back to a time well before the infamous Chorleywood process, which also uses a lot of yeast, in order to make a strong dough, because it is being made at unnaturally high speed. But when you are making bread at home, if you use a large quantity of yeast it increases the risk of failure, because the fermentation speeds up, and then the whole process is more difficult to control. Your bread will rise up crazily in the oven, but then collapse, and it will be doughy inside. So it is much better to use natural leaven, or a little yeast, and go for a longer, slower fermentation.

'There is a quite lazy method of bread-making that I really like to do myself at home, which is to use the fridge. Follow your recipe up to the point where you shape the dough, quite tightly, then start the second proving, but after around 30 minutes to 1 hour, when you can see that the dough is halfway through the rising, put it into the fridge overnight to finish. This slows the fermentation right down, and makes the texture of the dough strong and more tolerant. It is what, since I worked in Australia, I call a "no worries" method. Then next day you just check that the dough has risen to the right stage, heat your oven and you are ready to bake.

'You will also notice that we only knead these breads once, never after the first proving and fermentation. This, again, is different to many British recipes that are designed around stiffer doughs, high in yeast. Because we are progressing the dough as naturally as possible, we want to keep in the air that has been created by the first proving, not knock it out, so all we do is very gently "de-gas" it, by pressing down very briefly and lightly with the palms of our hands, then if we are adding extra ingredients, such as fruit, or vegetables, we fold them in quickly, and then shape the dough ready for baking.

'It is important to remember that when you make bread, you are dealing with something that is alive. It isn't like making a salad, or grilling a steak; the conditions in your kitchen, the humidity, everything you do can affect the outcome. Also every oven is different, so the temperatures are guidelines, and you might have to experiment and adapt them (remember too, that if you use a fan oven, this usually has a more intense heat, so the temperature will need to be lower).

'To be a good baker,' insists Eric, 'it is important to practise, and to fail sometimes, because that is part of the learning process. If you bake bread time and time again and it comes out just OK, you will never really understand the process, because you don't need to. But when something goes wrong, you need to be like a doctor and do a diagnosis, to really understand what has gone wrong and what you can do about it. And once you start to do this, then you will make really good bread.

'But, you know, the main thing is to have fun with your bread. It is only professional bakers, like me, who have to turn out bread day in, day out that is in tip-top condition. When you bake at home, however your bread comes out of the oven, it will still be good, something to be proud of, that you have made yourself, with love and care and that you can be very happy about.'

Squash, Honey and Sage Bread

This bread is baked at quite a low temperature, because at a higher heat the squash, honey and malt extract would caramelise and colour too quickly, so you would run the risk of the bread burning and tasting bitter.

180g strong white flour

20g butter, softened

10g sugar

35g milk

5g fresh yeast or 3g dried yeast

5g fine sea salt

50g butternut squash, coarsely grated

10g pumpkin seeds

5g malt extract

1 teaspoon honey

4 sage leaves, very thinly sliced

a little vegetable oil, for greasing the bowl and the clingfilm

Put the flour, butter, sugar, milk, yeast and salt into a bowl with 70g of lukewarm water and mix into a dough.

Turn out the dough on to your work surface and knead for 5 minutes.

Add the squash, pumpkin seeds, malt extract, honey and sage and knead for another 5 minutes (using extra flour if necessary), until you have a smooth and shiny dough.

Transfer to a lightly oiled bowl, cover with oiled clingfilm and allow to rise in a warm place, until doubled in size.

Turn out the dough and 'de-gas' by pressing down briefly and gently with the flat of your hand, to even out the bubbles of air, then shape into a ball. Transfer to a floured proving basket, or a baking sheet. Cover with a clean tea towel and again leave in a warm place to prove, until doubled in size.

Meanwhile preheat the oven to 180°C/gas 4. This might seem like a low temperature; however, this is a bread that colours very quickly.

If the dough has been resting in a proving basket, turn it out on to a baking sheet. If it has been resting on a baking sheet, finely dust the top with flour (if it has been in a proving basket it will already have this fine dusting).

Score the top of the loaf swiftly and cleanly with the blade of a sharp serrated knife (see page 318), put it into the oven and bake for about 25–30 minutes. If you throw some ice cubes into the bottom of the oven, this will create steam and enhance the crust.

The bread is ready when, if you tap the base, it sounds hollow.

Remove from the oven and place on a cooling rack.

Notes on ingredients and technique

When you make bread, accuracy of ingredients is important in a way that it isn't in general cooking, so weigh everything – including water.

Although most of these recipes are for one loaf, I find it much easier to bake at home if I am working with a bigger quantity of dough – so I recommend that you double or triple the quantities and make 2 or 3 loaves at a time, if possible. You can always put the bread that you don't need immediately into the freezer.

Don't automatically dust your work surface with flour before kneading your bread. Have some in a little bowl next to where you are working, but only use it if you really need to, and then use a very light dusting. Remember that if you use lots of extra flour you are adding this to your dough and altering the ratio of the ingredients.

The quantities of yeast are approximate, because the quality varies according to the brand; so find one that you like, experiment with it, then stick with that brand, so that you know how it will behave, rather than chopping and changing – there are enough variables in bread, without adding more.

A traditional proving basket – in France we call it a banneton – is a cheap but excellent piece of equipment to have in your kitchen, to hold loaves that are not being baked in a tin, while they are proving. Made of wicker and lined with cloth, the basket allows the air to circulate, so that the dough doesn't dry out, and if you dust it with flour, when you turn out the dough ready to bake, it will keep this fine dusting on the top, which will give the finished bread an attractive look.

Before you put your dough into the oven, you need to score the top with the blade of a sharp serrated knife, quickly and cleanly, so you don't drag the dough. The cuts don't need to be deep – only about 2mm – but they will create weak points in the surface of the forming crust, which will allow the gases that build up as the dough bakes to push against the crust and expand, allowing the bread to rise to its full potential. If you don't make any cuts, think of it as a volcano with a lid on it. What will happen is that eventually the crust will crack randomly under the pressure, but still not enough to allow the bread to rise as much as it would like.

When you score your bread, the simplest way to do it, for round loaves, is to make a wide cross on the top, and for longer loaves, to make a series of slashes along the top of the loaf. Always make your cuts as long as possible: the full width of the bread. When you become more comfortable with the whole process, you can be as imaginative with your scoring as you like – even draw pictures with your knife if you like. Sometimes I score breads with leaf patterns, for example.

I suggest that for most loaves, you throw a handful of ice cubes into the bottom of the oven as you put in the bread. The cubes evaporate instantly, without marking your oven, and the steam they create softens the top of the dough at the beginning of baking, allowing it to rise more, and give you a nice shiny crust at the end.

Eric Duhamel

Pumpernickel

'This is a very sticky dough that stays sticky, so, honestly, it can be easier to do the mixing and kneading in a mixer with a dough hook,' advises Eric. 'Mix the ingredients together on the first speed for 10 minutes, then knead for 3 minutes on the second speed, add the raisins and mix for another 3 minutes back on the first speed.

'The bread is only proved once, and the finished loaf will look more like a brick than a risen bread.' This is baked at quite a low temperature, for quite a long time, as it doesn't form a crust like many of the breads.

60g cracked rye

25g pumpkin seeds, plus 1 tablespoon for topping

15g sunflower seeds, plus 1 tablespoon for topping

10g linseeds

10g fine sea salt

60g strong white flour

120g dark rye flour

1 teaspoon instant coffee

60g molasses

12g fresh yeast

75g raisins

a little vegetable oil, for greasing your hands and the clingfilm

Put the cracked rye, all the seeds (except those for the topping) and the salt into a bowl and stir in 90g of lukewarm water. Leave to soak overnight.

Have ready a 15cm x 9cm loaf tin (if it is not non-stick, grease and line with greaseproof paper).

Put both flours into a bowl with the coffee, molasses and yeast and add the soaked seeds. Mix together, then turn out on to a lightly floured surface and knead for 10 minutes. Because the dough is naturally sticky, this is one occasion when you probably will have to use a little extra flour, as necessary. Alternatively, if you find it is really difficult to knead with your hands, leave the dough in the bowl, and use a wooden spoon to move it around in a kneading action.

Sprinkle the raisins over the dough and knead again for a few minutes, again with your hands, or a wooden spoon, until they are well distributed.

The dough will still be quite soft and sticky, so oil your hands to make it easier to handle, then form it into a rough ball, drop it into the prepared tin and press lightly down on the top. Scatter over the extra pumpkin and sunflower seeds.

Cover with a clean tea towel and leave in a warm place to prove for 1–2 hours, until it is about one and a half times the original size.

Meanwhile preheat the oven to 160°C/gas 3. Put in the tin and bake the bread for 45–50 minutes. For this bread, check as you would for a cake. Insert a metal skewer into the centre, and if it comes out clean, the bread is ready.

Turn out and cool on a rack.

Hot Cross Loaf or Buns

The idea for making a hot cross 'loaf' as a variation on
the classic buns came from the youngest baker of Eric
Duhamel's team, Matthew Dunning, whose family live not
far away in Milton-under-Wychwood and have regularly
visited Daylesford. At nineteen he applied for a job in the
bakery, and, says Eric, 'Like all of my team, he really cares
about making bread as well as he can; and because he
has learned – and is still learning – everything, here in the
bakery, he doesn't have any bad habits coming from the
famous, but bad, Chorleywood process that is taught in
bakery schools.'

The loaf is lovely, sliced and spread with a little good
butter, and jam.

500g strong white flour

10g fine sea salt

10g fresh yeast or 4g dried
yeast

75g butter, softened

25g golden syrup

110g milk

1 teaspoon mixed spice

2 teaspoons ground
cinnamon

90g currants

70g sultanas

70g mixed peel

1 egg, beaten, for brushing

a little vegetable oil, for
greasing the bowl and the
clingfilm

For the crossing paste:

60g plain flour

15g sunflower oil

For the glaze:

25g sugar

1 teaspoon liquid malt
(available from health stores)

1 teaspoon lemon juice

To make the dough, sift the flour and salt into a large bowl
with the yeast, butter, syrup, milk and 220g of lukewarm
water. Mix together to form a dough. Turn out on to your
work surface and knead for 10 minutes, or until smooth.

Roll the dough out with a rolling pin to about 2cm thick,
then sprinkle over the spices, fruit and peel. Knead again
until evenly distributed throughout the dough, then form

into a ball and put into a large oiled bowl. Cover with oiled clingfilm and leave to rise in a warm place for about 1–2 hours, until doubled in size.

Turn out the dough and 'de-gas' by pressing down briefly and gently with the flat of your hand, to even out the bubbles of air, then either shape into a ball and press gently into three 400g loaf tins, or, for buns, divide into 12 pieces. Form each one into a bun shape and place on a large baking tray. Cover with a clean tea towel.

Leave the loaf tins or buns in a warm place, again until doubled in size, then brush with beaten egg.

Preheat the oven to 210°C/gas 7 for buns, or 200°C for loaves.

While the loaves or buns are proving, make the crossing paste by mixing the flour and oil with 60g of water. Put it into a piping bag with a medium, plain nozzle.

To make the glaze, put the sugar, malt and lemon juice into a pan with 25g of water and heat, stirring, until boiling, then take off the heat and set aside to cool.

When the loaves or buns have doubled in size, pipe 'crosses' on the top of each one (one big cross for the loaves), then put into the preheated oven and bake for about 20–25 minutes, until golden. If you throw some ice cubes into the bottom of the oven, this will create steam and enhance the rising and look of the buns or loaves.

Remove from the oven (turn the loaves out of their tins) and, while still warm, brush the tops with glaze. Leave to cool on a rack or racks.

Baking with Natural Leaven

The oldest breads were fermented naturally using wild yeasts, long before the first commercial versions became available in the nineteenth century. Every baker has their own preferred way of making a leaven (sometimes also called a starter, mother, or ferment), which is a mixture of flour and water, and an ingredient like honey, yoghurt or fruit, in this case, grapes, which feeds the wild yeasts, and boosts the fermentation. As Eric says, 'You can take ten people, give them the same method for leaven, and the end result will be a little different, because they might use different flours, a little more or less liquid, slightly different times and temperatures of fermentation, and everything will be reflected in the leaven. But when you get used to working with these natural yeasts, you can evolve your own leaven in the way you want. These things take time and patience, though – it took me a year when I first started baking, to develop my leaven, and I like to think I am a fast learner.'

Many bakers have leavens that they have been feeding and tending for years. Eric has one that he brought all the way back from the artisan bakery where he was working in Australia to France, and finally to Daylesford. In order to keep it alive on the long flight from Australia, he dehydrated the leaven and ground it to a powder. You can imagine the questions that the customs officers asked when his little bag of white powder went through the X-ray machine at the airport!

Vladimir Niza, the chef who first set up the cookery school on the farm – but eventually took up an opportunity to teach in America – decided that the leaven should have a proper French name, so he christened it Jacqueline. Vlad was a real character, with a massive enthusiasm for food and teaching, and used to relish telling his captive audience in the school ever taller stories about how Eric's flight was held up, with all the passengers on board, while the customs people analysed his leaven.

Once you have made your leaven, you will need to refresh or 'feed' it with more flour and water every 2 days, and it will continue to grow, so unless you bake regularly – using some of the leaven each time – it will start to take over your fridge like a live monster. The answer? Keep baking.

Here is how to make your own leaven. The process will take around 7 days from start to finish.

Days 1–4
Start with 800g of grapes. Remove the stalks, then blend until smooth, put into a bowl and cover with clingfilm.

Leave in a warmish room at around 24–30°C for 3 days, during which time it will start to ferment. By day 3 it should be bubbling, and have an alcoholic, acidic smell.

Strain through a very fine sieve or coffee filter into a jug.

Days 4–5
Measure 200g of the fermented grape juice and put into a bowl. Mix in 200g of strong flour until smooth.

Cover with clingfilm and leave for 24 hours in a warm room (24–30°C again), after which the mixture should have fermented, have lots of bubbles, and have grown in size.

Days 5–6
Take 2 large tablespoons of the fermented mixture and weigh it. Add enough lukewarm water to bring the total up to 200g and whisk until smooth. Add 200g of strong flour and mix until well blended.

Cover with clingfilm and leave in a warm room (24–30°C) for another 24 hours.

Days 6–7
Take 2 large tablespoons of the fermented mixture and weigh it. But this time, you need to lower the hydration of

the leaven, ready for bread-making. So add only enough lukewarm water to bring the total up to 120g and whisk until smooth. Then add 200g of strong flour and mix until well blended.

Cover with clingfilm and leave in a warm room (24–30°C) for 1–2 hours, then put into the fridge for 24 hours, to stabilise it and finish the maturation as it cools down. By the next day it will be ready to use.

Day 7
You will now have 320g of your own leaven. From now on, you can use some for baking, and what is left over can be kept going indefinitely in a bowl in the fridge, as long as you continue to feed it every 2 days, in the same final ratio of 100 per cent flour and 60 per cent liquid. If you don't keep refreshing and re-activating it in this way, it will lose its properties.

All the following recipes are based on this natural leaven.

Sourdough

'When you make bread with natural leaven, it has an element of sourness to it that gives this style of bread its name,' says Eric. 'However, the degree of sourness and the style of bread varies from bakery to bakery. There are two kinds of acidity in a natural leaven, acetic and lactic. The acetic is the one you find in vinegar and is quite sharp, whereas the lactic is mainly found in yoghurt, and is more subtle and brings a sensation of freshness to the bread, without too much sourness, so it really stimulates the tastebuds. There is always some acetic acidity in the bread, but I prefer not to develop this too much, just to the point where you recognise that you have a sourdough; and to develop more of the lactic acidity, which makes the finished bread a little more refined. All this is a matter of adjusting your leaven, and experimenting, and this comes with time and practice. Don't worry, if you stick to this recipe, you should make a very good sourdough – you can refine it, play with it and personalise it, the more confident you become.'

530g strong white flour

10g fine sea salt

200g natural leaven (see page 328)

a little vegetable oil, for greasing the bowl and the clingfilm

Put the flour into a bowl with the salt and 350g of lukewarm water and mix to a dough.

Turn out the dough on to your work surface and knead for 5 minutes. Add the leaven and knead for another 5 minutes (using extra flour if necessary).

Transfer to a lightly oiled bowl, cover with oiled clingfilm and allow to rise in a warm place until it is one and a half times its original size.

Turn out the dough and 'de-gas' by pressing down briefly and gently with the flat of your hand, to even out the bubbles of air, then shape into a ball. Transfer to a floured proving basket, or a baking sheet. Cover with a clean tea towel and again leave in a warm place to prove, until it has increased by one and a half times in size.

Preheat the oven to 240°C/gas 9.

If the dough has been resting in a proving basket, turn it out on to a baking sheet. If it has been resting on a baking sheet, finely dust the top with flour (if it has been in a proving basket it will already have this fine dusting).

Score the top of the loaf swiftly and cleanly with the blade of a sharp serrated knife (see page 318), then put it into the oven and bake for about 30 minutes. If you throw some ice cubes into the bottom of the oven when the bread goes in, this will create steam and enhance the crust.

The bread is ready when, if you tap the base, it sounds hollow.

Remove from the oven and place on a cooling rack.

Seven Seeds Sourdough

The malted grain in the flour that we use is the seventh seed.

120g strong white flour

120g malted flour

10g pumpkin seeds

10g sesame seeds

10g linseeds

10g poppy seeds

10g millet seeds

10g sunflower seeds

10g fine sea salt

100g natural leaven (see page 328)

a little vegetable oil, for greasing the bowl and clingfilm

Put all the ingredients, apart from the leaven and the oil, into a bowl with 175g of lukewarm water and mix to a dough.

Turn out the dough on to your work surface and knead for 5 minutes. Add the leaven and knead for another 5 minutes (using extra flour if necessary).

Transfer to a lightly oiled bowl, cover with oiled clingfilm and allow to rise in a warm place until one and a half times its original size.

Turn out the dough and 'de-gas' by pressing down briefly and gently with the flat of your hand, to even out the bubbles of air, then shape into a tight bloomer (oval shape) and transfer to an oval-shaped floured proving basket, or a baking sheet. Cover with a clean tea towel and again leave in a warm place to prove, until it has increased by one and a half times in size.

Preheat the oven to 240°C/gas 9.

If the dough has been resting in a proving basket, turn it out on to a baking sheet. If it has been resting on a baking sheet, finely dust the top with flour (if it has been in a proving basket it will already have this fine dusting).

Score the top of the loaf swiftly and cleanly with the blade of a sharp serrated knife (see page 318), then put into the oven and bake for about 35 minutes. If you throw some ice cubes into the bottom of the oven when the bread goes in, this will create steam and enhance the crust.

The bread is ready when, if you tap the base, it sounds hollow.

Remove from the oven and place on a cooling rack.

Two Flowerpot Breads

These are fun to make, and look fantastic. We bake them at quite a low temperature, because a flowerpot is not designed for baking, and doesn't transmit the heat that well, so at a high temperature the top of the loaf always has the potential to brown and become over-baked before the rest is ready.

Red Onion, Cheddar and Chilli Bread

The almonds will help to protect the top of the bread, but if you find that it becomes a little too brown the first time you try this, next time dust the top of the dough with a little flour before baking.

Go lightly on the chilli and paprika, as these are meant to bring a delicate flavour, and not dominate the other ingredients, or add any real heat, in the case of the chilli.

Again, in this bread we use less leaven with a small quantity of fresh yeast, to help the lightness.

180g strong white flour

45g dark rye flour

5g salt

2g fresh yeast

90g natural leaven (see page 328)

35g chopped red onion

35g mature Cheddar cheese, grated

a good pinch of paprika

a good pinch of chilli flakes

15 flaked almonds

a little vegetable oil, for greasing the bowl and clingfilm

Put the flours, salt and yeast into a bowl with 160g of lukewarm water and mix to a dough.

Turn out the dough and knead for 5 minutes. Add the leaven and all the rest of the ingredients, except for the oil and the almonds, and knead for another 5 minutes.

Transfer to a lightly oiled bowl, cover with oiled clingfilm and allow to rise in a warm place until one and a half times its original size.

Have ready a clean terracotta flowerpot, lined with greaseproof paper.

Turn out the dough and 'de-gas' by pressing down briefly and gently with the flat of your hand, to even out the bubbles of air, then shape into a ball and press gently into the lined flowerpot. Cover with a clean tea towel and again leave in a warm place to prove, until it has doubled in size.

Preheat the oven to 180°C/gas 4.

Brush the top of the dough with a little water and sprinkle on the almonds, then put into the oven and bake for about 35–40 minutes.

If you throw some ice cubes into the bottom of the oven when the bread goes in, this will create steam and enhance the crust.

Tapping the base of this bread to check that it sounds hollow isn't such a good guide for this as with other breads, as the pot will help to keep in more moisture. But after 35–40 minutes it will be baked.

Remove from the oven, turn out of the flowerpot and place on a cooling rack.

Nettle Bread

'Nettles,' says Eric, 'are a perfect example of sustainable, nutritious food, full of proteins, fibres and minerals, and have been valued since antiquity, but make sure you harvest them from your own garden, or from a clean place, free of pesticides, and not from the side of the road, where they can be polluted. You need to wash and dry them, as you would salad leaves (it is best to wear gloves, as they sting) then lay them on a tray in a very cool oven (at its lowest setting) for a few hours until they are perfectly dry. Then it is easy to shred the leaves.'

260g strong white flour

6g salt

100g natural leaven (see page 328)

6g washed and completely dried nettle leaves, shredded (see introduction, above)

a pinch of anise seeds

a little vegetable oil, for greasing the bowl and clingfilm

Put the flour and salt into a bowl with 180g of lukewarm water and mix to a dough.

Turn out the dough and knead for 5 minutes. Add the leaven, nettles and seeds, and knead for another 5 minutes.

Transfer to a lightly oiled bowl, cover with oiled clingfilm and allow to rise in a warm place until one and a half times its original size.

Have ready a clean terracotta flowerpot, lined with greaseproof paper.

Turn out the dough and 'de-gas' by pressing down briefly and gently with the flat of your hand, to even out the bubbles of air, then shape into a ball and press gently into the lined flowerpot. Cover with a clean tea towel and again leave in a warm place to prove, until it has increased by one and a half times in size.

Preheat the oven to 180°C/gas 4.

Finely dust the top of the dough with flour, then put into the oven and bake for about 35–40 minutes.

If you throw some ice cubes into the bottom of the oven when the bread goes in, this will create steam and enhance the crust.

Tapping the base of this bread to check that it sounds hollow isn't such a good guide for this as with other breads, as the pot will help to keep in more moisture. But after 35–40 minutes it will be baked.

Remove from the oven, turn out of the flowerpot and place on a cooling rack.

CAKES
&
BREAKS

Honey and spice
Energy bars bursting with fruit and seeds
Chocolate decadence
Buttery shortbread
Old-fashioned festive favourites

English cakes have lasted the test of time for a reason: everyone loves them. We give traditional recipes a contemporary edge, and a lightness of touch, but we rarely deviate too far from classic recipes – and woe betide us, if we stop making a particular cake – just ask Benje Ward, a well-known and well-loved Daylesford character who has been serving cakes, especially for afternoon tea, in the café, for eleven years, and he knows every cake inside out. Amongst his personal favourites are the lemon drizzle cake on page 353, and the Manuka honey cake on page 348.

Cake time is also a good opportunity to make a refreshing tea, such as fresh mint – just leaves and hot water – or the Daylesford favourite, lemon and ginger, which we make with 2 slices of fresh lemon, 2 teaspoons of freshly grated ginger (with the skin left on), mixed into a cup of hot water, with a tablespoon of honey served separately on the side, so that people can dip in the spoon and sweeten the tea as much, or as little as they like.

Many of the cakes we serve for afternoon tea and in the farmshop were first made by pastry chef Jo Thompson, who eventually moved on to start her own artisan, organic patisserie, Once Bitten, in Chipping Norton. She made them all in small batches, completely by hand, 'just as you would at home. Originally,' she remembers, 'we even used the old "pound cake" method: a pound of flour to a pound each of sugar, butter and eggs.'

Biscuits too, are real crowd-pleasers, made to tried and tested recipes that we have been using for many, many years. Enjoy!

Chocolate Cake

We used to make a quite grown-up and very bitter chocolate cake, which was very popular with adults, but not so much with children, so this is a slightly sweeter one that everyone likes.

460g plain flour

a pinch of salt

1 teaspoon bicarbonate of soda

1 teaspoon vanilla extract

420ml milk

280g good dark chocolate (at least 70% cocoa solids)

380g butter, softened

330g caster sugar

330g light brown sugar

6 eggs

For the filling/glaze:

300g good dark chocolate (at least 70% cocoa solids)

125g butter

75g golden syrup

60ml sunflower oil

Preheat the oven to 180°C/gas 4 and grease and line two 20cm sandwich tins.

Combine the flour, salt and bicarbonate of soda. Stir the vanilla extract into the milk.

Put the chocolate into a heatproof bowl and place over a pan of gently simmering water (make sure the base of the bowl doesn't touch the water). Stir, and when melted remove from the heat.

In a bowl, cream the butter, caster sugar and brown sugar until pale and fluffy and then gradually beat in the eggs. Gently stir in the melted chocolate. Fold in half the flour, then half the milk, then fold in the rest of the flour and finish with the rest of the milk.

Spoon into the prepared tins and bake in the preheated oven for 30 minutes, or until a skewer inserted in the middle of the cakes comes out clean.

Remove from the tins and cool on a rack.

Meanwhile, to make the filling/glaze, put the chocolate into a heatproof bowl with the butter and golden syrup, place over a pan of gently simmering water (again, make sure the base of the bowl doesn't touch the water), and stir until the chocolate is melted and the mixture is smooth.

Take off the heat, then spoon off about a third of the mixture into a separate bowl and whisk in the sunflower oil. Allow to cool and firm up slightly, then spread over one of the sponges and sandwich them together.

Check that the remaining glaze is still pourable, and if not, put the bowl back over a pan of gently simmering water, as before, for just long enough to loosen it.

Keep the sandwiched cake on the rack, but put a plate or tray underneath to catch the drips, then pour and spread the remaining glaze over the top of the cake, making sure it also coats the sides.

Manuka Honey Cake

All good honey is said to have restorative, even healing properties, but certain batches of Manuka honey from New Zealand have been shown to have special antibacterial qualities – the Maoris traditionally put it on cuts to help fend off infection. This is admittedly not a cheap cake to make, but apart from being good for you it has a very distinctive, acquired flavour, quite potent and floral, from the Manuka, other honeys would just tend to make this cake sweet without adding notable flavour.

160g butter, plus a little extra for greasing the tin

100ml Manuka honey

100ml clear honey

65g light brown sugar

2 large eggs, beaten

220g self-raising flour

For the syrup:

2 tablespoons Manuka honey

1 tablespoon sugar

Preheat the oven to 170°C/gas 3. Grease and line a round 18cm cake tin that is about 6cm deep.

Melt the butter in a pan, then take off the heat, add the honeys and sugar, and stir until the sugar has dissolved.

Beat the eggs in a bowl, pour in the honey mixture, mix well, then whisk in the flour briefly until just combined. Pour into the prepared cake tin.

Put into the preheated oven and bake for about 40–50 minutes, or until a skewer inserted into the centre comes out clean. Remove from the oven and leave in the tin on a rack to cool slightly before turning out. Once turned out, return the cake to the rack, but put a plate underneath to catch any drips when you glaze it with syrup.

Make the syrup by putting the honey and sugar into a pan with 2 tablespoons of water and bringing to the boil. Take off the heat straight away and pour over the cake while it is still warm.

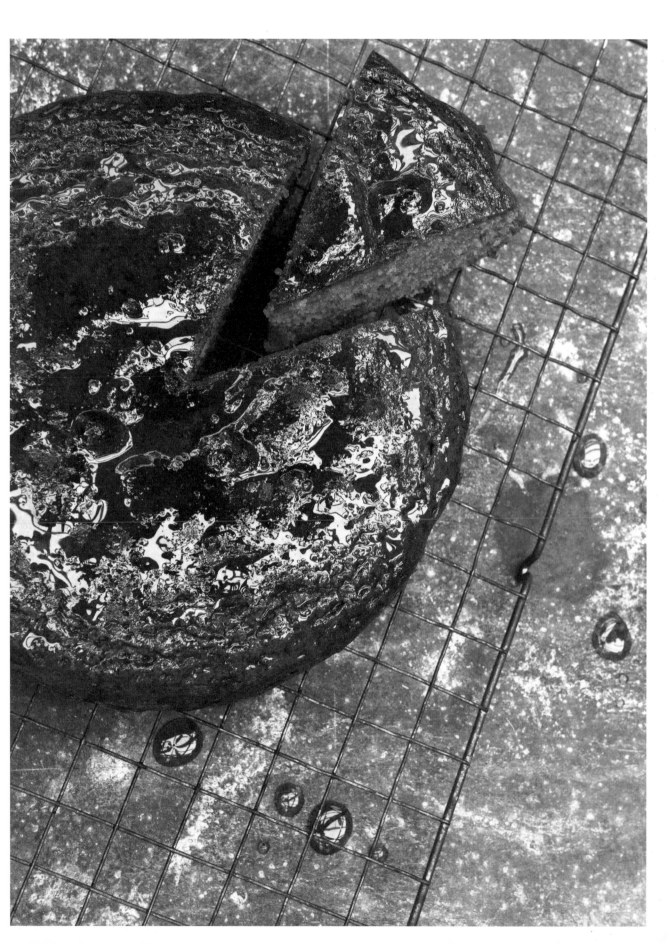

Spiced Apple Cake with Streusel Topping

Streusel is a German name for a crumble-style topping made with flour, sugar, butter and, in this case, chopped nuts, which is scattered over pies and cakes, particularly apple – like this quite autumnal, spiced apple cake.

As the cake bakes the juice will come out of the apples and make the mixture quite moist, so be sure to do the skewer test to check that it is fully baked all the way through. Otherwise, when you cut into it, the cake will be doughy in the centre.

Jez suggests using Egremont Russet apples for this – 'sweet, rich and dense'.

a little butter, for greasing the tin

2 eggs

100g caster sugar

120ml sunflower oil

120ml milk

150g plain flour

40g wholemeal flour

1 teaspoon bicarbonate of soda

2 teaspoons baking powder

2 teaspoons ground cinnamon

1 teaspoon ground nutmeg

160g peeled, cored and chopped apple (approximately 2 apples)

70g sultanas

For the streusel topping:

60g plain flour

60g light brown sugar

40g butter

40g roughly chopped pecan nuts

Preheat the oven to 160°C/gas 3 and grease a 1kg loaf tin lightly with butter.

To make the streusel topping, put the flour, sugar and butter into a bowl, rub together until the mix resembles breadcrumbs, then stir in the chopped pecan nuts. Put into the fridge to chill and harden for 30 minutes.

Meanwhile, to make the cake batter, whisk together the eggs and sugar in a bowl until combined but not aerated, then slowly add the sunflower oil and milk, whisking until they are mixed in. Finally fold in the flours, bicarbonate of soda, baking powder, cinnamon and nutmeg, until you have a smooth batter. Fold in the apples and sultanas and pour into the prepared loaf tin.

Take the streusel topping from the fridge and scatter over the top.

Put into the preheated oven and bake for about 25–30 minutes, until a skewer inserted into the centre comes out clean.

Take out of the oven and leave to cool in the tin before turning out.

Lemon Drizzle Cake

We have been making this since the farmshop opened.
It is a true English classic, but there are many different
opinions on how to make it. Often it is done with a glaze
of lemon icing over the top, whereas in a true drizzle cake,
the lemony sugary syrup should seep into the cake itself.
The secret is to pour or 'drizzle' the warm syrup over the
cake while it, too, is still warm, so that the cake absorbs
the flavour. Eat within a week, otherwise you lose that
zingy lemony freshness.

2 large eggs	1 teaspoon baking powder
130g caster sugar	zest of 1 lemon
80ml double cream	
50g butter, melted and cooled	For the syrup:
	juice of 1 lemon
125g plain flour	80g caster sugar

Preheat the oven to 170°C/gas 3. Grease and line a
15cm x 9cm loaf tin.

In a bowl, whisk the eggs and sugar until the sugar has
just dissolved. Stir in the cream and the melted and cooled
butter, mix well, then add the flour, baking powder and
lemon zest and whisk briefly until well combined.

Spoon into the prepared tin and bake in the preheated
oven for 30–40 minutes, until the cake is golden brown,
well risen, firm to the touch, and a skewer inserted into the
centre comes out clean. Remove from the oven and leave
the cake, still in its tin, on a cooling rack.

Meanwhile, make the syrup by combining the lemon juice
and sugar in a small pan and stirring over a low heat until
the sugar has just dissolved. Remove from the heat. Prick
the top of the cake all over with a skewer and pour the
syrup over it while still warm. Leave until the cake has
cooled, then remove from the tin.

Earl Grey Cake

In this recipe Earl Grey tea is used instead of alcohol or juice, to soak and plump up the fruit, so that the cake is kept moist. The tea has a strong aroma initially, but tones right down and just gives gentle floral background notes to the quite light cake. For the best flavour, use loose-leaf tea.

3g Earl Grey tea or 3 Earl Grey tea bags

200g raisins

200g sultanas

200g currants

200g plain flour

1 teaspoon baking powder

175g butter, softened

175g light brown sugar

3 eggs, beaten

1 teaspoon vanilla extract

Brew the Earl Grey tea by placing the tea leaves or tea bags in a large jug and pouring over 500ml of boiling water. Leave for 5 minutes. Put the dried fruit into a bowl, then strain the tea through a fine sieve over the top (or just remove the tea bags, if using). Cover (with muslin, ideally) and leave overnight, stirring occasionally when you can, to ensure the fruit absorbs the liquid.

Preheat the oven to 170°C/gas 3. Grease and line an 18–20cm round cake tin, and sift together the flour and baking powder.

In a bowl cream the butter and sugar until pale and fluffy. Gradually beat in the eggs and vanilla extract. If the mix looks like it's 'curdling', add a teaspoon of the measured flour.

Drain the soaked fruit and stir into the mixture. Gently fold in the flour and baking powder, then spoon into the prepared cake tin and smooth the top.

Bake in the preheated oven for about 1½ hours, or until a skewer inserted into the cake comes out clean. Leave the cake to cool down on a rack before removing the tin.

Variation: Simnel Cake

You can use this recipe as the base for the traditional Easter cake. Different towns historically made Simnel cakes in different shapes, with various decorations, but the best known has eleven balls of marzipan on top, representing the apostles – with Judas, the traitor, missing.

Just replace 100g of the combined weight of dried fruit with 50g each of mixed peel and morello cherries. For the decoration, divide 500g good natural marzipan into 3 equal pieces. Dust your work surface with a little icing sugar, and roll out the first piece into a circle just big enough to allow you to cut around the base of the cake tin. Repeat with the second piece of marzipan, so you have two discs. Divide the third piece of marzipan into 11 pieces and roll each one into a small ball. Cover all the marzipan with clingfilm to keep it moist until needed.

When ready to bake, spoon half the cake mixture into the tin, level the top, then cover with one of the discs of marzipan. Carefully spoon the remaining cake mixture on top and again gently level the surface, and bake as in the recipe. While the cake is cooling, make a glaze by heating 100g smooth apricot jam in a small pan with the juice of half a lemon and a tablespoon of water, stirring all the time until it bubbles up, then take off the heat and keep to one side. Have ready a beaten egg.

When the cake is cool, brush with the glaze and place the second marzipan disc on top. Brush with beaten egg, then gently press the balls of marzipan evenly around the edge of the cake. Brush the tops with the rest of the beaten egg. Put the cake under a hot grill until the marzipan is lightly toasted, or do this with a blowtorch.

Dark and White Chocolate Brownies

'These are iconic,' says Rosie Henderson. 'In the café and farmshop I feel as though I am the keeper of the brownies, so I take it upon myself to taste them pretty much every day, to make sure they are perfect!'

4 eggs	180g plain flour
150g caster sugar	1 teaspoon baking powder
150g demerara sugar	1 teaspoon vanilla extract
350g unsalted butter	380g white chocolate buttons
350g good dark chocolate (at least 70% cocoa solids)	

Preheat the oven to 160°C/gas 3 and line a 30cm square cake tin (or equivalent) with baking paper.

In a bowl, whisk the eggs and both sugars together until thick.

Put the butter and dark chocolate into a heatproof bowl over a pan of simmering water (make sure the base doesn't touch the water) and let the chocolate melt.

Let the chocolate cool a little, then add to the beaten eggs and sugar, and mix well. Gently fold in the flour, baking powder and vanilla extract, and when thoroughly combined add the chocolate buttons and mix in gently.

Spoon into the prepared tin and bake in the preheated oven for 20 minutes, making sure you don't overbake the brownies. They need to stay quite soft and moist in the middle, so they should be springy to the touch, and if you insert a skewer into the centre, it should come out sticky, not clean, as you would expect with a cake.

Take out of the oven and allow to cool in the tin before turning out on to a board or clean work surface and cutting into squares.

Energy Bars

We wanted something nice and light and healthy that visitors to the farmshop could have with a coffee or tea – and this was the result.

160g porridge oats	6 tablespoons (90g) honey
3 tablespoons sesame seeds	7 tablespoons (100g) golden syrup
3 tablespoons sunflower seeds	100g butter, softened
2 tablespoons pumpkin seeds	160g light brown sugar
2 tablespoons flax seeds	100g sultanas
2 tablespoons poppy seeds	80g dried apricots, chopped
70g desiccated coconut	1 teaspoon bicarbonate of soda
70g light rye flour	

Preheat the oven to 170°C/gas 3. Grease and line a 22cm x 22cm square tin that is about 5 cm deep.

Put the oats, 2 tablespoons of sesame seeds, 2 tablespoons of sunflower seeds, the pumpkin, flax and poppy seeds, the coconut and the rye flour into a mixing bowl.

Put the honey, syrup, butter and sugar into a small pan and heat gently. Add the sultanas and apricots and continue to heat until just bubbling, then take off the heat, stir in the bicarbonate of soda and pour over the oat mixture. Mix well, pour into the prepared tin, spread evenly and sprinkle with the remaining sesame and sunflower seeds.

Bake in the preheated oven for 35 minutes, then turn off the oven, open the door and leave the energy bars inside to dry out for 10 minutes. Remove the tin from the oven. Allow to cool before cutting into bars.

Three Cheese Biscuits

These little savoury biscuits are good to nibble on any time, or to put out with drinks.

Cheddar Biscuits

250g strong white flour

½ teaspoon baking powder

½ teaspoon sea salt

150g cold butter, grated

2 tablespoons double cream

1 egg yolk

150g Cheddar cheese, grated

Put the flour, baking powder and salt into a bowl with the butter, and rub together with your fingertips until the mixture resembles breadcrumbs. Add the cream, egg yolk and 100g of the cheese, and bring together gently into a dough.

Turn out on to a lightly floured work surface and divide the dough in half. Roll each half into a log shape, about 4cm in diameter. Wrap each one in clingfilm and put into the fridge to chill and firm up for about 30 minutes.

Preheat the oven to 180°C/gas 4.

Take the logs of dough from the fridge, and slice each one into 8 rounds. Lay them on a non-stick baking sheet (or alternatively line one with greaseproof paper) and put back into the fridge to rest again for another 30 minutes. Bake in the preheated oven for about 15 minutes, until golden brown.

Take out of the oven and, while still hot, scatter the tops with the remaining cheese. Leave to cool on the tray for a few minutes before transferring to a wire rack.

Blue Cheese and Walnut Biscuits

325g strong white flour

1 teaspoon baking powder

½ teaspoon salt

190g cold butter, grated

80ml double cream

250g blue cheese, grated
(or chopped, if soft)

1 large egg yolk

125g walnuts, chopped

Put the flour, baking powder and salt into a bowl with
the butter, and rub together with your fingertips until the
mixture resembles breadcrumbs. Mix in the cream, blue
cheese and egg yolk to form a dough.

Turn out on to a lightly floured work surface and divide
the dough in half. Roll each half into a log shape, about
4cm in diameter. Wrap each one in clingfilm and put into
the fridge to chill and firm up for about 30 minutes.

Preheat the oven to 180°C/gas 4.

Take the logs of dough from the fridge, and slice each one
into 12 rounds. Lay them on a non-stick baking sheet (or
alternatively line with greaseproof paper) and top each
round with some walnuts, pressing the nuts down slightly.
Put the baking sheet back into the fridge to chill again for
30 minutes. Bake in the preheated oven for about 15–20
minutes, until golden brown.

Leave to cool on the tray for a few minutes before
transferring to a wire rack.

Parmesan, Chilli and Marcona Almond Biscuits

170g butter, softened

100g Parmesan cheese, finely grated

75g mature Cheddar cheese, finely grated

170g plain flour

½ teaspoon sea salt

½ teaspoon smoked paprika

¼ teaspoon dried chilli flakes

150g roasted, salted Marcona almonds, roughly chopped

Put the butter, Parmesan and Cheddar into a bowl and cream together. Mix in the flour to form a stiff dough. Add the salt, paprika, chilli flakes and almonds and, when incorporated into the dough, turn out on to a lightly floured work surface and roll out into 6 log shapes, each about 4cm in diameter.

Wrap each log in clingfilm and put into the fridge to chill for at least 30 minutes.

Preheat the oven to 180°C/gas 4.

Take the logs of dough from the fridge and slice each log into rounds 0.5cm thick. Lay the rounds on a non-stick baking sheet or sheets (or alternatively line one with greaseproof paper) and put back into the fridge to rest again for another 30 minutes. Bake in the preheated oven for 10–15 minutes, until golden brown and crunchy.

Leave to cool on the tray for a few minutes before transferring to a wire rack.

Lemon Shortbread Biscuits

Sometimes we dip the finished biscuits into melted white chocolate, which makes them very decadent. Don't overwork the dough, as shortbread should be crumbly and buttery, almost melt-in-the-mouth. The more usual way to make shortbread is to pack the mixture into a baking tin, then cut it into fingers once it is baked. However, because we like to make round (or sometimes heart-shaped) biscuits, in advance of baking we put the dough into the fridge to firm up, before stamping it out with a biscuit cutter – otherwise the dough would just fall apart.

125g softened butter	65g rice flour
65g caster sugar, plus a little extra for sprinkling on top	a pinch of salt
	zest of 1 lemon
115g plain flour	

In a bowl, cream the softened butter with the sugar until pale and fluffy. Add the flours, salt and lemon zest and combine until the mixture comes together. Form this dough into a ball. Lightly flour a work surface and roll out the dough until it is 0.5cm thick. Lift carefully on to a flat baking sheet and put into the fridge for 1 hour to firm up.

Preheat the oven to 170°C/gas 3 and line a baking tray with greaseproof paper.

Take the dough from the fridge, slide it off the baking sheet on to your work surface, then, using a biscuit cutter of about 7cm in diameter, cut out 10–12 rounds (or similar-sized shapes of your choice). Lay the rounds on the prepared baking tray.

Bake in the preheated oven for 10–15 minutes, until a very light golden brown. Take out of the oven and leave the biscuits on the tray for a few minutes to firm up before carefully lifting them off with a fish slice or spatula and transferring them to a cake rack to cool. Dust with caster sugar before serving.

Ginger Biscuits

These contain stem ginger, so although they are crunchy on the outside they have little pockets of soft, sticky gingeriness on the inside.

150g butter, softened

100g caster sugar

3 tablespoons dark brown sugar

2 tablespoons molasses

2 whole eggs

170g plain flour

2 teaspoons bicarbonate of soda

2 teaspoons ground ginger

1 teaspoon ground cinnamon

1 teaspoon mixed spice

2 tablespoons stem ginger, chopped small (about 0.5cm)

a pinch of salt

caster sugar, for dusting

Preheat the oven to 180°C/gas 4 and grease two baking trays with butter.

Put the softened butter and sugars into a bowl and cream together until pale and fluffy. Add the molasses, then gradually beat in the eggs.

Fold in the flour, bicarbonate of soda, spices, stem ginger and salt.

Spoon dessertspoonfuls of the mixture on to the prepared baking trays and flatten slightly into rounds of about 1cm thick with the back of the spoon.

Put into the preheated oven and bake for about 10–15 minutes, until golden. Remove from the oven and lightly sprinkle with caster sugar while still warm.

Cool slightly before removing to a cake rack.

Double Chocolate Chip Cookies

These are at their best straight from the oven – and even after you have made them and they are cold, you can put them into the oven briefly just to warm them through. They stay quite rustic-looking, and don't have any real crunch, but are soft and melting in the middle.

250g butter	400g plain flour
175g caster sugar	2 teaspoons baking powder
160g light brown sugar	60g cocoa powder
1 large egg, beaten	250g white chocolate buttons

Preheat the oven to 180°C/gas 4 and line four baking trays with greaseproof paper (alternatively bake the cookies in batches).

Put the softened butter and sugars into a bowl and cream together until pale and fluffy, then beat in the egg.

Sift together the flour, baking powder and cocoa powder and fold into the butter mixture until you have a soft dough. Mix in the white chocolate buttons.

Take pieces of the mixture and roll into balls the size of a golf ball (you should have enough for 20). Place well apart on the prepared baking trays, as the mixture will spread a little during cooking, and squash and flatten them slightly.

Put into the preheated oven and bake, in batches if necessary, for about 12 minutes, until firm on the outside but soft in the middle. Take out of the oven and leave to cool on the trays.

Milk Chocolate, Almond and Espresso Fudge

When Jo Thompson first developed our fudge recipes, since she had a Scottish great-grandmother she began researching traditional condensed milk fudge. However, there was no such thing as organic condensed milk, so instead she began working with cream. 'The result,' she says, 'was a very clean-cut, smooth, simple fudge, not cloying at all, which has been a hit ever since. We made versions with various flavourings, including this one. Coffee and chocolate are natural partners – but the coffee element is quite subtle.'

If you don't have an espresso maker, make a very strong filter coffee using 5 parts boiling water to 1 part coffee.

400g good milk chocolate	75g whole blanched almonds, lightly toasted in a dry pan and roughly chopped
500ml double cream	
500g caster sugar	
50g golden syrup	75g toasted flaked almonds
75g unsalted butter	75ml espresso coffee, or strong filter coffee (see above)

Line a deep (2–3cm) tray, baking dish or container, about 20cm x 20cm, with greaseproof paper.

If you don't have a sugar thermometer, have ready a bowl of iced water.

Put the chocolate into a heatproof bowl over a pan of simmering water (make sure the base doesn't touch the water) and let the chocolate melt.

Put the cream, sugar, syrup and butter into a pan and bring to the boil, stirring continuously until you reach the 'soft ball' stage. This will be at 115°C, if you have a sugar thermometer. If not, to check it is ready, dribble a little of the mixture into the iced water, give it 10 seconds or so to

cool, then, with your fingers, see if you can roll it into a small ball. If you can it is ready.

As soon as it reaches this point, take the pan from the heat and carefully stir in the melted chocolate, along with the almonds and the coffee. Beat slightly with a spatula or wooden spoon until the mixture binds together.

Pour into the lined trays and allow to cool, then put into the fridge to solidify for 24 hours before cutting into squares.

Variation: White Chocolate and Cranberry Fudge

This fudge was first created by Jo Thompson one Christmas, when we decided to make a festive-looking fudge that people might like to give as a present, but it was so popular it has stayed constantly in the farmshop ever since.

It is made using the same method, but with different quantities.

To make 500g fudge, line a deep 20cm x 10cm tray, baking dish or container, as in the previous recipe, and melt 150g white chocolate in the same way. Follow the rest of the instructions, but use 200ml double cream, 200g caster sugar, 20g golden syrup and 30g unsalted butter.

As soon as the mixture reaches 'soft ball' stage, take the pan from the heat and carefully stir in 80g dried cranberries and the melted chocolate and continue with the recipe.

Two Christmas Favourites

Dried fruit plumping up in brandy, ready to fill mince pies, or bake in a traditional cake. It's the Christmas season.

Aunt Mimi's Mince Pies

'Aunt Mimi is my mother-in-law's sister, a great baker,' says Carole Bamford. 'I would make mince pies at home, and Anthony, my husband, would always say: "Not quite as good as Auntie Mimi's."'

Of course you can buy good mincemeat – but homemade is what makes the pies special. You will need to leave it to marinate in an airtight container for at least a week, but it can keep for up to 2 months.

If you can find individual candied orange and lemon peel, then use a ratio of two-thirds orange to one-third lemon, as this makes the mincemeat more floral than sharp.

For the mincemeat:

115g sultanas

115g raisins

70g currants

2 tablespoons flaked almonds

2 tablespoons dried cherries

115g crystallised ginger

35g mixed candied peel (see above)

500g grated Bramley apples (about 3)

85g soft light brown sugar

4 tablespoons Cognac

zest of 3 lemons

zest of 3 oranges

a pinch of mixed spice

a pinch of ground nutmeg

70g lard, grated, or suet

a pinch of sea salt

For the pastry:

800g plain flour

280g cold butter, grated, plus a little extra for greasing

120g cold lard, grated

200g caster sugar

a pinch of salt

12 egg yolks, plus 1 egg, beaten, for glazing (optional)

To make the mincemeat, mix together all the ingredients and allow to marinate in a lidded, airtight container in the fridge for 1 week.

Lightly butter two 12-hole tart trays.

Put the flour, butter and lard into a bowl, and rub with your fingertips until the mixture resembles breadcrumbs. Stir in the sugar and salt, then gradually add the egg yolks until combined and the mixture comes together in a dough. Form into a ball, wrap in clingfilm, and chill in the fridge for at least 1 hour before using. This is very short, crumbly pastry, so it needs this quite long chilling time to firm up and make it easier to roll.

Lightly flour your work surface. Cut the ball of dough in half, and keep the second ball in the fridge while you roll out the first one to about 4mm thick. Using a plain round cutter, 6.5cm in diameter, cut out 24 circles and press into the tart trays – take the time to do this gently and carefully, so that the pastry doesn't crack. Spoon 1 full tablespoon of mincemeat into each tart, making sure it domes slightly in the centre.

Roll out the remaining pastry, and cut out as above. Gently lay a circle of pastry over the top of each mincemeat-topped base and gently crimp the edges together all the way round, to seal. Brush with a little beaten egg if you like, then insert the tip of a knife into the middle of each pastry top, to make a tiny slit for steam to escape. Put the tins into the fridge to rest again for an hour.

When ready to bake, preheat the oven to 170°C/gas 3.

Remove the trays from the fridge and bake in the preheated oven for 20 minutes, until the pastry is golden brown. Take out of the oven and leave to cool in the trays before removing.

Christmas Cake

This is another family recipe special to Carole Bamford, who developed it along with baker Betty Thornton.

Traditionally the cake is made 4–6 months in advance of Christmas, then kept wrapped and in an airtight container, so that the flavours can mature over time. The key to keeping it moist is to 'feed' it regularly, by making holes in the cake with a skewer, spooning over a little brandy, and allowing the alcohol to seep through the cake.

However, there is no need to panic if you leave it to the last minute: just make sure that the fruit is soaked well in brandy, and properly plumped up, before you start to make your cake. You can leave it to soak for up to 3 days if you like: the longer the better.

Fashions in Christmas cakes come and go, so it is up to you whether you ice it in the more formal way, with marzipan and then white icing, or go for the more relaxed look, decorating the top with fruit and nuts in a contemporary take on an old-fashioned style – then tie a big ribbon around the cake.

If you are icing it, you can do this a couple of weeks before Christmas. However, if you opt for fruit and nuts, do this about 2 days before you want to cut the cake, because you are exposing it to the air, and there is more chance of it drying out than if the top and sides are sealed inside an airtight covering of marzipan and icing.

225g raisins

225g currants

225g sultanas

60g dried cherries

35g toasted flaked almonds

4 tablespoons mixed candied peel

zest and juice of 1 lemon

zest and juice of 1 orange

100ml brandy

170g butter, softened, plus a little for greasing the tin

170g soft light brown sugar

1 tablespoon treacle or molasses

1 teaspoon vanilla extract

3 medium eggs

170g plain flour

½ teaspoon mixed spice

½ teaspoon ground ginger

½ teaspoon ground nutmeg

½ teaspoon ground cinnamon

½ teaspoon ground cardamom

Put all the dried fruit, nuts, peel, citrus zest and juice into a bowl with the brandy, mix well, then cover (with muslin, ideally) and leave to soak overnight.

The next day, preheat the oven to 160°C/gas 3. Grease an 18cm round tin (with a removable base) with butter and then line it with a double layer of greaseproof paper.

Cream together the softened butter and sugar in a mixing bowl until pale and fluffy, then gradually beat in the treacle or molasses, vanilla extract and eggs. When all is incorporated, add the soaked fruit, flour and spices and gently fold in.

Spoon into the prepared cake tin and smooth the top. Put into the preheated oven and bake for about 2½–3 hours, or until a skewer inserted into the centre comes out clean.

While the cake is still warm, pierce with the skewer and 'feed' with brandy, two or three times – more if you like – as the cake matures.

'It isn't pretentious, it isn't fancy, or about the ego of the chef;
it is all about the quality of the produce.'
John Hardwick, The Kitchens

Daylesford is a real learning curve for a chef. Not everyone understands it, but when you do, it changes the way you think about food and cooking completely. We have a number of chefs coming into the kitchens, with great CVs, but they just can't get to grips with the simplicity of what we do. It isn't pretentious, it isn't fancy, or about the ego of the chef, it is all about the quality of the produce: just real, proper, good honest cooking of fresh ingredients, put simply on a plate. And there is just as much skill in that as there is in using half a dozen processes in every dish.

When we write a menu the first port of call is Jez in the vegetable garden, to find out what is available, and what is going to be coming into season soon. Just walking around and looking at what he is growing gives you inspiration. Then again, sometimes he will come in and say, 'Sorry, we've had a bad frost . . .' And there will be times in winter, when, in terms of the kind of exciting ingredients that chefs like to play with, the garden is pretty barren, so you have to be on your toes and really work hard to be creative with root vegetables and pulses – but that is proper seasonality and proper farming. We have gone back in time really, to the way it would have been in the old days. If something isn't available, that's that. We aren't going to fly it in from Argentina.

In many kitchens you just decide what dishes you want to cook and order the ingredients from the supplier's list. So you would think nothing of picking up the phone and asking for asparagus to make soup in February. If I am honest, I didn't used to think much about seasonality beyond strawberries and lighter dishes in summer and root vegetables and heavier food in winter. I don't think most chefs do, because it is only relatively recently that restaurants have started prioritising local food. But here you really look forward to the venison coming in in the autumn, the purple sprouting broccoli, or the first tender broad beans – even if, by the end of the season, when everyone has been double-podding mountains of broad beans for months, we are all saying, 'If I never see another broad bean . . . !'

In recent years the fashion in food has moved away from refined, fussy assemblies and into more rustic cooking, and named producers and breeds of animals on menus, but when I first arrived here in 2002 to help Tom Aikens set up the farmshop, Carole Bamford was already driving it into everyone that it was all about home-grown ingredients, at their prime, and doing very little with them.

I found it intriguing, but quite alien at first. Like Tom, I came from a background of Michelin-starred kitchens, having worked with chefs like Phil Howard at the Square and John Burton-Race at L'Ortolan, and I had spent time working in France, so I was used to complex processes, layers of intricate components in every dish, and immaculate presentation.

I had had a taste of a different way of cooking when I took on my first head chef job for Stephen Bull at his Blandford Street Restaurant in the late nineties. Stephen wasn't impressed by Michelin stars, and the emphasis was all on flavour, much less on the look. Suddenly instead of foie gras and truffles, I was looking at a whole different larder of cheaper cuts and pulses. But at Daylesford simplicity was being taken so much further.

What we had at the beginning was a small affair with a café on the side: little more than a few tables and chairs. We spent weeks making pickles, chutneys and jams to stock the shelves and hand-tying labels; and we made a small offering of terrines, pâtés and sandwiches for people to have for a snack or lunch. The bakery was right alongside, so people could see the fresh bread and savoury and sweet tarts being pulled from the oven every day, and the shop was full of wonderful aromas. The farm was producing some vegetables, small quantities of beef and lamb and the Sasso chickens that Tom researched, and the creamery had been established for about a year, so we had great Cheddar, the jewel in the crown.

Since then we have constantly evolved and grown, but we are still guided by traditional English farmhouse cooking, with a bit of a twist, and an emphasis on lightness and healthiness.

When new chefs arrive, the first thing we tell them is, 'We don't do foams, or spherifications, or *sous vide* cooking.' I have yet to be convinced that cooking a piece of meat in a bag in a water bath for hours and hours, then rolling it around in a pan, can be nicer than roasting and caramelising it, in the old-fashioned way, allowing the fat to melt through the meat and tenderise it. Chefs like *sous vide* because it gives you consistent results every time, but to me it is a lazy method. Cooking is about smells and sounds, and using your eyes and touch, and constantly tasting to get something just right, rather than just setting a timer.

When I was training, it was drummed into you that every tomato had to be skinned, deseeded and diced, and I have worked in kitchens where the head chef would throw chives back at you because every one wasn't cut to an identical length, which seems quite comical now. When new chefs from a similar background come into the kitchens, I say to them, 'Have you ever had someone in a restaurant saying to a waiter: "Take back this plate immediately: there is a piece of skin on my tomato." Or: "This piece of chive is twice as long as the others!"' Of course we want our food to look inviting, but simplicity and flavour are more important than vanity.

There are no vans arriving in the early morning, delivering ingredients ready-prepped and all the same shape and weight. Instead Jez, in his wellies, brings you vegetables straight from the gardens still caked in mud, so there is a lot of work to do, washing and chopping. Most chefs have never been so close to a farm, let alone one where the herds of rare breed, heritage animals that you see in the fields will be on your butcher's block one day. I have genuinely never cooked with better lamb or venison, and the Gloucester beef, in particular, is unbelievably marbled with fat, which melts into the meat as it cooks and makes it beautifully succulent and tender.

In most kitchens you learn about particular produce by talking to knowledgeable suppliers, but here you are surrounded by people who eat, sleep and breathe the rearing of the animals, growing fruit and vegetables, making cheese and baking artisan bread – putting together every piece of the kitchen jigsaw – and their enthusiasm rubs off on everyone.

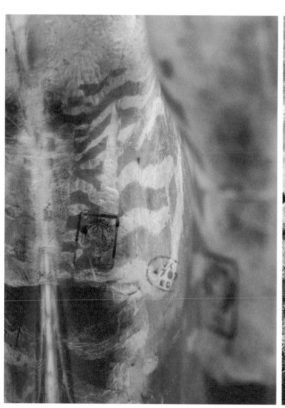

STAPLES

Fresh dressings and pesto
Herb-rich mayonnaise
Sauces, pickles and chutneys for the store cupboard
Jams bursting with fruit

A collection of fresh dressings, pestos, mayonnaise and sauces that can be kept in the fridge; bottled sauces for your storecupboard; and chutneys, pickles and jams that make the most of seasonal fruit and vegetables when they are at their prime, capturing their flavours for another day.

French Dressing

3 tablespoons white wine vinegar

juice of 1½ lemons

1 tablespoon honey

3 tablespoons Dijon mustard

200ml grapeseed or vegetable oil

200ml extra virgin olive oil

sea salt and freshly ground black pepper

In a bowl whisk together the vinegar, lemon juice, honey and mustard until blended. Combine the oils in a jug and very slowly start adding to the bowl: just a few drops, at first, then work up to a slow, steady trickle, whisking constantly until all the oil is incorporated and the dressing will coat the back of a spoon. Season with salt and lots of freshly ground black pepper. Put into the fridge and chill.

Mayonnaise

2 egg yolks

1½ tablespoons Dijon mustard

1 tablespoon white wine vinegar

juice of ¼ of a lemon

500ml grapeseed or vegetable oil

sea salt and freshly ground black pepper

In a bowl whisk together the egg yolks, mustard, vinegar and lemon juice until blended. Very slowly start adding the oil: just a few drops, at first, then work up to a slow, steady trickle, whisking constantly until all the oil is incorporated, and you have a thick, creamy mayonnaise. If you add the oil too quickly the mayonnaise will split, but if this happens, you can rescue it by putting a tablespoon of water into a clean bowl, and then whisking in the split mixture drop by drop, until properly emulsified.

Season with salt and lots of freshly ground black pepper. Chill until ready to use. It will keep in the fridge for up to a week.

Salsa Verde Mayonnaise

This is an amalgamation of two classics: mayonnaise, and salsa verde, the famous Italian green sauce, full of herbs, and made piquant with capers and anchovies. You could add the flavourings to a good bought mayonnaise, or see page 381, if you want to make your own. Serve it as a dipping sauce with fresh vegetable crudités – when we do this we also put out a pot of hot Cheddar sauce (see page 387), for a real contrast of temperatures and flavours.

Once made, this will keep for up to a week in the fridge.

40g fresh parsley leaves, roughly chopped

20g fresh mint leaves, roughly chopped

30g rocket leaves, roughly chopped

1 clove of garlic, roughly chopped

3 tablespoons capers

4 heaped teaspoons Dijon mustard

160ml olive oil

4 anchovy fillets

160ml mayonnaise

Mix all the ingredients apart from the mayonnaise in a bowl and leave to stand for 10 minutes to allow the flavours to infuse into one another. Blend to a coarse paste (or do this with a pestle and mortar).

Put the mayonnaise into another bowl and slowly whisk in the blended herb mixture, a little at a time. Do this slowly, to avoid the mayonnaise separating. Chill in the fridge until needed.

Herb Mayonnaise

A simpler herb mayonnaise, which is good with steamed vegetables, chicken or fish.

1 heaped teaspoon chopped
fresh parsley

1 heaped teaspoon chopped
fresh tarragon

2 heaped teaspoons chopped
fresh mint

1 heaped teaspoon chopped
fresh chives

125ml mayonnaise (see page
381)

sea salt and freshly ground
black pepper

Mix the chopped herbs into the mayonnaise, taste and season as necessary, then chill in the fridge until needed.

Watercress or Wild Garlic and Pumpkin Seed Pesto

Great spooned into a bowl of soup or with grilled fish or meat.

130g watercress leaves or
sliced wild garlic leaves

1 clove of garlic, thinly sliced

130ml olive oil

3 tablespoons pumpkin seeds,
lightly toasted in a dry pan

25g Parmesan cheese, grated

sea salt and freshly ground
black pepper

In a bowl mix half the watercress or wild garlic with the garlic clove and olive oil and leave to stand for 10 minutes, then transfer to a blender and whiz to a smooth paste. Add the remaining watercress or wild garlic, the pumpkin seeds and Parmesan and pulse for a few seconds until you have a coarse pesto. Taste and season as necessary. Put into the fridge to chill (for up to a week) if not using straight away.

Minted Aioli

The classic garlic mayonnaise is freshened up with loads
of mint, so is great with roast lamb, and especially the
pressed lamb on page 235.

It is at its best chilled in the fridge for 24 hours, so
that the flavour of the mint can really infuse all the way
through.

4 egg yolks	250ml olive oil
2 cloves of garlic, crushed	250ml rapeseed oil
juice of 1 lemon, strained	4 tablespoons chopped fresh mint leaves
sea salt and freshly ground black pepper	

In a bowl whisk together the egg yolks, crushed garlic,
lemon juice, sea salt and freshly ground black pepper.

Very slowly start adding the oil: just a few drops, at
first, then, as the mixture starts to thicken, work up to a
slow, steady trickle, whisking constantly until all the oil
is incorporated and the aioli is thick and creamy. Add a
little water (1–2 tablespoons) if necessary to get the right
consistency, then gently stir in the chopped mint. Taste and
adjust the seasoning as necessary. Spoon into a bowl and,
ideally, leave in the fridge for 24 hours before serving.

Hot Cheddar Sauce

We put pots of this out, together with some salsa verde mayonnaise (see page 382), whenever we serve crudités from the garden – but it is also great just with good bread for dipping into it, at the start of a meal. The sauce will keep for up to a week in the fridge.

2 egg yolks

300g crème fraîche

60g Cheddar cheese, finely grated

40g Parmesan cheese, finely grated

sea salt and freshly ground black pepper

Put the egg yolks and crème fraîche into a heatproof bowl over a pan of simmering water (making sure the base of the bowl doesn't touch the water) and whisk constantly until the mixture becomes hot and slightly thick. Take off the heat, add the grated cheeses, gently mix until all the cheese has melted (this will thicken the sauce fully), then check for seasoning.

If not using immediately, pour into a small container and leave to cool, then put into the fridge.

When you want to use it, reheat it very gently over a low heat, stirring constantly until just hot. Take care not to let it boil, or the sauce will curdle and have the consistency of scrambled egg.

Notes on jars and bottles

To sterilise your preserving jars or bottles, place them, open, on a tray in the oven at 100°C/gas ½ for 10 minutes. Fill them, while still hot, with hot chutney, jam or sauce, then close the jars or bottles.

If you are only making a small quantity to be eaten in a matter of weeks, then this is all you need do, but if you are making use of a glut of fruit or vegetables and making larger quantities to keep, it is best to have the jars or bottles good and airtight, to stop any air getting in and mould growing. If you happen to have a steam function on your oven, as we do in our kitchens, put the closed jars in for 20 minutes to create a vacuum and seal them. Take out using a tea towel, and retighten the lid on each jar. Otherwise, boil the jars on the hob. Line a large pan with a cloth or tea towel at the base, which will stop the glass of the jars cracking, then put in your jars, so that they aren't touching one another. Pour in enough boiling water to cover the jars completely, then put a lid on the pan and simmer for 10 minutes. Leave them in the pan until cool enough to touch, or lift out using tongs, again retightening the lids (if using screw caps) as they come out, then dry the jars, label and store.

John Hardwick

Pickled Vegetables

When we have a glut of different vegetables, we often pickle them together, just poaching them in the pickling liquid, so they retain their essential flavour, look very pretty in the jar, and are lovely just run through a salad, or with cold meats. You can vary the vegetables, but choose mainly crunchy ones, with a few slightly softer ones, so that you have an interesting mix of textures. You can add small onions if you like – put them in at the same time as the fennel.

Stored in a cool, dry place, these will keep for up to 6 months.

Selection of vegetables, for example:

1 fennel, cut into chunks

2 carrots, sliced at an angle

1 small cauliflower, cut into florets

2 celery stalks, sliced at an angle

1 red pepper, deseeded and sliced

1 yellow pepper, deseeded and sliced

2 courgettes, sliced

For the pickling liquid:

500ml white wine

250ml white wine vinegar

100ml olive oil

115g caster sugar, preferably unrefined

2 tablespoons salt

3 cloves of garlic, halved

5cm piece of fresh root ginger, chopped

2 sprigs of fresh rosemary

2 sprigs of fresh thyme

1 bay leaf

1 teaspoon black peppercorns

½ teaspoon pink peppercorns

4 whole cloves

1 teaspoon fennel seeds

1 teaspoon coriander seeds

½ teaspoon juniper berries

1 star anise

First make the pickling liquid. Put all the ingredients into a large pan with 1.5 litres of water, bring to the boil, then turn down to a simmer for 5 minutes. Take off the heat and leave to infuse for 3 hours, then remove all the halved garlic cloves and discard.

Put the pan back on the heat and bring back to the boil, then add the vegetables a variety at a time, at 1-minute intervals, starting with the crunchiest ones (in this case the fennel) and finishing with the softest (the courgette), so that each one retains its crunch or bite.

Have ready your hot, sterilised jars (see page 388). Lift out the hot vegetables with a slotted spoon and divide between the jars, then top up with the hot pickling liquid (keep in the herbs and spices). Close the jars, then seal in a pan of boiling water (see page 388).

Variation: Piccalilli

We also pickle vegetables in a classic piccalilli. We make ours with chopped shallots and onions, cauliflower and cucumber, but you can add broccoli, green beans, peppers, or whatever you like, so long as it has a good crunch.

For about 2kg, cut 1 large cauliflower into small florets, chop 2 medium white onions small (about 1cm), and cut 350g small shallots into quarters. The key is to draw as much moisture out of the vegetables as possible, so that the piccalilli doesn't become too liquid, so put the cauliflower, onions and shallots into a bowl with 3 teaspoons of sea salt and leave in the fridge for 24 hours, then drain in a colander under the cold tap, to wash off the salt, and leave to 'drip dry'. De-seed and chop ½ cucumber (again about 1cm), repeat the salting process with another 3 teaspoons, but just for 20 minutes, drain, rinse and leave to dry.

To make the sauce, put 350ml white wine vinegar and ½ chopped red chilli, (with seeds) into a medium heavy-based pan and bring to the boil, then turn off the heat, leave to infuse for 20 minutes, and pass through a fine sieve, to remove the chilli (keep the pan, as you will need it again shortly). Next put 250g caster sugar into a bowl with 25g English mustard powder, 1 tablespoon ground turmeric and 1½ tablespoons cornflour and whisk in half the infused vinegar, smoothing out any lumps.

Pour the remaining infused vinegar into the reserved pan and bring to the boil, then add the vinegar and flour mixture, bring back to the boil and whisk until the mixture starts to thicken, taking care not to let it get lumpy. Take it off the heat, and while still hot pour over the vegetables.

Have ready your hot, sterilised jars (see page 388), fill them with the hot piccalilli, close the jars, then seal in a pan of boiling water (see page 388).

Chutneys

A good chutney is about the balance of sweet and sour flavours: you don't want it to be overpoweringly vinegary or sugary, because you should be able to taste all the key ingredients.

Use a stainless steel pan, which won't react with the acidity in the vinegar (and could give a metallic taste to the chutney), and stir regularly during the cooking, so that the chutney doesn't catch and burn on the bottom of the pan.

Once potted in sterilised and sealed jars all these chutneys will keep for a couple of years, and become richer and more mellow as they mature. As with any preserves, though, use your eyes and nose, and if you think anything is wrong when you open the jar, discard the contents – however, it is very rare to have a problem with a chutney, as the very nature of it is that it is high in acidity (from the vinegar) and sugar: two things that bacteria don't like.

Apple and Chilli Chutney

This recipe dates back to the opening of the farmshop back in 2002, when John Hardwick and Tom Aikens between them made 22,000 jars of jams, pickles and chutneys from a standing start, in small batches with just a single pan on the stove. This one works beautifully in a ploughman's-style sandwich, made with good bread, Cheddar and ham; and is equally good with pork, and terrines.

Over the years it has been made with many different varieties of apple from the orchards – some cookers, some eating apples, some heritage varieties – whatever has tasted right at the time of making. Cookers are easiest to get hold of at home, but if you want to experiment with varieties other than Bramleys, essentially you want an apple that will break down a little, not stay intact, but will give some good acidity, as a cooking apple does. Jez suggests Newton Wonder, Howgate Wonder or Blenheim Orange, the classic dual-purpose apple which is quite tart around the end of September to October but sweetens later. These won't soften quite as much as Bramleys, which are much bigger. The rule of thumb with apples is that the bigger the fruit and the larger its cells, the more it will disintegrate.

The chilli just gives a background, fragrant spiciness, rather than a kick of heat, as you don't want it to dominate the other ingredients. Generally the smaller the chillies, the hotter they are, so chose a medium-sized one. That said, all chillies vary in their heat levels, so taste a little raw, before you start making the chutney, and then you can use more or less, accordingly.

2kg cooking apples, peeled, cored and chopped	2 tablespoons ground ginger
350g sultanas	3 medium red onions, thinly sliced
750g demerara sugar	6 cloves of garlic, finely chopped
50g yellow mustard seeds	
2 red chillies, deseeded and chopped	500ml white wine vinegar

Put all the ingredients into a heavy-based pan with 250ml water and bring to the boil, stirring frequently to prevent sticking on the bottom of the pan, then turn down the heat and simmer for 1–1½ hours – again stirring regularly – until the mixture is soft and most of the liquid has evaporated. Take off the heat.

Have ready your hot, sterilised jars (see page 388), fill them with the hot chutney, close the jars, then seal in a pan of boiling water (see page 388).

Butternut Squash Chutney

Choose a butternut squash with a really bright orange flesh, rather than a pale one, if possible, as otherwise the tomatoes, brown sugar and raisins will dull down the colour. Also look for a tight flesh, not loose and broken, as this way you will get a bit more texture to your chutney.

2 large butternut squash (about 1.5 kg), peeled, seeds removed, flesh finely chopped

500g tomatoes, roughly chopped

500g onions, finely chopped

500g cooking apples, finely chopped

500ml cider vinegar

500g soft brown sugar

250g raisins

2 teaspoons sea salt

1 teaspoon mixed spice

½ teaspoon black pepper

Put the squash, tomatoes, onions, apples, vinegar, and all the rest of the ingredients into a heavy-based pan with 250ml of water. Bring to the boil, stirring frequently to prevent sticking on the bottom of the pan, then turn down the heat and simmer for 1½ hours – again stirring regularly – until the mixture has thickened and there is only a little liquid left in the pan. Take off the heat.

Have ready your hot, sterilised jars (see page 388), fill them with the hot chutney, close the jars, then seal in a pan of boiling water (see page 388).

Red Tomato Chilli Jam

This is a fantastic way of using up ripe tomatoes that are becoming too soft to use for salads. Because you cook the jam quite quickly it retains a beautiful colour and looks almost translucent in the jar. The kick of chilli offsets the sweetness, and it works best with something pungent like a mature Cheddar or even a goat's cheese.

1kg ripe red tomatoes, roughly chopped

2 red chillies, finely chopped (keep in the seeds)

1kg caster sugar

1 bay leaf

1 teaspoon cumin seeds

1 teaspoon fennel seeds

1 teaspoon black peppercorns

½ teaspoon cayenne pepper

2.5cm piece of fresh root ginger, very finely chopped

3 cloves of garlic, finely chopped

2 teaspoons salt

juice of 1½ lemons

650ml red wine vinegar

Put the tomatoes and chillies into a bowl, cover with the sugar, stir and leave in the fridge overnight.

When ready to make the jam, put a saucer into the fridge and get it really cold, ready to test the setting point.

Make a little spice bag by laying the bay leaf in the centre of a small square of muslin, add the cumin and fennel seeds, peppercorns and cayenne pepper, then gather up and tie securely.

Transfer the tomato and chilli mixture to a heavy-based pan, along with the ginger and garlic, salt, lemon juice and vinegar, and add the spice bag.

Bring to the boil, then turn down the heat to a simmer, stirring regularly to ensure the mixture doesn't burn on the bottom of the pan as it thickens. After about 30 minutes, test to see if the jam has reached setting point. Take the

pan off the heat, and the cold saucer from the fridge.
Spoon out a tablespoon of jam on to it, wait a minute,
then push your finger through the middle of it. If it leaves
a line that stays clean (i.e. the jam doesn't run back into it)
and the jam wrinkles slightly, it has reached setting point.
If not, continue to boil, and keep testing.

Have ready your hot, sterilised jars (see page 388), fill
them with the hot jam, close the jars, then seal in a pan of
boiling water (see page 388).

Two Bottled Sauces

The nation's favourites – even better if you make them yourself.

Tomato Ketchup

1 teaspoon black peppercorns	900g onions, peeled and finely chopped
1 teaspoon whole allspice berries	1kg cooking apples, peeled, cored and chopped
½ teaspoon cloves	800g caster sugar, unrefined
½ teaspoon cayenne pepper	1 litre malt vinegar
3.5kg tomatoes, roughly chopped	1 tablespoon sea salt

Make a little spice bag by heaping the peppercorns, allspice, cloves and cayenne pepper in the centre of a small square of muslin, then gather up and tie securely.

Put the tomatoes, onions, apples and sugar into a large heavy-based pan with the muslin spice bag. Add the vinegar and the salt. Bring to the boil, then turn down to a simmer for about 2 hours, stirring from time to time to make sure the mixture doesn't stick, until you have a pulp.

Remove from the heat and leave to cool a little. Purée in a blender, a little at a time, until smooth. Strain through a medium sieve into a clean pan and bring back to the boil for 2–3 minutes, stirring constantly to prevent catching and burning.

Have ready your hot, sterilised bottles (see method for jars on page 388). Pour the ketchup, through a funnel, into the bottles and close up, then seal in a pan of boiling water (see page 388).

Brown Sauce

'This is a great sauce,' says John Hardwick. 'The recipe comes from Ivan, our sous chef in the farmshop, and we had to prise it from him. It gives HP a run for its money, and is great with corned beef hash (see page 34).'

Jez suggests Blenheim Orange, Bountiful and the English Golden Delicious apples. 'People have a blinkered view of this apple because of the flabby French variety of the seventies and eighties,' he says. 'Whereas the English variety is a marvellous apple – hard, dense and sweet.'

250g pitted prunes	2 teaspoons grated nutmeg
850ml malt vinegar	750g (about 4 medium) onions, chopped
50g sea salt	
1 teaspoon cayenne pepper	1kg apples (see above), peeled and chopped
1 tablespoon ground allspice	500g caster sugar, preferably unrefined
2 teaspoons ground ginger	

Put all the ingredients into a large, heavy-based pan and bring to the boil, then turn down to a simmer for about 2 hours, stirring from time to time to make sure the mixture doesn't stick, until you have a pulp.

Remove from the heat and leave to cool a little. Purée in a blender, a little at a time, until smooth. Strain through a medium sieve into a clean pan and bring back to the boil for 2–3 minutes, stirring constantly to prevent catching and burning.

Have ready your hot, sterilised bottles (see method for jars on page 388). Pour the ketchup, through a funnel, into the bottles and close up, then seal in a pan of boiling water (see page 388).

Two jams, a conserve and marmalade

All our jams are set naturally without any added pectin, so we rely on what is naturally in the fruit and on the method of reducing the mixture of fruit, sugar and water right down until there is no liquid left, by which time the jam should have reached setting point. The downside is that there is a small window between the jam retaining its bright colour, and looking darker. You also need to watch it all the time, to make sure it doesn't catch and burn. We have tried all kinds of traditional methods to add pectin, including blitzing together lemon pith and flesh, and adding it to the jam pan in a muslin bag, or asking the bakery to keep back all the apple skins after they have made spiced apple cakes, and adding these too, in muslin bags, but the reality is, you need masses of all of these trimmings to make a real difference.

As a rule the more tart the fruit, the more pectin it contains, which is why we have chosen most of the fruits in the recipes that follow. And because they are quite tart to begin with they can cope with the concentrated sweetness that comes from reducing the jam right down. The exception is strawberry, which we make as a conserve, rather than a jam – as it demands less sugar, and has a slightly softer set.

Rhubarb and Ginger Jam

Rhubarb can be quite low in pectin, despite its tartness, and it does tend to break down into a purée as it cooks, so the texture is a little different to other jams, but the flavour is wonderful. It is best made with early-season, pink forced rhubarb, rather than the red-skinned later varieties, which are usually quite green inside and make a terrific crumble, but look less pretty in a jam.

1.6kg rhubarb, washed and cut into 2.5cm pieces

1.3kg granulated sugar

juice of 2 lemons

25g fresh root ginger, very finely chopped

The day before you want to make the jam, put the rhubarb, sugar and lemon juice into a bowl and leave to macerate in the fridge overnight. Just before cooking, stir in the chopped ginger.

When ready to make the jam, put a saucer into the fridge and get it really cold, ready to test the setting point.

Transfer the macerated rhubarb into a large, heavy-based pan with 300ml of water, and bring to the boil, skimming off any scum with a slotted spoon. Turn down to a simmer, stirring regularly to avoid catching and burning. Remove the scum as it appears.

After about 30 minutes, test to see if the jam has reached setting point. Take the pan off the heat, and the cold saucer from the fridge. Spoon out a tablespoon of jam on to it, wait a minute, then push your finger through the middle of it. If it leaves a line that stays clean (i.e. the jam doesn't run back into it) and the jam wrinkles slightly, it has reached setting point. If not, continue to boil, and keep testing.

Have ready your hot, sterilised jars (see page 388). Take the pan from the heat and leave the jam to stand for 5 minutes before filling and closing the jars, then seal in a pan of boiling water (see page 388).

Gooseberry and Elderflower Jam

The combination of gooseberries and elderflowers is an English classic. With gooseberries, the best are always mid-season: not too hard and sour, as the earliest can be, and not too soft and verging on the sweet, as in the late ones. Gooseberries are high in pectin, so it is easy to get this jam to set.

1.4kg gooseberries, topped and tailed

juice of 1 lemon

1.4kg granulated sugar

200ml elderflower cordial

Put a saucer into the fridge and get it really cold, ready to test the setting point of the jam.

Wash the gooseberries really well and put them into a large heavy-based pan over a medium heat with the lemon juice and 250ml of water. Cook gently, ensuring the sugar doesn't burn before the fruit has turned to pulp, stirring regularly to avoid sticking.

Add the sugar and cordial and bring to the boil, skimming off any scum with a slotted spoon, then turn down to a simmer and stir regularly to avoid catching and burning. After about 30 minutes test to see if it has reached setting point. Take the pan off the heat, and the cold saucer from the fridge. Spoon out a tablespoon of jam on to it, wait a minute, then push your finger through the middle of it. If it leaves a line that stays clean (i.e. the jam doesn't run back into it) and the jam wrinkles slightly, it has reached setting point. If not, continue to boil, and keep testing.

Have ready your hot, sterilised jars (see page 388). Take the pan from the heat and leave the jam to stand for 5 minutes before filling and closing the jars, then seal in a pan of boiling water (see page 388).

Strawberry and Vanilla Conserve

The difference between a jam and a conserve is the ratio of sugar to fruit. A jam must have a minimum of 65 per cent sugar, which is fine for quite acidic fruit, like gooseberries, blackcurrants, rhubarb and even raspberries, but can be too sweet for delicate fruits like strawberries. So in this recipe we have lowered the sugar slightly to let the delicate flavours of the vanilla and strawberries come through – but because of this lower sugar content, we have to label it a conserve.

The butter helps to stop the quite loose and syrupy watery mix from boiling over at the beginning of cooking.

1.8kg strawberries, washed well, hulled and stalks removed	1 small knob of butter
1.4kg granulated sugar	2 vanilla pods, split, each pod cut so that you have 1 piece per jar
juice of ½ lemon	

Forty-eight hours before you want to make the conserve, put 500g of the strawberries into a bowl and mix with the sugar. Leave to macerate in the fridge.

When ready to make the conserve, put a saucer into the fridge and get it really cold, ready to test the setting point.

Put the rest of the strawberries into a large heavy-based pan with the lemon juice and 300ml water and cook gently for a couple of minutes.

Add the sugared berries and the butter, and bring to a rapid boil, skimming off any scum with a slotted spoon. Continue to boil (it is important to cook quickly to maintain the colour and stop the berries from breaking up), stirring regularly to avoid catching and burning. After about 5 minutes put in the vanilla pods, scraping in the seeds too. Then, after another 5–6 minutes, test to see if the conserve has reached setting point. Take the pan off the heat, and the cold saucer from the fridge. Spoon out a

tablespoon of conserve on to it, wait a minute, then push your finger through the middle of it. If it leaves a line that stays clean (i.e. the conserve doesn't run back into it) and the conserve wrinkles slightly, it has reached setting point. If not, continue to boil, and keep testing.

Have ready your hot, sterilised jars (see page 388). Take the pan from the heat and leave the conserve to stand for 5 minutes before filling, making sure a piece of vanilla pod goes into each jar, and closing the jars, then seal in a pan of boiling water (see page 388).

Seville Orange Marmalade

This recipe works equally well with grapefruit. At Christmas we make a festive version with a glug of brandy or whisky added just before we take the marmalade off the heat. You can also add some mulled wine spices in a muslin bag during the cooking.

1.3kg Seville oranges, washed	juice of 1½ lemons
1.3kg granulated sugar	

Put a saucer into the fridge and get it really cold, ready to test the setting point of the marmalade.

Put the whole washed oranges into a large heavy-based pan with 2 litres of water, bring to a simmer, and cook gently until they are soft. Lift out the oranges from the pan with a spoon and cool slightly. Let the liquid in the pan bubble up, reduce by a third, then take off the heat, strain through a sieve into a bowl and then pour back into the pan.

Top, tail and halve the cooled oranges and scoop out the flesh, keeping the peel and pith intact. Trim off all but a thin lining of pith, weigh the peel so that you have 150g, then shred into strips about 3mm wide.

Put the orange flesh, complete with pips, into a blender and blend to a purée. Strain through a fine sieve into the reduced liquid from cooking the oranges. Add the strips of peel, the sugar and the lemon juice and bring to the boil. Boil rapidly, stirring occasionally to avoid catching and burning on the bottom of the pan.

After about 30 minutes, test to see if the marmalade has reached setting point. Take the pan off the heat, and the cold saucer from the fridge. Spoon out a tablespoon of marmalade on to it, wait a minute, then push your finger through the middle of it. If it leaves a line that stays clean

(i.e. the marmalade doesn't run back into it) and the marmalade wrinkles slightly, it has reached setting point. If not, continue to boil, and keep testing.

Have ready your hot, sterilised jars (see page 388). Take the pan from the heat and leave the marmalade to stand for 5 minutes before filling and closing the jars, then seal in a pan of boiling water (see page 388).

'In my mind two things symbolise sustainable food production: the soil, and the bees. If you have a healthy soil and happy bees, you are in business.'
Tim Field, The Environment

The soil is the essence of everything. If you look after it and encourage the microbial and earthworm activity, you end up with a rich, light, aerated soil, which can retain moisture, but won't get compacted and heavy, and that doesn't need chemicals. But bees, too, have an incredibly important role to play; they are a key species. In my mind two things symbolise sustainable food production: the soil, and the bees. If you have a healthy soil and happy bees, you are in business.

We have two beekeepers on the farm: one based in the market garden, and one producing estate honey, in small quantities, but in which you can really taste individual flowers or herbs at certain times of the year. In the market garden, the beekeeper has a policy of minimal intervention, so we let the queens and their colonies leave their hives and go where they need to: perhaps a hollow in a tree, or a chimney pot, or with any luck a vacant hive, where we encourage them to take up residence, so we can continue to harvest their honey. It is fascinating to study their behaviour and the way they will sometimes select a new queen, and then the colony will follow her everywhere.

Only once, in 2012, have we had a problem with swarming, and then, after a beautiful March, followed by a horrendous wet April, when there was a lack of pollen and nectar, we suddenly had a warm week in May and the bees decided to take off in a bid to move house. It was the day before our summer festival, and so on the morning when thousands of people were due to arrive and stroll around the market garden, I was chasing bees. It was a real heart-in-mouth moment, but we relocated them all, and when the visitors arrived, no one was any the wiser.

I'm a Cotswold boy, always lived in the country, and as a kid I was forever digging ponds and hunting for newts, and there would always be tadpoles in a jam jar on my windowsill. At university I studied Environmental and Behavioural Biology, looking at the impact of farming on the environment, and trying to fathom out the most sustainable way to feed the world. After I finished my degree I was working as an environmental consultant, when the chance came up to join Daylesford. They had already been farming organically here for years, but Carole Bamford wanted to push sustainability as far as it is possible to go. So everything we do is geared towards that goal. On top of composting and recycling we now have 1,000 solar panels, which in high summer can generate all the electricity we need to power the bread ovens, the creamery, the dairy, the refrigeration, all from the sun. We have an energy capsule which catches the heat above the log-fired oven in the kitchens, and heats the water for the kitchens, and our own sustainable rainwater system, which will eventually be used for all of the farm, so one day we can be completely off-grid in terms of energy and water.

I remember on the day I arrived, Richard Smith took me around, and there was a soggy wet patch in one of the fields by the river, really weedy, and he said he wanted to do something with it. For someone who grew up digging ponds it was the continuation of a theme for me. And now we have a wetlands area for wildfowl, wading birds and kingfishers, and we have an otter running through, wreaking havoc. Wetlands used to be an important part of our environment, that has been lost through the intensification of farming, so it feels good to see it thriving.

There are two elements that feed the soil: green matter and brown matter. Green matter includes nitrogen-rich elements that build up fertility and can come from chicken manure, grass cuttings, or crops like mustards, which are grown on bare patches of ground for their dual value as ground cover, and for digging in and adding fertility. Brown matter, which signifies carbon-rich elements, can come from straw, newspaper or leaf material.

We compost all the fruit and vegetable trimmings from the kitchens and the Black Barn, which we mound up and turn once a week, until it becomes a rich, black, friable mix. It is a wonderful cyclical process, in which nothing travels further than a few hundred yards: the produce goes from the market garden to the kitchens, and then the scraps go to the compost and back on to the gardens again, with a by-product of happy people eating food that is full of goodness and flavour, in between.

But much of the composting is also done in the garden itself. If Jez is harvesting leeks, cutting off the roots and heads, he will just drop the trimmings there, where they will rot and be dug into the soil, ready for another crop of a different vegetable . . . as the rotation system ensures that you don't grow the same crop in the same place again for four years, so that you remove the risk of pests and disease which attack specific crops.

Organic systems also rely on beneficial predator insects that control pests, and so we could plant all sorts of wildflower meadow strips to attract them, but actually we don't need to, since the diverse way that Jez crops does more than anything else to attract the 'good' insects naturally, because throughout the year there are hundreds of different fruits and vegetables all flowering or producing seed heads or leaf material at different times.

I have foraged and fished all my life, and now I also manage the wild deer around Daylesford. Our farmed venison all comes from Staffordshire, but here in Gloucestershire we have wild Muntjac deer, which are a species originally from South East Asia that were brought over to Woburn Abbey in the early part of the twentieth century, and are now over-running the countryside, decimating the woodland flora, destroying bluebells and rare orchids; and while everyone likes to see a few deer around the farm, you have to keep the populations down. Their meat is delicious, very lean and healthy like all venison, and high in iron, so we use it in the cookery school, and in the Summer Solstice Garden, which was designed for the Chelsea Flower Show and then re-built in the market garden, where we hold demonstrations and run courses.

I show people how to butcher and cook wild food and game, from pigeon and rabbit to venison, pheasant, partridge, and duck from the wetlands. Or I will introduce people to foraging for wild food, which is something I have always done. We go around the farm, picking berries and nuts and wild herbs, and then we come back and make something delicious from them. There is so much we can supplement our everyday grocery lists with, by just getting out there and foraging in the hedgerows and woods and fields.

I teach people how to prepare wild game, and then we will make something like a herb-encrusted loin of venison . . . perhaps to follow a wild crayfish pasta or risotto, made with crayfish caught from the river.

I am on something of a game crusade, since I know people are scared of cooking it sometimes, and it can be harder to do well than lamb or beef, because it is so much leaner, and vulnerable to drying out, and it has a stronger flavour, which not everyone likes. If I am cooking venison loin, it has to be pink … sometimes when I have friends around I barbecue steaks, marinated with a little chilli and garlic, so you get the meat a little charred on the outside, and even my friends whose palates generally aren't up to strong game enjoy that. Personally, though, I don't think you can beat a rich, slow-cooked stew, with venison shoulder, with some fruits put in to balance the stronger flavour of this cut. A good trick if you are worried about the gaminess is to mix in some shin of beef or stewing steak, which balances out and tones down the flavours. A little pancetta or bacon to add some smokiness helps too.

I also love to cook game birds like pheasant, but for me, the worst way to cook a bird like this is to roast it whole, because it is difficult to get the timing right so that the legs and breast are cooked perfectly. So I will often take off the breasts and cook them alone, more accurately, then confit the legs separately. Or I might make a casserole with some of Jez's cider, some tarragon from the

garden, and serve it with beetroot, tossed in balsamic vinegar, olive oil and thyme and roasted in the oven. I'm a sucker for the farm cheese too, so I would have some leeks from the market garden on the side, in a Cheddar and mustard sauce.

In the Summer Solstice Garden, Jez will also teach people how to grow vegetables, or make cider, and we have bee-keeping and hen-keeping courses. What excites me most, though, is the food sustainability projects we do with children, through our own Foundation and as part of the Food for Life partnership, working with schools, helping teachers to set up organic gardens, bringing children on to the farm, and engaging them in where their food comes from. Food for Life have a wonderful clip of children trading Brussels sprouts in an inner city playground in London. They had set up their own garden, busily planting, raking, weeding and pruning, and then when it came to harvesting, the children were trading sprouts, like sweets. Just brilliant.

Notes on stocks

Never waste a vegetable, or a bone: make stock! Making stock is so easy, and so satisfying. It is really just about getting into the habit of automatically using up whatever vegetables you have left over in the fridge, or saving the chicken or beef carcass after a roast, ready to boil up, rather than wasting it.

The key with meat stocks is to bring them to the boil, then turn down to a simmer, and spend a good 10 minutes skimming off the 'scum', i.e. all the impurities and grease that rise to the surface, in what I call 'the first throw'. If you don't turn down the heat, and leave the stock boiling at this point, the fats will emulsify into the stock. There is no real flavour in the stock yet, so you are taking nothing away in terms of taste, whereas if you leave it until later, you will be losing flavour. As the stock continues to simmer over a few hours, a tiny bit more scum will probably kick up to the surface, now and then, but you can skim that off easily without harming the flavour.

Once you have made your stock, you can keep it in the freezer, in bags or ice cube trays, ready to pull out at any time for a soup or casserole, and it will make all the difference to the flavour. Above all, you will know exactly what is in your stock: nothing but pure goodness.

Vegetable Stock

You can vary the vegetables as much as you like but avoid green vegetables, apart from leeks, as they tend to colour the water, which will eventually turn brownish in the way that it always will if you overcook greens, and the stock will lose some of its fresh flavour.

To make about 3 litres, chop ¼ of a celeriac, 2 large carrots, 1 leek, 1 large onion, 3 sticks of celery, ½ a head of fennel, 1 sweet potato, and ¼ of a butternut squash and put into a large pan. Cover with 5 litres of water and add 2 sprigs of fresh thyme, ½ teaspoon of sea salt and 1 teaspoon of black peppercorns. Bring to the boil, then turn down the heat and simmer for 1 hour. Take off the heat and leave to stand for 2 hours, to improve the flavour. Remove the vegetables from the pan with a slotted spoon and throw them away. Pass the liquid through a fine sieve into a clean container, using a ladle. Either keep in the fridge (for up to a week), or freeze.

Chicken Stock

In our kitchens we tend to use chicken stock for most of our cooking, even if we are making a casserole of lamb or beef, because it is lighter and allows other flavours in a dish to come through more than, say, a beef stock. We make a white (light) chicken stock, which is good for soups and chicken casseroles; and a roast or 'brown' one, which we use in dark meat casseroles, and for gravies and sauces – however you can vary the latter recipe to use any meat bones, such as beef, lamb, duck or turkey.

White (light) chicken stock
To make 3.5 litres, put a 1.2kg chicken carcass into a large pan, cover with 4.5 litres of water and add 2 teaspoons sea salt. Bring slowly to the boil, then reduce the heat to a simmer and skim off the scum and grease from the surface with a slotted spoon. Add 2 peeled and quartered onions, 1 leek, washed well, split and halved; 3 halved sticks of celery; 6 cloves of garlic, 2 tablespoons chopped fresh thyme leaves, and 1 tablespoon black peppercorns, and bring back to the boil, then turn down the heat and simmer for about 1 hour, carefully skimming off any more scum that rises to the surface from time to time.

Turn the heat off and leave to cool for 30 minutes. Remove the carcass and vegetables from the pot with a small sieve or slotted spoon and discard, then strain the liquid through a fine sieve into a clean container. Either put into the fridge until ready to use (it will keep for 2 days), or freeze.

Roast (brown) chicken stock
To make 3.5 litres, preheat the oven to 200°C/gas 6. Chop up a 1.2kg chicken carcass (or use the equivalent weight in chicken wings) and put into a roasting tin. Drizzle with 1 tablespoon of vegetable oil and put into the oven for about 30–40 minutes, or until golden brown. Meanwhile, roughly chop 2 onions, 2 large carrots, 3 sticks of celery, and break a head of garlic into cloves.

Heat 3 more tablespoons of vegetable oil in a large pan, then add the vegetables and cook over a medium heat, stirring occasionally, until they are golden brown, adding the garlic towards the end, so that it doesn't burn and become bitter. Add 2 tablespoons tomato purée and continue to cook for another 5 minutes, making sure to scrape the bottom of the pan or the tomato purée will burn.

Remove the roasting tin from the oven and, with tongs, add the roasted bones or wings to the pan and pour off any excess fat from the tin, keeping back the juices (you can keep the fat for the Sunday roast). Add a few tablespoons of water to the roasting tin and stir until all the roasting juices are released, then add these to the pan and cover with 4.5 litres of water. Bring to the boil, then reduce the heat to a simmer. Skim off the scum and grease from the surface with a slotted spoon, then add 4 sprigs of fresh thyme, a tablespoon of sea salt and a teaspoon of black peppercorns and continue to simmer for 2 hours, carefully skimming off any more scum that rises to the surface from time to time.

Take off the heat, allow to cool a little, then lift out the bones and vegetables with a small sieve or slotted spoon and discard. Strain the liquid through a fine sieve into a clean container. Either put into the fridge until ready to use (it will keep for 2 days), or freeze.

John Hardwick

Weights and Measures

DRY MEASUREMENTS

Metric	US cups	Metric	Australian cups
150g	1 cup flour	125g	1 cup flour
225g	1 cup caster/granulated sugar	225g	1 cup caster/granulated sugar
175g	1 cup brown sugar	200g	1 cup brown sugar
225g	1 cup butter	220g	1 cup uncooked Arborio rice
200g	1 cup uncooked Arborio rice		

WEIGHTS

Metric	Imperial
10g	½oz
25g	1oz
50g	2oz
75g	3oz
110g	4oz
225g	8oz
450g	1lb

LIQUID MEASUREMENTS

Metric	Imperial	US cups
30ml	1 fl oz	⅛ cup
60ml	2 fl oz	¼ cup
125ml	4 fl oz	½ cup
185ml	6 fl oz	¾ cup
250ml	8 fl oz	1 cup
500ml	16 fl oz	2 cups

Acknowledgements

This book is dedicated to my grandchildren: Tilly, Caspian, Teddy and Scarlet. It is a celebration of good food by our passionate team here at Daylesford, and a compilation of favourite café and family recipes and styling details, and there are so many people to thank. I hope they all share my pride when they look through the pages.

A huge thank you to Louise Haines of Fourth Estate for her endless care with the detailed production of this book. To Sheila Keating for her patience and for being so gentle. To photographers Sarah Maingot and Martin Morrell for their beautiful photography – both are a joy to work with. To Anna Jones and Emily Ezekiel, who prepared the food so sympathetically for photography, and to Joby Barnard for pulling everyone's ideas together in the design. To Georgia Mason at Fourth Estate, for keeping everyone focused and on track, Annie Lee for her meticulous editing, and Ben Curtis of Daylesford who brought the whole project together, and to whom I am eternally grateful.

This book would never have been possible without John Hardwick, our trusted chef for many years: thanks for his support and for all the time he has put into the book on top of his Daylesford day job. As John says, the food at Daylesford has evolved over the years, and many chefs who have worked in the kitchens have contributed to the dishes and recipes we enjoy today. In particular we would like to thank the following people for their inspiration and input: head chef Gaven Fuller and Black Barn chef Andy Wheeler; Paul Collins, Karl MacEwan, Kuttiya Nimcean, Chris Webb, Alex Holder, Ivan Reid, Tom Kitchin, and Tom Aikens. A big thank you too, to Robin Gosse, Adam Caisley, Annabelle Briggs and Marianne Lumb for fine-tuning all the recipes so carefully for the home kitchen.

Thanks to Richard Smith for farming our land so well, and to everyone in the butchery and bakery, patisserie and production kitchens; to Jez Taylor and his team, for growing all the wonderful vegetables in the market garden, John Longman and his fellow cheese-makers in the creamery, and Eric Duhamel and his dedicated bread-makers, who know that good cheese and good loaves needs love, care, and above all, time. And to Tim Field, our environmental scientist, who helps guide us in our efforts to be as self-sustaining and ethical in our food production as is possible.

Thanks to Brooke Litchfield – always a source of inspiration for me; and the team at the Mothership who are really the heartbeat of Daylesford, especially Mark Bright and Rosie Henderson; and to my PA, Michele, who manages to fit everything in the diary and without whom I couldn't perform.

Special thanks go to all the suppliers and food producers – many small and artisan – who help to make Daylesford what it is today, and to our many friends for their support and enthusiasm, particularly Rose Prince, Carlo Petrini, Raymond Blanc and Patrick Holden.

To my children Alice, Jo and George for all the help they have given in their own ways: they have always told me when something was good, and I hope they will be proud of this book and all we have achieved at the farm.

And finally a huge thank you to Anthony for his never-ending patience, especially during the making of this book, when every time he went into the kitchen, he would find yet another recipe being tried and tested. Without his support none of this would have been possible.

Carole Bamford

Index

Almonds
apricot and almond tart 297–99
green beans with almonds, parsley
and garlic butter 132–33
Jerusalem artichoke risotto with
garlic and almond breadcrumbs
149–51
milk chocolate, almond and espresso
fudge 367–69
Parmesan, chilli and Marcona
almond biscuits 362
purple sprouting broccoli, spelt,
crispy garlic and toasted almond
salad 108–9

Apples
apple and chilli chutney 394–95
blackberry and apple crumble tart
295
brown sauce 402
celeriac and apple soup 60
poached apple and pear jelly with
crumble topping and prune cream
282–84
spiced apple cake with streusel
topping 350–51
vanilla rice pudding with apple and
blackberry compote 290–92
venison cottage pie with beetroot
and apple salad 268–69
wild rice, red cabbage, apple and
toasted cobnut salad 120–21

Asparagus
asparagus, spelt, pea and mint salad
84–85
garden vegetables with hot Cheddar
sauce and salsa verde mayonnaise
9–11
Oddington goat's cheese and
asparagus tart 170–71
pearl barley, asparagus and pea
shoot risotto 156–57

Basil
sardines on toast, with tomato,
basil and caper relish 18–20
tomato and sourdough salad, with
red pepper, onion and basil 90

Beans see individual bean names

Beef
beef, ale and barley casserole 264
braised brisket with lentils 260–61
corned beef 262–63
corned beef hash with brown sauce
34–35
featherblade of beef with creamed
wild mushrooms 256–57

roast rib of beef with Dijon mustard
and balsamic sauce 249–51
smoky slow-cooked shin of beef
chilli 258–59

Beetroot
beetroot, bacon and crème fraîche
soup 55–57
beetroot, swede and potato bake
138–40
grilled mackerel with roasted
beetroot and spiced lentils 199–201
raw beetroot, kidney beans and
mustard leaf with horseradish
dressing 114–15
venison cottage pie with beetroot
and apple salad 268–69

Biscuits
blue cheese and walnut biscuits 361
cheddar biscuits 360
double chocolate chip cookies 366
ginger biscuits 364–65
lemon shortbread biscuits 363
Parmesan, chilli and Marcona
almond biscuits 362

Blackberries
blackberry and apple crumble tart
295
vanilla rice pudding with apple and
blackberry compote 290–92

Bledington Blue Cheese and broccoli
tart 172–73

Broad beans
broad bean, bulgar wheat and herb
salad 79–81
broad bean, pea and watercress
risotto 147–48
broad bean, pea, mint and feta
toasts 12–14
smashed broad beans, peas and mint
128–29

Broccoli
Bledington Blue Cheese and broccoli
tart 172–73
chestnut, quinoa, kale and broccoli
salad 106–7
purple sprouting broccoli, spelt,
crispy garlic and toasted almond
salad 108–9
brown sauce 402

Butter beans
lamb and butter bean casserole with
tomatoes, caperberries and olives
229–31

spiced pumpkin, butter bean and
spinach casserole 141

Butternut squash
butternut squash chutney 396–97
butternut squash, goat's cheese and
olive salad 96–99
butternut squash, honey and sage
soup 62
butternut squash and kale tart
176–77
squash, honey and sage bread 316–17
see also squash

Cabbage
bubble and squeak with fried egg
27–29
crushed, buttered root vegetables
and cabbage 135
wild rice, red cabbage, apple and
toasted cobnut salad 120–21

Cashew nuts
mixed raw vegetables and cashew
nuts in chilli, soy and ginger
dressing 91–93

Casseroles, notes on 238–39

Cauliflower
curried cauliflower, red pepper and
nigella seeds salad 103–5

Cavolo nero
Jerusalem artichoke and cavolo
nero tart 178
venison and cavolo nero lasagne
265–67

Celeriac
celeriac and apple soup 60
mushroom, celeriac, truffle honey
and toasted pine nut salad 118–19

Cheddar cheese
Cheddar biscuits 360
Cheddar, potato and onion pie
184–86
hot Cheddar sauce 387
pan haggerty with mustard, egg and
caper mayonnaise 31–33
red onion, Cheddar and chilli bread
338–39
Welsh rarebit and chutney 21–22

Cheese 304–5 see also under
individual types of cheese

Chicken
chicken and apricot curry 243–44

chicken Caesar salad **122–23**
chicken casserole with a splash of brandy **240–42**
chicken, leek and bacon pie **187–88**
chicken (or turkey), ginger and vegetable broth **58–59**
chicken stock **417–18**
ten vegetable and two grain minestrone **63–65**

Chickpeas
pickled pear and hazelnut salad with chickpeas, quinoa and Daylesford Blue **100–102**

Chillies
apple and chilli chutney **394–95**
mixed raw vegetables and cashew nuts in chilli, soy and ginger dressing **91–93**
red tomato chilli jam **398–400**
smoky slow-cooked shin of beef chilli **258–59**
venison terrine with tomato and chilli jam **44–45**

Chocolate
chocolate cake **345–47**
dark and white chocolate brownies **356–57**
double chocolate chip cookies **366**
milk chocolate, almond and espresso fudge **367–69**

Christmas cake **372–73**

Christmas pudding **303**

Chutney
apple and chilli chutney **394–95**
butternut squash chutney **396–97**
Welsh rarebit and chutney **21–22**

Cobnuts
wild rice, red cabbage, apple and toasted cobnut salad **120–21**

Cod
cod with lemon, parsley and tomato butter **209–11**

Coffee
coffee jelly with brown bread ice cream **285–86**
milk chocolate, almond and espresso fudge **367–69**

Courgettes
griddled courgettes and pine nuts in yoghurt and mint dressing **86**

Crab
hot Dorset crab on toast **16–17**

Cucumbers
chilled tomato, cucumber and fennel soup **52–54**

Daylesford Blue
lentils, tomato, Daylesford Blue and red onion salad **110**
pickled pear and hazelnut salad, with chickpeas, quinoa and Daylesford Blue **100–102**

Earl Grey cake **354**

Eggs
bubble and squeak with fried egg **27–29**
garden vegetables with hot Cheddar sauce and salsa verde mayonnaise **9–11**
notes on eggs **30**
pan haggerty with mustard, egg and caper mayonnaise **31–33**
Rita's baked eggs and onions **24–26**
Welsh rarebit and chutney **21–22**

Fennel
chilled tomato, cucumber and fennel soup **52–54**

Feta cheese
broad bean, pea, mint and feta toasts **12–14**
tomatoes and feta with mint and lemon dressing **88–89**

Fish *see under individual names of fish*

Flowerpot breads, two **336–37**

French dressing **381**

Fruit *see individual fruit names*

Fudge
milk chocolate, almond and espresso fudge **367–69**

Garlic
Jerusalem artichoke risotto with garlic and almond breadcrumbs **149–51**
leek and wild garlic pesto risotto **152**
potato wedges with garlic and rosemary butter **134**
purple sprouting broccoli, spelt, crispy garlic and toasted almond salad **108–89**

Goat's cheese
butternut squash, goat's cheese and olive salad **96–99**
Oddington goat's cheese and asparagus tart **170–71**

Gooseberries
gooseberry and elderflower jam **405**
gooseberry fool with shortbread **273–75**

Halibut with Morecambe Bay shrimp butter sauce **212–14**

Ham hock terrine with piccalilli **37–39**

Hazelnuts
pickled pear and hazelnut salad, with chickpeas, quinoa and Daylesford Blue **100–102**

Honey
butternut squash, honey and sage soup **62**
Manuka honey cake **348–49**
squash, honey and sage bread **316–17**

Hot cross loaf or buns **323–25**

Jams
gooseberry and elderflower jam **405**
red tomato chilli jam **398–400**
rhubarb and ginger jam **404**
strawberry and vanilla conserve **406–08**

Jars and bottles, notes on **388**

Jellies
coffee jelly with brown bread ice cream **285–86**
notes on **276**
orange-poached rhubarb jelly **278**
poached apple and pear jelly with crumble topping and prune cream **282–84**

Jerusalem artichokes
Jerusalem artichoke and cavolo nero tart **178**
Jerusalem artichoke risotto with garlic and almond breadcrumbs **149–51**

Kale
Adlestrop cheese and kale tart **169**
butternut squash and kale tart **176–77**
chestnut, quinoa, kale and broccoli salad **106–7**

Kedgeree
baked salmon, spinach and smoked haddock kedgeree **218–19**

Kidney beans
raw beetroot, kidney beans and mustard leaf with horseradish dressing **114–15**

Lamb
lamb and butter bean casserole with tomatoes, caperberries and olives **229–31**
pressed lamb **235–37**
slow-cooked lamb shoulder with white beans and salsa verde mayonnaise **232–34**

Lasagne
    venison and cavolo nero lasagne
    265–67

Leaves, notes on 111–12

Leeks
    chicken, leek and bacon pie 187–88
    cider baked leeks 141–42
    leek and potato soup 66–67
    leek and wild garlic pesto risotto 152

Lemons
    cod with lemon, parsley and tomato
        butter 209–11
    lemon drizzle cake 352–53
    lemon refresher 40
    lemon shortbread biscuits 363
    tomatoes and feta with mint and
        lemon dressing 88–89
    wilted spinach with toasted pine nuts,
        sultanas and lemon zest 130–31

Lentils
    braised brisket with lentils 260–61
    grilled mackerel with roasted
        beetroot and spiced lentils 199–201
    lentils, tomato, Daylesford Blue
        and red onion salad 110

Mackerel
    grilled mackerel with roasted
        beetroot and spiced lentils
        199–201
    smoked mackerel pâté with
        Daylesford toasts 36

Manuka honey cake 348–49

Marmalade
    Seville orange marmalade 409–11

Mayonnaise 381
    herb mayonnaise 385
    salsa verde mayonnaise 382–83

Mint
    asparagus, spelt, pea and mint
        salad 84–85
    broad bean, pea, mint and feta
        toasts 12–14
    chilled pea and mint soup 50–51
    griddled courgettes and pine nuts
        in yoghurt and mint dressing 86
    minted aioli 386
    smashed broad beans, peas and
        mint 128–29
    tomatoes and feta with mint and
        lemon dressing 88–89

Mozzarella
    grilled peaches, spelt, pea, rocket
        and mozzarella salad 82–83

Mushrooms
    featherblade of beef with creamed
        wild mushrooms 256–57
    mushroom, celeriac, truffle honey
        and toasted pine nuts 118–19
    woodland mushroom shepherd's pie
        136–37

Mustard leaves
    raw beetroot, kidney beans and
        mustard leaf with horseradish
        dressing 114–15

Nettle bread 340–41

Olives
    butternut squash, goat's cheese and
        olive salad 96–99
    crushed new potatoes with olives,
        capers and herbs 127
    lamb and butter bean casserole with
        tomatoes, caperberries and olives
        229–31

Onions
    Cheddar, potato and onion pie
        184–86
    lentils, tomato, Daylesford Blue and
        red onion salad 110
    onion purée 146
    red onion, Cheddar and chilli bread
        338–39
    red onion tarte tatins with Baywell
        cheese 182–83
    Rita's baked eggs and onions 24–26
    tomato and sourdough salad, with
        red pepper, onion and basil 90

Oranges
    blood orange and polenta cake with
        orange whipped cream 300–302
    mulled wine and orange trifle
        279–81
    orange-poached rhubarb jelly 278
    Seville orange marmalade 409–11

Parsley
    cod with lemon, parsley and tomato
        butter 209–11
    green beans with almonds, parsley
        and garlic butter 132–33

Pastry
    savoury 167–68
    sweet 293–94

Pea shoots
    pearl barley, asparagus and pea
        shoot risotto 156–57

Peaches
    grilled peaches, spelt, pea, rocket
        and mozzarella salad 82–83

Pearl barley
    beef, ale and barley casserole 264
    pearl barley, asparagus and pea
        shoot risotto 156–57
    ten vegetable and two grain
        minestrone 63–65

Pears
    pickled pear and hazelnut salad,
        with chickpeas, quinoa and
        Daylesford Blue 100–102
    poached apple and pear jelly with
        crumble topping and prune cream
        282–84

Peas
    asparagus, spelt, pea and mint salad
        84–85
    broad bean, pea and watercress
        risotto 147–48
    broad bean, pea, mint and feta
        toasts 12–14
    chilled pea and mint soup 50–51
    garden vegetables with hot Cheddar
        sauce and salsa verde mayonnaise
        9–11
    grilled peaches, spelt, pea, rocket
        and mozzarella salad 82–83
    smashed broad beans, pea salad and
        mint 128–29

Peppers
    curried cauliflower, red pepper and
        nigella seeds salad 103–5
    tomato and sourdough salad, with
        red pepper, onion and basil 90

Pesto
    watercress or wild garlic and
        pumpkin seed pesto 385

Piccalilli 390–91
    ham hock terrine with piccalilli
        37–39

Pine nuts
    griddled courgettes and pine nuts in
        yoghurt and mint dressing 86
    mushroom, celeriac, truffle honey
        and toasted pine nut salad 118–19
    wilted spinach with toasted pine
        nuts, sultanas and lemon zest
        130–31

Pollock
    pan-roasted pollock with crushed
        potatoes and watercress
        mayonnaise 202–4
    traditional fish pie 207–8

Potatoes
    beetroot, swede and potato bake
        138–40
    bubble and squeak with fried egg
        27–29
    Cheddar, potato and onion pie
        184–86
    corned beef hash with brown sauce
        34–35
    crushed new potatoes with olives,
        capers and herbs 127
    leek and potato soup 66–67
    pan haggerty with mustard, egg
        and caper mayonnaise 31–33

pan-roasted pollock with crushed
potatoes and watercress
mayonnaise 202–4
potato wedges with garlic and
rosemary butter 134
venison cottage pie with beetroot
and apple salad 268–69
woodland mushroom shepherd's pie
136–37

Pumpernickel 320–22

Quinoa
chestnut, quinoa, kale and broccoli
salad 106–7
pickled pear and hazelnut salad,
with chickpeas, quinoa and
Daylesford Blue 100–102

Rhubarb
orange-poached rhubarb jelly 278
rhubarb and ginger jam 404
rhubarb queen of puddings
287–89

Risotti
broad bean, pea and watercress
risotto 147–48
Jerusalem artichoke risotto with
garlic and almond breadcrumbs
149–51
leek and wild garlic pesto risotto
152
pearl barley, asparagus and pea
shoot risotto 156–57
spelt, garden vegetable and herb
risotto 153–55

Roasts, notes on 245–48

Sage
butternut squash, honey and sage
soup 62
squash, honey and sage bread
316–17

Salmon
baked salmon, spinach and smoked
haddock kedgeree 218–19
salmon and smoked haddock
fishcakes 205–6
traditional fish pie 207–8

Sauces
brown sauce 402
hot Cheddar sauce 387

Shortbread
gooseberry fool with shortbread
273–75
lemon shortbread biscuits 363

Simnel cake 355

Smoked haddock
baked salmon, spinach and smoked
haddock kedgeree 218–19

salmon and smoked haddock
fishcakes 205–6
squash and smoked haddock
chowder 61
traditional fish pie 207–8

Sourdough 331–32
garden vegetables with hot Cheddar
sauce and salsa verde mayonnaise
9–11
seven seeds sourdough 333–35
tomato and sourdough salad,
with red pepper, onion and basil
90
Welsh rarebit and chutney 21–22

Spelt
asparagus, spelt, pea and mint salad
84–85
grilled peaches, spelt, pea, rocket
and mozzarella salad 82–83
purple sprouting broccoli, spelt,
crispy garlic and toasted almond
salad 108–9
spelt, garden vegetable and herb
risotto 153–55
ten vegetable and two grain
minestrone 63–65

Spinach
baked salmon, spinach and smoked
haddock kedgeree 218–19
Single Gloucester, spinach and
smoked bacon tart 174–75
spiced pumpkin, butter bean and
spinach casserole 141
wilted spinach with toasted pine
nuts, sultanas and lemon zest
130–31

Squash
squash, honey and sage bread
316–17
squash and smoked haddock
chowder 61
see also butternut squash

Steak, notes on cooking 252–53

Stocks
chicken stock 417–18
notes on 416
vegetable stock 416

Swede
beetroot, swede and potato bake
138–40

Terrines
ham hock terrine with piccalilli
37–39
venison terrine with tomato and
chilli jam 44–45

Toasts
broad bean, pea, mint and feta
toasts 12–14

hot Dorset crab on toast 16–17
notes on 15
sardines on toast, with tomato,
basil and caper relish 18–20
smoked mackerel pâté with
Daylesford toasts 36

Tomatoes
chilled tomato, cucumber and fennel
soup 52–54
cod with lemon, parsley and tomato
butter 209–11
garden vegetables with hot Cheddar
sauce and salsa verde mayonnaise
9–11
lamb and butter bean casserole with
tomatoes, caperberries and olives
229–31
lentil, tomato, Daylesford Blue and
red onion salad 110
notes on 87
red tomato chilli jam 398–400
sardines on toast, with tomato, basil
and caper relish 18–20
three tomato tart 179–81
tomato and sourdough salad, with
red pepper, onion and basil 90
tomato ketchup 401
tomatoes and feta with mint and
lemon dressing 88–89
venison terrine with tomato and
chilli jam 44–45

Tuna
cold rose veal with tuna and caper
mayonnaise 23

Veal
cold rose veal with tuna and caper
mayonnaise 23

Venison
venison and cavolo nero lasagne
265–67
venison and cranberry pies 189–90
venison cottage pie with beetroot
and apple salad 268–69
venison terrine with tomato and
chilli jam 44–45
Wootton Estate game pie 191–95

Walnuts
blue cheese and walnut biscuits 361

Watercress
broad bean, pea and watercress
risotto 147–48
pan-roasted pollock with crushed
potatoes and watercress
mayonnaise 202–4
watercress or wild garlic and
pumpkin seed pesto 385

White beans
slow-cooked lamb shoulder with
white beans and salsa verde
mayonnaise 232–34